Guide to California's
Wine Country

By the Editors of Sunset Books and Sunset Magazine

Old Bale Mill—Napa

273740

Lane Publishing Co. • Menlo Park, California

Research and Text: Bob Thompson

Supervising Editor: Barbara J. Braasch

Special Consultant: Margaret Smith,
Sunset Magazine
Design: Cynthia Hanson
Illustrations: Rik Olson

Hours, telephone numbers, and highway designations in this book are accurate as of August 1979.

Maps have been provided in each chapter for the special purpose of highlighting significant regions, winery locations, routes, and attractions in the area. Check automobile clubs, insurance agencies, and chambers of commerce or visitors bureaus in major cities for detailed highway maps.

Cover: Sylvan setting is archetypical vineyard scene at Rutherford in the Napa Valley. Photographed by Fred Lyon.

Editor, Sunset Books: David E. Clark

First Printing August 1979

Contents

Good wine *begins in a vineyard, ends in a glass.*

Introduction

The pleasures of going to see wine where it is made

Touring the wine country is not a new idea. Visitors have been crossing threshholds into California wine cellars for more than two centuries, 1969 having been the official bicentennial. But if the paths are well worn, they are more inviting than ever.

California's first wineries, adjuncts to the Franciscan missions, were spaced a hard day's ride apart, from San Diego to Sonoma. Nearly all of their wine went to sacramental use, but some was also used to welcome neighbors, and some to settle the dusty thirst of summer travelers or drive the chill from winter visitors.

When the Franciscans abandoned their California winemaking in the 1830s, others were there to pick up the reins, not only in the original districts, but in areas farther north, and, above all, farther east in the great Central Valley. In essence, winemaking in California had its present geographic shape by the late 1880s. Prohibition dimmed the outline from 1918 to 1934, but did not erase it.

From the viewpoint of visitors, however, there has been a tremendous revolution in the state's wineries since 1968, when the first edition of this book appeared. For example, the original edition described 18 wineries in the Napa Valley and the same number in Sonoma County. The current edition shows 65 for Napa and 55 for Sonoma. Even more striking: Monterey had but one winery in 1968, and Santa Barbara had none, while between the two of them, the total vineyard acreage ranged around 30. In this edition, Monterey shows 5 and Santa Barbara 7 wineries open to visitors, while Monterey's grape acreage surpasses 34,000 and Santa Barbara's exceeds 6,000.

Mere numbers aside, there has been another great change for visitors. The old-line cellars, the ones that were around for the first edition, were, in a great majority of cases, of a size to run formal visitor facilities, including tour guides and special tasting rooms. Some of the new names have followed their model, but a great majority are too small to have either guides or tasting rooms, so they welcome visitors only by appointment and offer tastes only when there is a bit of wine to spare.

One logical visitor approach to this situation is to use the cellars with developed tour programs as sources of primary information, saving the appointment-only places for a time when an hour's talk about the fine points of winemaking does not require a taste to be worthwhile. The other logical approach is to choose wineries whose wines are personal favorites, no matter what size or shape the cellar.

Whatever approach is taken to the state's wineries, they are rewarding for their diversity. Over the course of two centuries, California has acquired winemakers from every corner of the globe. They have contributed differing notions about how grapes should be grown, how wine should be made, how buildings should be designed, and even what kind of dog should stand sentry.

Someone bent on record-setting could visit as many as 20 cellars a day in some districts . . . but should not. Such a visitor would miss all the details, and details are what wine is all about. Experienced travelers in the vineyards limit themselves to three, or at most four, stops a day.

About This Book

These explanations will help make *California's Wine Country* a more useful and reliable guide.

Each map has accompanying tour information for the wineries located within the area shown. The hours listed for each winery are subject to change. In the case of small family wineries, hours may change on any day because of one or another necessity. Most wineries close for major holidays.

Abbreviations used in the tour information accompanying the maps may be translated as follows: *IT* (informal tour; in most cases it means no guide or at least no guarantee of one); *GT* (guided tour); and *Ta* (tasting). If picnic areas are provided, they are noted, along with reservation policies.

In the cases of both map entries and main text, the wineries are presented alphabetically rather than in any geographical sequence. Subchapters within main chapters group wineries that are within easy driving range of one another.

Each winery described in the main text has some of its wines listed as part of the description. The listings are in no sense meant as buyer guides or preferences but only as indications of the main focus of production in each case. (In this and in other descriptions we have tried to preserve some discoveries for the visitor.)

Vintage Calendar

For most wine buffs, thoughts of the calendar revolve around the vintage. September and October are the months of most dramatic activity in vineyard and cellar alike, and also a season of agreeable weather. But the annual cycle of winegrowing has crucial moments all through the year, with reasons to visit the wine country in every season. In an important sense, a vintage begins in March, when a pale fringe of new leaf

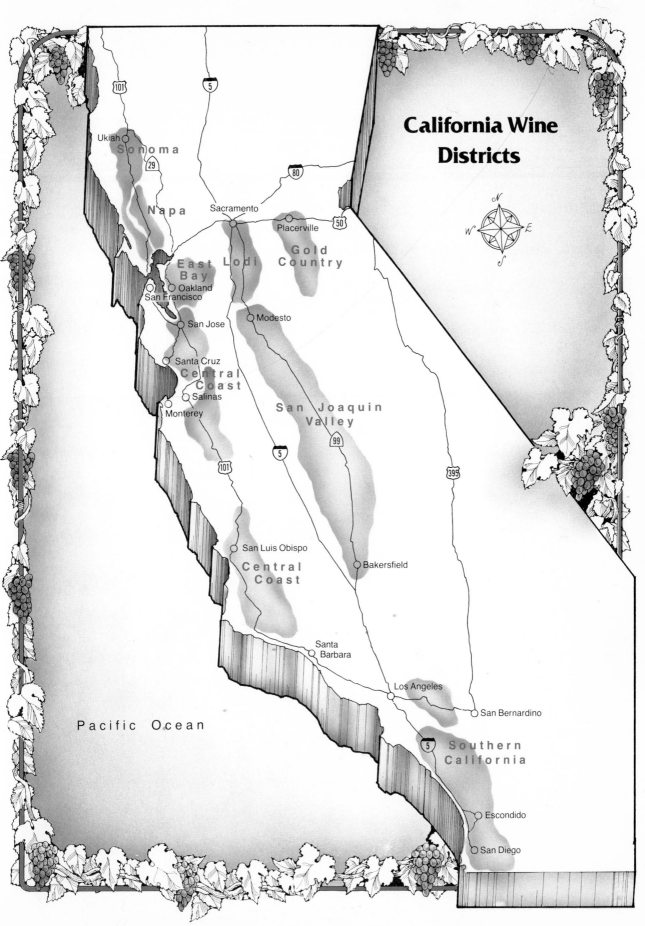

California Wine Districts

Ukiah

Sonoma

29

Napa

Sacramento

Placerville

Gold Country

East Bay

Lodi

Oakland

San Francisco

San Jose

Modesto

Santa Cruz

Central Coast

Salinas

Monterey

San Joaquin Valley

San Luis Obispo

Central Coast

Bakersfield

Pacific Ocean

Santa Barbara

Los Angeles

San Bernardino

Southern California

Escondido

San Diego

Wine is made *ofttimes in grand buildings such as The Christian Brothers Greystone Cellars (above). However, outsides matter less than insides, for equipment reveals more about what the winemaker thinks. The cellar scene (right) is at J. Pedroncelli.*

begins to cover the bare bones of the winter vines. Since it is a true beginning, this calendar starts there, too.

Spring. In many ways, March—the month of great transitions—has as much drama as the harvest. Early in the month, the winter cover crop still flourishes everywhere. In the coast counties, from Mendocino down to Santa Cruz, this takes the form of dazzling seas of mustard. In the Sierra foothills, the cover is less flowery, but vineyardists there turn fleecy white sheep out among the vines to mow the grasses. By mid-month, the flowers begin to fade, tractors begin to disc under whatever vegetation is left, and new leaf begins to peek out on the vines, each variety of grape hewing to its own timetable.

From March through May, the vines play their annual game of tag with frosts and hailstorms. One night of frost can do away with 10 percent of a grower's crop. A long siege of freezing nights can wipe out his whole season.

Cold as the nights may be, daytimes often reach into the balmy 70s—lower 20s on a Celsius thermometer.

For landscape painters or photographers, this is the best season of the year. First there are the winter cover crops. After them come the new grape leaves, luminous green against the brown of fresh-turned earth, the canes still short enough to make each row stand out separately. (Late in summer, canes lengthen, leaves darken, and vineyards tend to photograph as seas of dusty spinach.) Furthermore, spring skies yield the year's best collections of puffy white clouds.

Summer. In a way, summer is the least of times and the most of times. It is the least of times because little happens: the vines have made their growth, the cellars tend to be as idle as they get.

And yet, there are moments. By June, the fruit buds look very much like clusters of miniature grapes. Then, in the middle third of the month, these buds unfold into one of the most insignificant floral displays in all of botany. Though no feast for the eyes, this flowering marks a critical stage in growing wine grapes. To set a full crop, the vines must now have 10 to 14 days of dry, moderately warm weather. Rain is a disaster. Extreme heat is not much better.

Visitors, flocking in their peak numbers, wish all summer long for moderate temperatures. But many will come to know how much heat goes into ripe grapes, for all but a handful of districts experience at least a few days of 100°F/38°C during June, July, and August.

Autumn. The vintage builds toward a peak as September moves to a close. A few grape varieties ripen early in the month—even in August—and a few straggle into November, or, in Monterey, December. But most California grapes ripen in the last three weeks of September and the first three of October. At the peak of the harvest, pickers go into the vineyards before the sun gets up, racing in the cool dawn air so they can slow down in the heat of the day.

The crushing of grapes to make wine is messy. Ton upon ton of pulped fruit is not quite the same thing as a few pounds of berries on the way to becoming jelly. Still, as soon as fermentations get going, matters begin not only to look better, but to smell just fine. A fermentation that smells sweet is sure to yield good wine

for drinking regardless of how it looks at the time.

Demands upon winemakers at this time are incredible. They must help each variety follow its distinct path in fermenting. Moving wines along to make room for later arrivals requires no small amount of midnight work, so a tank will be ready when the first loads of a new day arrive.

Autumn, along with spring, is an enormously photogenic time, but for people at work rather than for landscapes: pickers rushing, crushers and presses in motion, and—hard to catch but worth a wait—the seething of a fermentation in full flight.

Winter. After Thanksgiving comes the quiet season in the vineyards. From December through March, pruners shear away last year's canes, leaving gnarled gray trunks to poke up out of grasses that deepen with each rain.

In the cellars, there is a great deal of work but not much bustle. New wines are racked clear, a tedious process for cellarmen who huddle over slow pumps, moving wine from one big tank to another. The first fresh wines of the past harvest begin going to bottle for release in early spring. Of considerable interest to wine buffs, this is a season for releasing many age-worthy wines from earlier vintages.

The crowds of summer and fall dwindle, leaving winery hosts more time to answer hard questions.

There is a price: December through February is the rainy season. Skies can be bleak, temperatures in the 40sF/4°C at midday, in the 20sF/−4°C at night. However, with luck, visitors can catch the tail end of a storm and be treated to showy weather . . . hillsides cloaked in wisps of cloud, lemon-hued sun lighting new grass, and just enough warmth to promise spring.

How Wine Is Made

In broad outline, winemaking is extremely simple. Ripe grapes are harvested and crushed. Yeast causes the juice to ferment. After fermentation, time and gravity make the wine clear, and ready to drink.

If that were the whole story, connoisseurs would not become passionate proponents of one cellar's wine over that of its neighbor. But it is not the whole story. At every stage in winemaking, dozens of subtle choices lead to tastable differences in the finished product. Examining these choices provides much of the intrigue in winery touring.

Many of the choices a winemaker elects are visible in the forms of equipment—an air-pressure press versus a continuous one, new barrels versus old casks— but these external signs explain only so much. How a winemaker uses any piece of equipment has at least as big an effect on the resulting wine as the basic nature of the gear.

This schematic diagram on pages 8 and 9 outlines the major steps in winemaking, showing some of the alternatives. At no winery will it serve as a precise model, but it may help form a base of understanding so that the differences make sense. Since whites and reds are fermented differently, they are shown separately.

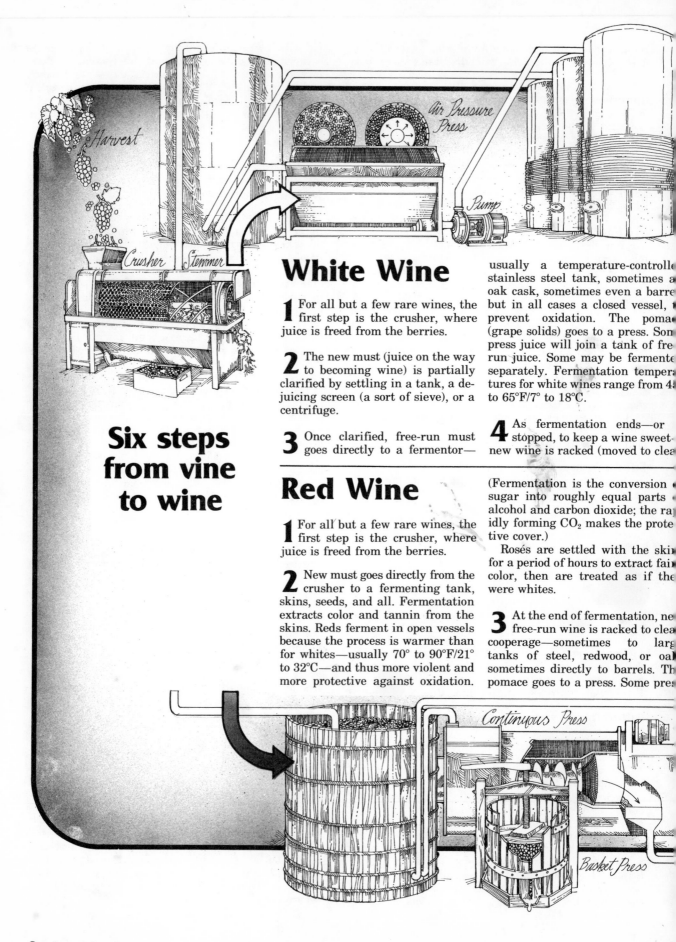

White Wine

1 For all but a few rare wines, the first step is the crusher, where juice is freed from the berries.

2 The new must (juice on the way to becoming wine) is partially clarified by settling in a tank, a de-juicing screen (a sort of sieve), or a centrifuge.

3 Once clarified, free-run must goes directly to a fermentor—

usually a temperature-controlle[d] stainless steel tank, sometimes a[n] oak cask, sometimes even a barre[l] but in all cases a closed vessel, t[o] prevent oxidation. The poma[ce] (grape solids) goes to a press. Som[e] press juice will join a tank of fre[e-] run juice. Some may be fermente[d] separately. Fermentation tempera[-] tures for white wines range from 4[5°] to 65°F/7° to 18°C.

4 As fermentation ends—or [is] stopped, to keep a wine sweet—new wine is racked (moved to clea[n]

Six steps from vine to wine

Red Wine

1 For all but a few rare wines, the first step is the crusher, where juice is freed from the berries.

2 New must goes directly from the crusher to a fermenting tank, skins, seeds, and all. Fermentation extracts color and tannin from the skins. Reds ferment in open vessels because the process is warmer than for whites—usually 70° to 90°F/21° to 32°C—and thus more violent and more protective against oxidation.

(Fermentation is the conversion [of] sugar into roughly equal parts [of] alcohol and carbon dioxide; the ra[p-]idly forming CO_2 makes the prote[c-]tive cover.)

Rosés are settled with the ski[ns] for a period of hours to extract fai[nt] color, then are treated as if the[y] were whites.

3 At the end of fermentation, ne[w] free-run wine is racked to clea[n] cooperage—sometimes to larg[e] tanks of steel, redwood, or oa[k,] sometimes directly to barrels. Th[e] pomace goes to a press. Some pre[ss]

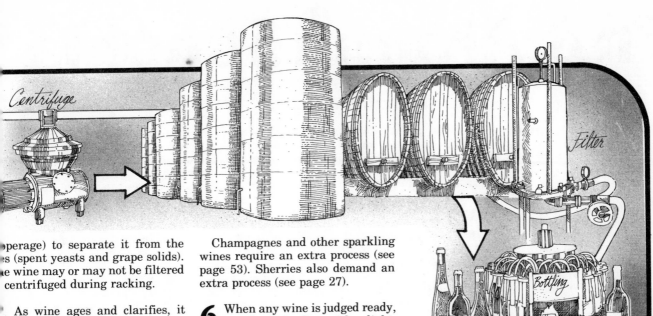

Centrifuge

Filter

Bottling

operage) to separate it from the
lees (spent yeasts and grape solids).
The wine may or may not be filtered
or centrifuged during racking.

As wine ages and clarifies, it
may be racked again. Clarify-
ing is done by time and gravity, or
by a fining agent such as a fine clay
called "bentonite." Fresh white
wines—those meant to be drunk in
their youth—may age entirely in
stainless steel or other neutral cooperage. Wine meant for keeping in
bottle often ages in small oak.

Champagnes and other sparkling
wines require an extra process (see
page 53). Sherries also demand an
extra process (see page 27).

6 When any wine is judged ready,
it is bottled, often with a light,
or polish filtration just as it goes to
the bottling line. Sweet whites may
be given a sterile filtration in a mil-
lipore filter, so yeasts cannot start
a refermentation in the bottle.

---

wine may be added to free-run wine
from the same fermentation. Some
will be kept for blending with other
(often weaker) wines. Some wines
are filtered at this point.

4 Most red wines are racked twice
or more to help clarify them.
They also may be fined with bentonite or albumen (egg white) to speed
clarification.

5 Some wineries rack their wine
more than once in order to flavor it with more than one kind of
wood—or to limit its exposure to

wood. Woods, like grapes, have regional and varietal characteristics.
These are pronounced in new cooperage, then fade with succeeding
uses.

6 When any wine is judged ready,
it is bottled, often with a light,
or polish filtration just as it goes to
the bottling line.

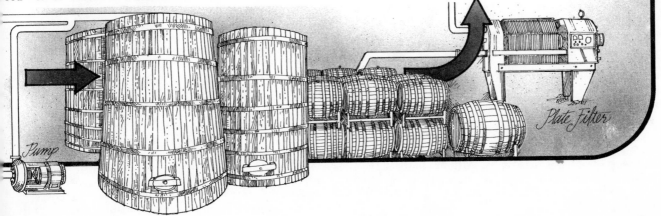

Pump

Plate Filter

In & Around Sonoma

Rich in California history as well as vines

Few districts have more of the character of old California than Sonoma County. The town of Sonoma sprang up around the last of the Franciscan missions in the 1830s. Already the Russians had founded and abandoned their fur-trading outpost on the coast at Fort Ross. After Sonoma's mission days, the town served as headquarters for Mariano Vallejo during his term as governor of Mexico. The Bear Flag Revolt, a triggering incident in the union of California with the United States, unfolded on Vallejo's doorstep.

Later, horticulturist Luther Burbank did much of his work in and around Santa Rosa to prove that this region is a veritable garden spot, while author Jack London labored at his home in the hills above Glen Ellen to prove that no place is a pure paradise.

Grapes and wine have been companions through all these historic episodes, a part of Sonoma from the beginning. The mission had vineyards in the 1830s. Vallejo took them over, along with the rest of the property, and ran a lively competition with Agoston Haraszthy to see who was the better winemaker. (In the judgment of history, Vallejo's fame is mainly political while Haraszthy is remembered for his long reign as father of California winemaking.) Burbank grew grapes experimentally but never drank, while London refused to grow grapes but was eager to sample wine.

Today, the historical heart of Sonoma winemaking is but a small part of the county's vineyard, statistically speaking. By far the greatest acreage of vines and by far the greatest number of wineries are strung out on either side of U.S. Highway 101, from Santa Rosa north to the county line near Cloverdale. Healdsburg is the hub of the larger district, nearly all of it within the watershed of the Russian River. All told, the county had a shade more than 25,000 acres of vines in 1979. Wineries numbered in the 60s.

Mendocino County, Sonoma's neighbor to the north, in the past has been an appendage of the Russian River district. The wineries are still not numerous enough in this district to require a separate chapter, so it continues to be an adjunct to Sonoma in this travel book, although connoisseurs of wine began to think of it separately early in the 1970s. Ukiah, on U.S. 101, is one focal point of Mendocino's winemaking. Philo, near the coast, is another.

Sonoma

In a world often indifferent to yesterday, the town of Sonoma clings to much of its past. The town plaza was the heart of things when Fra José Altimira founded the mission in 1832. It remained the heart when the secular government of Mariano Vallejo supplanted the mission, and again when the Bear Flaggers did away with the Mexican regime. It remains the heart of town.

Time has changed the details of the plaza but not its essence. A good many of the adjacent buildings had weathered before California gained statehood in 1850. Most of the rest have had a chance to weather since. The square itself remained a patch of bare ground only until 1910, when the sizable city hall was built in its center using a buff-colored local sandstone. Sheltering trees have since grown up to shade the benches on which townsfolk and visitors take their ease in summer's heat.

West and north, a string of resort towns reaches back to the turn of the century, surviving in spite of losing their original purpose. The hot springs that made the district a favored spa for fog-chilled San Franciscans of the Gay Nineties cooled after the earthquake of 1906, never to heat up again. In spite of that, aged hotels and cottages in these towns cling to existence. A few have even been renovated with an eye to a growing clientele of winery visitors.

Encircling the town of Sonoma and stretching away to the north beyond the resorts, vineyards and wineries were and are integral parts of the Sonoma Valley.

The Wineries

Winegrowing north of San Francisco had its beginnings at Sonoma. Today, the wineries—like the rest of the valley—reflect old times and new in their architecture, sometimes even in their equipment.

In the spring of 1979, seven local cellars welcomed visitors freely, and another three offered somewhat more restricted opportunities for visiting. Plans were afoot to expand the roster of local cellars by at least five before the harvest of 1980.

Buena Vista has endured various fortunes since Agoston Haraszthy founded the winery in 1857.

Haraszthy, the now-a-colonel, now-a-count Hungarian who is widely credited as being the father of the modern California wine industry, set a tone. He brought the first really sizable importations of classic European vines to California, but, because he had unacceptable political affiliations, he never received payment from the state for his effort in its behalf. The hapless Haraszthy disappeared in Nicaragua just a few years before phylloxera began to play havoc with his vines.

Haraszthy's sons and others carried on after his departure until the 1906 earthquake severely damaged the winery buildings. Finally, Buena Vista closed its doors. The old stone buildings were abandoned until 1943, when newspaperman Frank Bartholomew bought the property and started reconditioning the place.

The long-of-memory might have crossed their fingers when they saw the first new vines in very crooked rows. (They were planted by World War II submarine crews on rehabilitation leave, presumably without their nav-

Autumn foliage *lends a fiery light to venerable vineyard at Davis Bynum winery.*

Plan a picnic

Sonoma County is a pleasing test of California's capacity for contrast. Its coast, however beautiful, leans toward cool and foggy summers rather than the warm, dry ones of its valleys.

At the expense of 2 or 3 hours' driving in pastoral countryside, a visitor can have a look at winemaking, cheesemaking, and oystering, crabbing, or clamming. At the expense of eight or ten dollars, he can assemble a picnic that combines all the joys of fermentation as company to a main course of seafood.

A well-warmed valley dweller can scoot west from U.S. Highway 101 at Santa Rosa on the Bodega Highway or take a slightly longer route from Sonoma west on State Highway 116 to Petaluma, then west on the Petaluma-Point Reyes Station Road ('D' Street). The latter route has few peers. It is its own pastoral symphony.

In the morning, with the dew still on the grapes, the valleys offer a kind of stillness. Just west of Sonoma, State 116 follows a curving course through dry, spaciously arranged hills, little populated and beginning to warm.

Once Petaluma is behind and the 'D' Street extension begins to be Point Reyes Station Road, the grass is greener and it begins to be dairy country. In the midst of these spacious rolling hills, the Marin French Cheese headquarters come into view. Here, especially if a bottle of wine and a loaf of bread are already aboard, is the place to lay in a stock of cheese and have a look at how it is made. From the cheese company, it is but a short jump after the retreating morning fog to Marshall and one of the Tomales Bay oyster markets.

What to take? Small individual cutting boards, steak knives (to double as personal cheese knives), wine glasses, and a corkscrew are the only utensils required for this picnic, though a large tray will come in handy.

---

igation officers.) It was not a bad omen, however. Buena Vista has enjoyed prosperous good health since its reopening.

Before Bartholomew sold the winery in 1968, he restored it to something very much like the original. The eucalyptus trees were much taller, and workaday wooden sheds did not reappear on the fronts of the two finely made stone buildings. Otherwise, the tranquility of the 1860s was recaptured intact.

The current owner, Young's Market Co. of Los Angeles, has expanded Buena Vista, but not at the expense of the old site. In 1975, the company constructed a new producing winery in the Carneros district, near its vineyards on the Sonoma-Napa county line, leaving the original stone buildings to serve as a wine aging facility.

The larger of the stone buildings houses the tasting room, as well as barrels placed in tunnels carved into the sandstone hill by Chinese laborers. This is also the building which visitors explore at their own pace, with signs and photographs as guides.

Outside are two picnic grounds, one directly in front of the larger building, the other set between the two buildings. In summer, this is the place to picnic on French bread from the bakery on the town plaza, fresh fruit from the market next door, cheeses from the factory diagonally across from them, and wine from the obvious source.

Buena Vista wines include Zinfandel (from a grape possibly imported by the Count himself), Pinot Noir, Cabernet Sauvignon, Chardonnay, Gewürztraminer, and Johannisberg Riesling. The winery also offers port and sherry types.

Chateau St. Jean has set out to look as romantically French as any place could, given the fact that Sugarloaf Ridge, which looms up just behind the winery, is a classic California coastal hill.

A mock medieval tower is to become the architectural focal point of the winery. In 1979, it had yet to be built, but no matter. The property has a head start on romance in the form of a one-time country estate house that would look at home on the Seine above Paris.

When it is built, the tower will be more than ornamental. Its purpose will be to provide a central vantage from which visitors can look down on the entire winemaking process. In the meantime, visitors with appointments can walk around to see the working cellar, from its large collection of small stainless steel fermenting tanks to its barrel aging cellar and bottling line.

The old estate house is already more than an ornament. It houses the tasting and sales in a pair of elegant wood-panelled rooms.

Founded in 1974, Chateau St. Jean emphasizes wines from individual vineyards, especially Chardonnays and late-harvest Johannisberg Rieslings, but the list also includes Fumé Blanc, Cabernet Sauvignon, Merlot, and *methode champenoise* sparkling wines.

The description of Riesling or other white wine as "late harvest" means that it was made from grapes affected by *Botrytis cinerea,* more romantically known as The Noble Mold. When harvest season weather produces exactly the right sequences of moisture and drying warmth, Botrytis has the curious effect of concentrating the juice within grapes to a super sweetness. It also creates intense fruit flavor, but does not produce any moldy taste. Sauternes from France and Ausleses and their sweeter kin from Germany also are Botrytised wines.

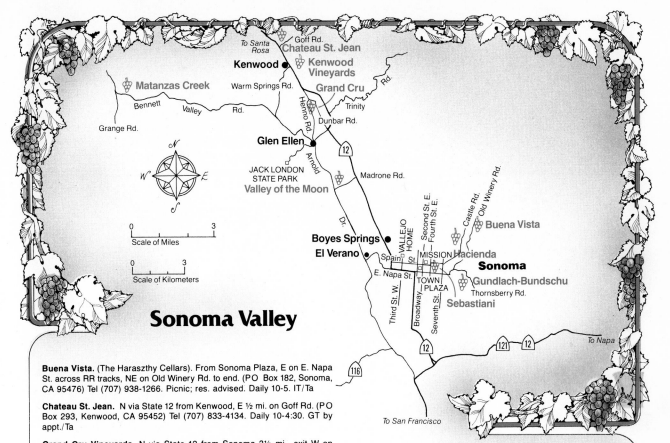

Sonoma Valley

Buena Vista. (The Haraszthy Cellars). From Sonoma Plaza, E on E. Napa St. across RR tracks, NE on Old Winery Rd. to end. (PO Box 182, Sonoma, CA 95476) Tel (707) 938-1266. Picnic; res. advised. Daily 10-5. IT/Ta

Chateau St. Jean. N via State 12 from Kenwood, E ½ mi. on Goff Rd. (PO Box 293, Kenwood, CA 95452) Tel (707) 833-4134. Daily 10-4:30. GT by appt./Ta

Grand Cru Vineyards. N via State 12 from Sonoma 3½ mi., exit W on Arnold Dr., N on Dunbar Rd., then W on Henno Rd. 1/5 mi., S on private rd. (No. 1 Vintage Ln., Glen Ellen, CA 95442) Tel (707) 996-8100. Sa, Su, holidays 10-4. Tours by appt./Ta

Gundlach-Bundschu. From Sonoma Plaza, E on E. Napa St., N on Old Winery Rd., E on Lovall Valley Rd., E on Thornsberry Rd. (PO Box 1, Vineburg, CA 95487) Tel (707) 938-5277. Sa, Su 10-4:30 or by appt. IT/Ta

Hacienda Wine Cellars. From SE corner of Sonoma Plaza, E on E. Napa St., N on 7th St. E., then Castle Rd. to winery gate, continue on private lane. (1000 Vineyard Ln., Sonoma, CA 95476) Tel (707) 938-2244. Picnic. Daily 9-5. Tours by appt./Ta

Hanzell. (18596 Lomita Ave., Sonoma, CA 95476) Tel (707) 996-3860. Tours by appt. only. No tasting. (Not on map)

Kenwood Vineyards. Opposite Warm Springs Rd. in Kenwood on E side of State 12. (PO Box 447, Kenwood, CA 95452) Tel (707) 833-5891. Picnic, groups must reserve. Daily 9-5. Tours by appt./Ta

Matanzas Creek. From State 12 (Farmers Ln.) in Santa Rosa, S 4 mi. on Bennett Valley Rd. (6097 Bennett Valley Rd., Santa Rosa, CA 95404) Tel (707) 542-8242. Tours by appt.

Sebastiani Vineyards. From NE corner of Sonoma Plaza, E 3 blocks on E. Spain St. to 4th St. E. (389 Fourth St. E., Sonoma, CA 95476) Tel (707) 938-5532. Daily 10-5. GT/Ta

Valley of the Moon. N via State 12 from Sonoma 4 mi., W on Madrone Rd. 3/4 mi. (777 Madrone Rd., Glen Ellen, CA 95442) Tel (707) 996-6941. Daily except Th 10-5. /Ta

Key: GT (guided tour); IT (informal tour); Ta (tasting).

Not incidentally, the name "Jean" is pronounced as in "blue jeans" rather than in the French fashion, because the cellar is named in honor of the wife of one of the trio of owners.

Grand Cru Vineyards exemplifies several aspects of wine in contemporary California.

It is one of several wineries located in old cellars restored to use after decades of vacancy. It is one of several partnerships in which scientists form the leadership, bringing with them extremely sophisticated notions about equipment and techniques. And it is a company that started almost as a weekend hobby, but quickly grew into a good-sized, full-time organization.

Specifically, Grand Cru is located in, on, and alongside the bunkerish old stone and concrete tanks of the Lemoine Winery, which date to 1886. In 1970, the new proprietors erected a battery of stainless steel fermentors right next to the concrete originals, an instructive

sight and, no doubt, a daily source of relief to the cellarmen. The old concrete storage tanks, with doors cut into them, have become surprisingly elegant vaults for the oak tanks and barrels in which Grand Cru wines age.

The mechanically minded will want to have a close look at Grand Cru. To give just one example, the crusher and Willmes pneumatic presses look conventional enough, but are powered by variable-speed hydraulic systems rather than conventional direct-drive electric motors. Other touches are just as refined.

Originally, the tasting room was in an A-frame building perched atop part of the old Lemoine fermentors. In 1979, construction began on a new building set atop the other old concrete works. The new structure is designed to house the tasting room, bottling room, and other storage while the old A-frame becomes offices.

In addition to the tasting room, there are oak-shaded picnic tables in a lawn that looks both straight into the

Size *is a major factor in winery visitor policies. Tiny Hanzell (above) requires appointments; larger Simi (right) has full-time tour guides for vineyard viewing (below) and regular tasting.*

crushing and fermenting area, and out to a vineyard.

Wines produced here include Chenin Blanc, Pinot Noir Blanc, Cabernet Sauvignon, and a specialty, a sweet Gewürztraminer with induced Botrytis. All but the latter may be tasted for a small fee.

Gundlach-Bundschu

Gundlach-Bundschu was a famous winery name in Sonoma's early history. In 1976, its traditional label, still owned by the founding family, re-entered the ranks of the modern-day Sonoma wine community.

Jacob Gundlach and son-in-law Charles Bundschu had a world-wide market for their wines from the 1850s until the 1906 earthquake (and ensuing fire in their San Francisco warehouse), followed by Prohibition, caused them to close their doors. Though the Bundschus went out of the wine business, they retained ownership of their vineyards and orchards in Sonoma.

In 1970, the fifth generation (Jim Bundschu and brother-in-law John Merritt) began rebuilding on one of the original winery sites. In the summer of 1976, they formally re-opened the cellars to the public.

Behind a quarried stone facade, they have filled a building with equipment and cooperage, and have even spilled out beyond the back wall. Just behind the front wall, tall stacks of barrels loom above a small tasting room. Behind the barrels come stainless steel fermentors, the press, a centrifuge, and other processing gear. Beyond these and the rear wall, a cluster of insulated stainless steel storage tanks nestles into an oak grove.

Many of the grapes come from the original vineyards, first planted in 1858. The varietal wines from the old vineyard (and a newer one nearby) include Sonoma Riesling, Gewürztraminer, and Chardonnay in whites; Carbernet Sauvignon, Merlot, and Zinfandel in reds. A particular specialty is a white called Kleinburger, from a little-known German grape variety.

Hacienda Wine Cellars

Hacienda Wine Cellars looks more at home than any of its peers in Sonoma's old Spanish colonial settlement because it is housed in a textbook example of Spanish colonial architecture.

The winery dates from 1973, when it was founded by the same Frank Bartholomew who restored Buena Vista to life in the 1940s. (Though Bartholomew still has a hand in the winery, the principal owner is now the veteran grape grower A. Crawford Cooley.) The building goes back to 1926, having formerly been the community hospital.

Tours of the well-equipped cellars are by appointment only, but the richly furnished tasting room is open daily. At the one end of it, tasters can look through an iron grill to see the barrel aging cellar. The crusher, press, and fermentors are outdoors at the rear; oak tanks and the bottling department are in an added wing next to the fermenting tanks.

Hacienda maintains a spacious picnic lawn next to the winery. Some of its tables are in plain sun, some nestle beneath oaks, but all look downslope to the town of Sonoma and the valley floor.

The winery produces Chardonnay, Gewürztraminer, Pinot Noir Blanc, Cabernet Sauvignon, and Zinfandel, among other vintage-dated varietal wines.

Hanzell Vineyards

Hanzell Vineyards is the property of Barbara De Brye of London. With Bob Sessions as winemaker, Hanzell continues the revolution launched in the late 1950s by founder James D. Zellerbach.

The notion was and is that California can equal some of the great wines of Burgundy. The architectural statement of intent is a facade copied after that part of the Clos de Vougeot that comes into view at the end of the entrance tunnel. Inside the winery the effort becomes more concrete with a cellar full of barrels made from oak harvested in the forest of Limoges and coopered in Beaune.

But Hanzell is not mere copying. The production is so carefully planned that the crusher can handle exactly as many grapes per hour as are required to fill one stainless steel fermentor with must, and so on, through the whole sequence of winemaking.

A visit is both instructive about thoughtful winery design and a sort of pilgrimage to a place where California wine found a new impetus toward a distinctive style. Hanzell is so small that appointments are required and tasting is not possible. Students of vinous California make the journey gladly to see the place and to buy Chardonnay or Pinot Noir when some of the small annual supply is available.

Kenwood Vineyards

Kenwood Vineyards, just off State Highway 12 on the south side of Kenwood, seems at first glance to be a typical country winery. Weathered, whitened, board-and-batten buildings snug into a hillside just a few hundred yards east of the highway, behind a vineyard and amid a shading grove of trees, mainly oaks.

It never was quite typical, though, and in recent years has not been country.

The place was built in 1906 by the Pagani Brothers, John and Julius, who were more than typically thoughtful. One example: the big crusher-stemmer rests in a notch cut into a bank between two roads. The proprietors can dump grapes into the crusher without lifting them very high and let stems mound up below, out of the way of work.

Under the Pagani proprietorship, this was purely a country winery that sold red and white wines, mostly in bulk but also in jugs for the local trade.

In 1970, the premises were purchased by a partnership, most of its members also members of a San Francisco family named Lee. By 1977, they had completed a shift over to varietal wines, nearly all vintage-dated. The old redwood tanks of Pagani days had given way to a collection of temperature-controlled stainless steel fermentors and two cellars full of American and French oak barrels. Presses and other winemaking equipment also are up to the minute. Tours are possible with appointments. Tasting needs no appointment.

The tasting room, in a front corner of the main building, is finished with old wood and decorated with cut-glass windows and watercolors by local artists. Kenwood focuses on Cabernet Sauvignon and Zinfandel, but also has Chardonnay, Chenin Blanc, and Johannisberg Riesling among whites.

Matanzas Creek Winery

Matanzas Creek Winery crushed its first grapes in the harvest of 1978. Technically, it is just far enough into the hills west of the Sonoma Valley to be a part of the Russian River watershed rather than that of Sonoma Creek, but it is closer to the Valley of the Moon than to the larger Russian River area north and west of Santa Rosa.

(Continued on next page)

Vallejo Home

. . . *Continued from page 15*

In any case, the cellar is built into and around a one-time small dairy. The old cold room is now stacked with rows of French oak barrels for the fermenting and aging of Chardonnay, and the aging of several other varietal wines. (This is one of several wineries, both large and small, that have taken to fermenting Chardonnay in barrels rather than in stainless steel.)

Outdoors are the temperature-controlled stainless steel fermentors, crusher, press, and other modern processing gear.

The proprietors, David and Sandra Steiner, cannot offer tours or tasting freely because of zoning restrictions, but do conduct scheduled open houses during the year for mailing list customers.

In addition to Chardonnay, wines on the list include Pinot Blanc, Cabernet Sauvignon, and Pinot Noir.

Sebastiani Vineyards anchors the northeast corner of settled Sonoma, starting at Fourth Street East and Spain Street and fanning out in several directions, but mostly northward toward the sharply rising hills.

The main wood aging cellars, with the tasting room in one corner, are on the east side of Fourth Street, next to a railroad track. In a corner opposite the tasting room, the Sebastiani family has gathered a small crusher, a basket press, and a single 500-gallon oak cask. With this equipment, the first Samuele Sebastiani made his first wine, a Zinfandel, circa 1895. Here is the place to set a perspective for the astonishing changes that have come since then.

From this vantage, orderly rows of varnished, red-hooped redwood tanks extend in an astonishingly long perspective. Behind them is a spanking new fermenting room filled with stainless steel tanks for the white wines. Behind this building, in an open space, are the crushers. Behind them, in a separate building, are the red wine fermentors. Still farther along is an enormous building filled with small oak barrels in which are stored the best of the Sebastiani reds. Across the railroad track from all of this is the largest building of them all: the stainless steel storage cellar where wines that are ready await their turns for bottling.

Samuele no doubt bottled his early wine at any handy bench and table—when he bottled wine at all. Today,

bottling and case storage require yet a fifth building, across Fourth Street from the others.

In spite of the growth, the sizable collection of small barrels stacked outside the main cellar is not there because the Sebastianis ran out of space within, but because they prefer to bake their sherry types with the warmth of the sun.

The tour does not take in all of these points. It would tax the endurance of a Sherpa guide if it did. Rather, it focuses on some of the crucial elements. There is an elevated walkway around the white wine fermentors that gives unobstructable views of the crushers and continuous presses as well as the fermentors. (Visitors in harvest season can tarry as long as they wish to see how wine begins.) In addition, the tour takes in an encyclopedic collection of cooperage in the main cellar.

Samuele Sebastiani died in 1946, leaving a prosperous but generally anonymous business to his son August. Most of the wines had gone into the world under other labels. In the mid-1950s, August started abandoning that role in favor of having the family name on the family product. That trend continues with new help from August's sons, Sam and Don.

A full range of table, appetizer, and dessert wines is on hand in a tasting room handsomely crafted from old wine tanks. Barbera is a signature among reds, as is Green Hungarian among whites. Gamay Beaujolais is another specialty.

Valley of the Moon Winery, an agreeable collection of sturdy wood-frame buildings, perches on the banks of Sonoma Creek.

Enrico Parducci bought the old vineyard property in 1941, and eventually turned over the reins to his son Harry (whose son, in turn, is coming up in the business). The vineyards go back to the 1850s, and were, for a time, owned by Senator George Hearst.

There is no tour of the new-in-1978 stainless steel fermentors, nor of the wood aging cellar with its well-used cargo of redwood uprights, oak ovals, and oak barrels. But there is tasting in a cool, dark room shaded by a huge California bay laurel that also serves as a sort of trademark for the Valley of the Moon label. This winery has long been a source of generic jug wines, but is also becoming a place to find varietal wines, including French Colombard, Semillon, Pinot Noir, and Zinfandel.

Other Than Wineries

On the old Sonoma Plaza and all around it, visitors may consort with the shades of history. Sonoma's mission on the northeast corner of the plaza is but one part of a complex State Historic Monument. The chapel no longer serves a religious purpose but has been preserved in its original state or nearly so. Other rooms in the lengthy adobe building house collections of memorabilia, including Indian arrowheads, civic documents, mission appointments, and photographs of early fire departments. The building is open daily.

Facing the mission across Spain Street and flanking it to the west, several adobe buildings stand as reminders of pueblo days. Some of these now contain antique shops. Others, within the monument, have been restored to demonstrate their original functions.

Several blocks away at Third West and Spain streets the old Vallejo home has been restored and made a state historical museum. Its name, Lachryma Montis, after a spring on the property, also went on the label for the wines Vallejo made in the mid-1800s.

Many rooms in the old Vallejo house, open daily 10 A.M. to 5 P.M., are filled with the belongings of General Mariano Vallejo and family.

Sonoma Plaza becomes truly populous only when the town stages the oldest of the state's vintage festivals. It usually comes the last weekend in September.

The festival puts considerable emphasis on local history. Many Sonomans allow themselves to be conscripted for on-stage or backstage service in a historical pageant or in one of the parades that celebrate the careers of the mission fathers, the Vallejo family, and the Haraszthys.

The wineries themselves play a quiet role. They elaborate on their daily welcome to visitors but do not invade the serenity of history. The effect is startlingly uncommercial.

Nearby is a memento of much more recent history. It is the old Jack London home, now a state park, on a hillcrest west of Glen Ellen. The turn off State Highway 12 is clearly marked.

Back in the town of Sonoma, a narrow-gauge railroad rambles around a meadow just south of the town plaza on State 12. It is the most suitable relief in the area for youngsters who have gone through more wineries than they cared to visit. The privately owned park is called Train Town.

Plotting a Route

Sonoma lies 45 miles north of San Francisco. U.S. Highway 101 across the Golden Gate is the main northward artery. It connects with State Highway 37 just north of Hamilton Air Force Base. That road runs east to an intersection with State Highway 121, which leads north toward the town of Sonoma. There is one more turn, clearly marked, onto State Highway 12, which runs right into the plaza.

The main approach from the north is State 12, which cuts inland from U.S. Highway 101 at Santa Rosa.

Coming from the east on Interstate Highway 80, turn onto State Highway 37 at Vallejo. That road runs directly across the desolate north margin of the bay to its intersection with State Highway 121.

All of these roads carry heavy traffic. U.S. Highway 101 is a freeway. The others are two-lane roads, but straight enough for fairly fast driving.

The Sonoma Valley is connected with other parts of the world by unhurried roads, too. These provide scenic if slightly slow access to the Pacific shore on one side and the Napa Valley on the other. Sonoma's handy central location makes it a logical part of many weekend trips north of San Francisco.

On any day of touring both Sonoma and Napa wineries, the back road from Sonoma through Vineburg to State Highway 12-121 offers not only scenery but the opportunity to pick up fresh honey in Vineburg.

Another alternative is the Trinity-Oakville road between State Highway 12, near Glen Ellen, and State Highway 29 at Oakville on the Napa side. It crosses a

steep-sided set of hills, the Mayacamas Range. In either direction the climb is slow and grinding, and the descent is heavy on the brakes. The rewards are superlative panoramas of both valleys and some pleasing smaller views in between.

The Russian River Valley

Between Geyserville and Forestville, the Russian River suffers a period of extreme indecision before it turns west in its serious and successful bid to reach the Pacific Ocean.

Its meanderings create a whole string of hillsides and benches favorable to the growing of fruit, especially apples and grapes. North of Santa Rosa, fruit growing remains the principal business of an agricultural district of considerable physical charm.

U.S. Highway 101 slices straight up the Russian River Valley, offering a surprisingly pleasant introduction to the charms of the region as its goes. But the truly joyous scenery is reserved for those who dawdle along the two-lane country roads flanking the highway on either side.

Aside from the commercial center of Santa Rosa and the agreeable small towns of Healdsburg, Geyserville, and Cloverdale, back-road driving is what this quiet part of the world has best to offer, especially when it can be coupled with winery touring. Water sport along the Russian River is a bonus.

The Wineries

The Russian River watershed supports a dizzying mixture of wineries, from the gigantic Italian Swiss Colony to the tiny Trentadue.

From the end of Prohibition until the end of the 1960s, this was mainly a region of middle-sized family wineries that sold most or all of their production to bigger firms with well-advertised labels. During the late 1960s, there began a two-pronged shift. One prong was the development of several sizable firms, owned by corporations and attuned to the production and marketing of vintage-dated varietal wines. The other was the increase of small, mostly privately owned cellars dedicated to small-lot winemaking, often of single-vineyard wines. Their arrival caused many of the old-line firms also to turn to vintage-dated varietal wines. With the advent of the newcomers, this has become one of the most visitable of California's wine districts.

The wineries come in a string and three clusters. The string reaches from Windsor to Cloverdale along either side of U.S. Highway 101. The regularly visitable wineries include, from south to north: Landmark, Sonoma Vineyards, Sotoyome, Foppiano, Cambiaso, Simi, Souverain, Trentadue, Geyser Peak, Nervo, Pastori, Italian Swiss Colony, and Rege.

The cluster west of Santa Rosa, in the area of Forestville, includes Davis Bynum, Hop Kiln, Korbel, Mark West, and Russian River. Another cluster, west of U.S. Highway 101, is in or near Dry Creek Valley. Its members include Dry Creek, Lambert Bridge, Mill Creek, Pedroncelli, and Rafanelli. The last cluster is east of the freeway, U.S. Highway 101, in Alexander Valley.

(Continued on next page)

. . . Continued from page 17

The roster includes Alexander Valley Vineyards, Field Stone, Johnson's of Alexander Valley, and Sausal.

As the listing under "More wineries" at the end of this section indicates, a good many more cellars will join these ranks within the next two years.

The alphabetic listing covers a region a shade more than 30 miles long and as much as 15 miles wide.

Alexander Valley Vineyards manages to bring

several major historic themes in California winemaking together into one quietly attractive piece of architecture.

Set at the rear of its sizable block of home vineyard, the cellar building uses adobe block and weathered wood to evoke thoughts of colonial Spain, the Old West, and contemporary California. It was built in 1975.

As for the working winery, it offers a mixture of typical and original ideas to those who take the guided tour. The typical ideas are an outdoor crusher-stemmer and Willmes basket press, and an indoor room full of temperature-controlled stainless steel fermentors. The original ideas are embodied in a lower cellar that is kept cooler and moister than one on the upper level. The lower one is full of French oak for Burgundian varieties, especially Chardonnay, while the upper one is full of American oak for the aging of Cabernet Sauvignon. The notion, as old European hands will recognize, is to duplicate the environment of a *cave* in Beaune on the one hand and a *chai* in Bordeaux on the other.

Tasting of Alexander Valley Vineyards' Chardonnay, Chenin Blanc, Gewürztraminer, Johannisberg Riesling, Cabernet Sauvignon, and Pinot Noir goes on indoors or—not infrequently—outdoors, on a shaded porch overlooking the press and a block of wines. Picnickers may obtain permission to use the outdoor tables.

History buffs may wish to wander up a grassy knoll behind the winery to the family gravesite of Cyrus Alexander, the pioneer for whom the valley is named, and whose sprawling ranch had its homestead on what is now the winery property of Harry Wetzel, Jr., and Harry Wetzel III.

Davis Bynum Winery has evolved a good deal in

getting to its present location in a one-time hop barn above a bend in the Russian River west of Healdsburg.

The property of a former San Francisco newspaperman, Davis Bynum started in 1965, in an ordinary store front on a busy commercial street in the East Bay town of Albany, feinted once in the direction of the Napa Valley, then moved to its current location in 1974.

Bynum's sturdy, white, wood-frame buildings alongside West Side Road house a well-equipped cellar. Visitors are mildly discouraged from taking tours because the old building is not easy to get through, but they are warmly welcomed in the tasting room.

Wines under the Bynum label come mainly from local grapes, but include some from as far away as San Luis Obispo County. The roster of varietals includes Chardonnay, Fumé Blanc, Cabernet Sauvignon, Merlot, Petite Sirah, and Zinfandel.

Cambiaso Vineyards sits near the top of a round

hill in the southeast quarter of Healdsburg at the end of a narrow and twisting lane.

Visitors who remember the place from 1974 or earlier may recall a couple of weathered wood barns and a squat winery covered with corrugated iron, a classic vision of the country jug cellar. It is no longer that.

Today, Cambiaso has a big, ultramodern cellar full of stainless steel fermentors and storage tanks, and an equally modern structure for its bottling line and bottled wine warehouse. The old cellar now holds the redwood tanks, a growing collection of oak tanks and barrels, and a retail sales desk.

The winery dates from 1934, when Giovanni and Maria Cambiaso started making wine in a wooden barn. The great expansion followed the winery's sale to Four Seas Investment Corporation by the second generation of Cambiasos.

The wine list still has jug generics, but emphasis is shifting toward varietals, notably including Chenin Blanc, Sauvignon Blanc, Cabernet Sauvignon, Petite Sirah, and Zinfandel.

Because neither the winding lane nor the sloping site permits many visitors at one time, Cambiaso offers neither tours nor tasting, but only sales.

Dry Creek Vineyards is located, appropriately

enough, in Dry Creek Valley several miles west of Healdsburg.

The winery was founded in 1972. Proprietor David Stare completed the first stage of his handsome concrete block building in time for the harvest of 1973. In 1978, a new wing, set perpendicular to the original building, doubled the size of the cellars.

Although the tasting room is open daily, tours without appointment are chancy, depending on the availability of someone from the small staff. Diligent scholars may wish to make an appointment, for this is an instructive small winery.

Temperature-controlled stainless steel fermentors and other processing gear are along one outside wall of the original building. Inside is the oak barrel aging cellar. The new wing holds stainless steel storage tanks, the bottling line, and stored cases awaiting sale to the retail market. The new wing also holds the tasting room. The whole sequence of the winemaking process can be walked through in a few minutes' worth of touring.

Visitors are also welcome to picnic at tables set on a lawn in the angle formed by the two wings.

Dry Creek wines include Chardonnay, Chenin Blanc, Fumé Blanc, Cabernet Sauvignon, and Zinfandel.

Field Stone Winery is dedicated to efficiency in sev-

eral ways. First, it is built underground in a small hill just west of State Highway 128, toward the southern end of the Alexander Valley. It is not quite a cave: it was set in a trench cut into the earth, and then was covered with soil. Because they are underground, the cellars are naturally stable in temperature.

Second, the place is a veritable study in using every inch of space. For example, the stainless steel fermenting tanks are clustered so tightly together that a cat would have a hard time getting between them. However, the gates and valves are turned in just such a way that the cellarmen can reach five tanks without moving a step.

Finally, the processing winery is set up to handle must that is not only field crushed, but also field pressed.

(Continued on page 23)

Fifteen years of progress *have filled the Alexander Valley with more vines and more than twice as many wineries as in the 1960s. The vineyards (above), planted in 1969, belong to Alexander Valley Vineyards. The new-in-1974 winery (right) is Souverain Cellars.*

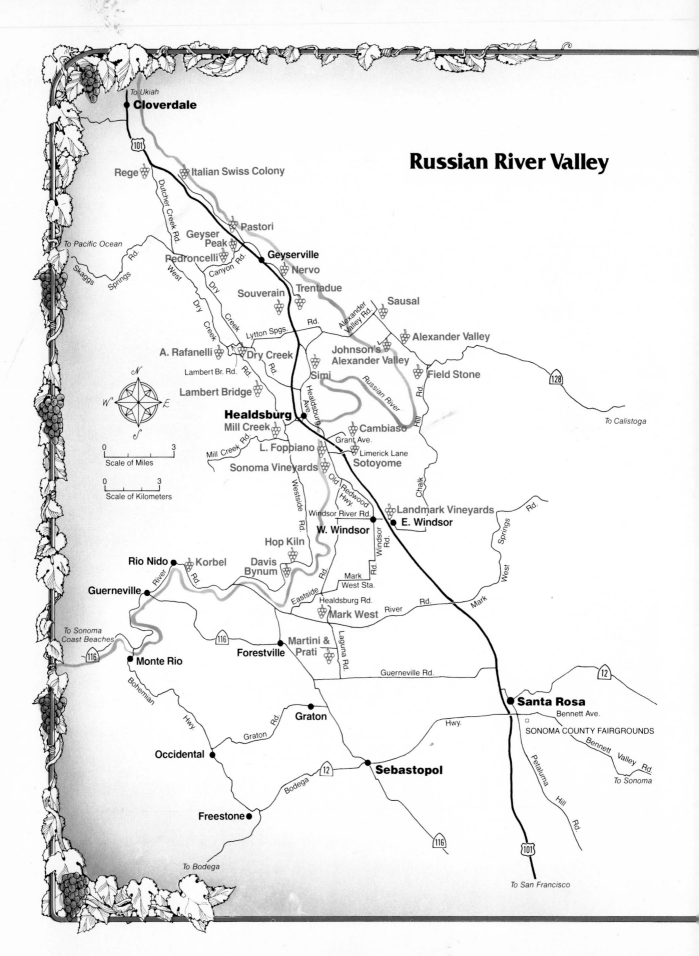

Russian River Valley

To Ukiah

● **Cloverdale**

101

Rege

Italian Swiss Colony

Dutcher Creek Rd.

Pastori

To Pacific Ocean

Geyser Peak

Pedroncelli

● **Geyserville**

Nervo

Skaggs Springs Rd.

West Dry Creek Rd.

Canyon Rd.

Souverain

Trentadue

Sausal

Alexander Valley Rd.

Rd.

Alexander Valley

Dry Creek Rd.

Lytton Spgs. Rd.

A. Rafanelli

Dry Creek

Johnson's Alexander Valley

Russian River

Field Stone

128

To Calistoga

Lambert Br. Rd.

Lambert Bridge

Simi

Hill Rd.

N
W · E
S

Healdsburg Ave.

● **Healdsburg**

Mill Creek

Cambiaso

Chalk

Scale of Miles
0   3

L. Foppiano

Grant Ave.

Limerick Lane

Sotoyome

Mill Creek Rd.

Scale of Kilometers
0   3

Sonoma Vineyards

Old Redwood Hwy.

Landmark Vineyards

Springs Rd.

Westside Rd.

Windsor River Rd.

● **E. Windsor**

W. Windsor

Windsor Rd.

West Springs Rd.

Hop Kiln

Rio Nido ●

Korbel

Davis Bynum

River Rd.

Mark West Sta.

Eastside Rd.

Mark West

Healdsburg Rd.

River Rd.

Mark Rd.

Guerneville ●

To Sonoma Coast Beaches

116

116

● **Monte Rio**

Bohemian Hwy.

116

Martini & Prati

Forestville ●

Laguna Rd.

Guerneville Rd.

● **Santa Rosa**

Bennett Ave.

12

Graton ●

Hwy.

SONOMA COUNTY FAIRGROUNDS

Bennett Valley Rd.

Occidental ●

Graton Rd.

12

● **Sebastopol**

Petaluma Hill Rd.

To Sonoma

Bodega Hwy.

Freestone ●

116

101

To Bodega

To San Francisco

Alexander Valley Vineyards. From intersection of Alexander Valley Rd. with State 128, 2 mi. E then S on State 128 to winery drive, E ¼ mi. to winery. (8644 Hwy. 128, PO Box 175, Healdsburg, CA 95448) Tel (707) 433-6293. Ltd. picnic. M-F 10-5, Sa-Su 12-5. GT/Ta

Davis Bynum Winery. From U.S. 101, Healdsburg Ave. exit, W on Mill St. to Westside Rd., S 8 mi. to winery. (8075 Westside Rd., Healdsburg, CA 95448) Tel (707) 433-5852. Daily 9-5, except in winter weekends only. GT by appt. /Ta

Cambiaso. From U.S. 101, Old Redwood Hwy.-Healdsburg Ave. exit, E ¼ mi. to Grant Ave., E on Grant Ave. to end, continue to end of lane. (1141 Grant Ave., Healdsburg, CA 95448) Tel (707) 433-5508. F-Tu.

Clos du Bois. (Office: 503 D St., San Rafael, CA 94901) Tel (415) 456-7315. (Not on map.)

Dehlinger Winery. (6300 Guerneville Rd., Sebastopol, CA 95472) Tel (707) 823-2378. (Not on map.)

Dry Creek Vineyard. From U.S. 101 W on Dry Creek Rd. 2½ mi., then S on Lambert Bridge Rd. (PO Box T, Healdsburg, CA 95448.) Tel (707) 433-1000. Daily 10-5. IT/Ta

Field Stone Winery. On W side of State 128 .2 mi. N of Chalk Hill Rd. (10075 Hwy. 128, Healdsburg, CA 95448) Tel (707) 433-7266. Picnic. Daily 9-5. GT/Ta

L. Foppiano. From U.S. 101, Old Redwood Hwy. exit, W ½ mi. (12707 Old Redwood Hwy., Healdsburg, CA 95448) Tel (707) 433-1937. Daily 9-5. Tours by appt. /Ta

Geyser Peak. 1 mi. N of Geyserville via U.S. 101, W side of hwy. at Canyon Rd. (Geyserville, CA 95441) Tel (707) 433-6585. Daily 10-5. /Ta

Hop Kiln Winery. From U.S. 101, Healdsburg Ave. exit, W on Mill St., S on Westside Rd. 6 mi. (6050 Westside Rd., Healdsburg, CA 95448.) Tel (707) 433-6491. Weekends & holidays or by appt. 10-5. IT/Ta

Italian Swiss Colony. From U.S. 101, Asti exit, E ¼ mi. (PO Box 1, Asti, CA 95413) Tel (707) 894-2541. Daily 9-6 summer, 9-5 winter. Group picnic by res. GT/Ta

Jade Mountain. (1335 Hiatt Rd., Cloverdale, CA 95425) Tel (707) 894-5579. (Not on map.)

Johnson's Alexander Valley Winery. From intersection of Alexander Valley Rd. with State 128, 1¾ mi. E then S on State 128 to winery drive, W ½ mi. to winery. (8333 Hwy. 128, Healdsburg, CA 95448) Tel (707) 433-2319. Daily 10-5. IT/Ta

Jordan Vineyard and Winery. (PO Box 878, Healdsburg, CA 95448) Tel (707) 433-6955. (Not on map.)

Korbel. From Santa Rosa, 4 mi. N on U.S. 101 to River Rd. exit, then W 14 mi. (Guerneville, CA 95446) Tel (707) 887-2294. Daily. GT (9:45-3:45)/Ta

Lambert Bridge. From U.S. 101, Healdsburg Ave. exit, W on Mill St. to W. Dry Creek Rd., N 3.7 mi. to winery. (4085 W. Dry Creek Rd., Healdsburg, CA 95448) Tel (707) 433-5855. M-Sa 9-4. Tours by appt.

Landmark Vineyards. From U.S. 101, E. Windsor exit to frontage rd., N .3 mi. to winery. (9150 Los Amigos Rd., Windsor, CA 95492) Tel (707) 838-9466. W & F 1-5, Sa-Su 10-5, or by appt. GT/Ta

Lytton Springs Winery. (650 Lytton Spring Rd., Healdsburg, CA 95448) Tel (707) 433-7721. By appt. M-F 8-5. (Not on map.)

Mark West Vineyards. From U.S. 101, River Rd. exit, W 5½ mi. to Trenton-Healdsburg Rd., N .1 mi. to winery. (7000 Trenton-Healdsburg Rd., Forestville, CA 95436) Tel (707) 544-4813. By appt.

Martini & Prati. From Santa Rosa, W on Guerneville Rd. 7 mi., N on Laguna Rd. 1.1 mi. (2191 Laguna Rd., Santa Rosa, CA 95401) Tel (707) 823-2404. M-F 9-4. IT/Ta

Mill Creek Vineyards. From U.S. 101, Healdsburg Ave. exit, W on Mill St./Westside Rd. to winery. (1401 Westside Rd., Healdsburg, CA 95448) Tel (707) 433-5098. M-F 10-4:30. Tours by appt.

Nervo Winery. E side U.S. 101 via Independence Ln. exit, 4 mi. N of Healdsburg. (19585 Old Redwood Hwy. S., Geyserville, CA 95441) Tel (707) 857-3417. Picnic. Daily 10-5. /Ta

Pastori Winery. From U.S. 101, 1 mi. N of Geyserville, Canyon Rd. exit to Asti Rd., then N 1.5 mi. to winery. (23189 Redwood Hwy., Cloverdale, CA 95425) Tel (707) 857-3418. Daily 9-4. /Ta

Pedroncelli. From U.S. 101, 1 mi. N of Geyserville, W on Canyon Rd. 1 mi. to winery. (1220 Canyon Rd., Geyserville, CA 95441) Tel (707) 857-3619. Daily, 10-5. IT/Ta

Preston Winery. (9282 W. Dry Creek Rd., Healdsburg, CA 95448) Tel (707) 433-4748. (Not on map.)

A. Rafanelli Winery. From U.S. 101, W on Dry Creek Rd. 3 mi. to Lambert Bridge Rd., S on Lambert Bridge 1 mi. to W. Dry Creek Rd. (4685 W. Dry Creek Rd., Healdsburg, CA 95448) Tel (707) 433-1385. Case sales by appt.

Rege. From U.S. 101 S of Cloverdale, Dutcher Creek Rd. exit, W on Dutcher Creek Rd. ½ mi. (26700 Dutcher Creek Rd., Cloverdale, CA 95425) Tel (707) 894-2953. Daily 10-5. IT

Sausal Winery. From intersection of Alexander Valley Rd. with State 128, E then S .7 mi. to winery drive, E .1 mi. (7370 Hwy. 128, Healdsburg, CA 95448) Tel (707) 433-2285. Tours by appt. only.

Simi Winery. From U.S. 101, Dry Creek Rd. exit E to Healdsburg Ave., N 1 mi. (PO Box 946, Healdsburg, CA 95448) Tel (707) 433-6981. Picnic. Daily 10-5. GT/Ta

Sonoma Vineyards (Windsor). From U.S. 101, West Windsor exit, W to Old Redwood Hwy., then N 3 mi. to winery. (PO Box 57, Windsor, CA 95492) Tel (707) 433-6511. Daily 10-5. GT/Ta

Sotoyome Winery. From U.S. 101, Healdsburg Ave. exit, S ½ mi. on Old Redwood Hwy. to Limerick Ln. E ½ mi. (641 Limerick Ln., Healdsburg, CA 95448) Tel (707) 433-2001. By appt.

Souverain. 5 mi. N of Healdsburg, W of U.S. 101 via Independence Lane exit. (PO Box 528, Geyserville, CA 95441) Tel (707) 433-6918. Daily 10-4.

Robert Stemmler Winery. (Lambert Bridge Rd., Healdsburg, CA 95448) Tel (707) 433-6334. (Not on map.)

Joseph Swan Vineyards. (2916 Laguna Rd., Forestville, CA 95436) Tel (707) 546-7711. (Not on map.)

Trentadue Winery. 3½ mi. N of Healdsburg, E via Independence Lane exit ½ mi., then E and S on private lane. (19170 Redwood Hwy., Geyserville, CA 95441) Tel (707) 433-3104. Daily 10-5. /Ta

Viña Vista Vineyard. (Office: 2680 Bayshore Frontage Rd., Mountain View, CA 94040) Tel (415) 969-3160. (Not on map.)

Key: GT (guided tour); IT (informal tour); Ta (tasting).

More than a tour *and a taste, wineries offer a variety of agreeable experiences to visitors. A good many cellars have picnic tables. The example above is at Sonoma Vineyards. A few maintain restaurants; the one shown (right) is at Souverain Cellars near Geyserville.*

... Continued from page 18

Nothing is surprising about this, for the principal owner of Field Stone is Wallace Johnson, a pioneer developer of mechanical harvesters some years ago, and the inventor of a field press first used in 1977.

The field-pressed wines include Chenin Blanc, Gewürztraminer, Johannisberg Riesling, Rosé of Cabernet, and Rosé of Petite Sirah. The winery also makes reds in the traditional way. These include Cabernet Sauvignon and Petite Sirah. All are available for tasting in a comfortable, wood-walled room inside the cellar building.

Foppiano Wine Company perches directly alongside the Old Redwood Highway, not far south of its exit from the freeway, U.S. Highway 101, at Healdsburg.

The aged building, plain-faced and wearing a gray brown paint job, houses some surprises. Not least among them is a fermenting room full of stainless steel tanks, which the family moved into place by the simple expedient of removing the roof and lowering them in with cranes. Another new addition is a steadily growing collection of oak barrels. Among the traditional touches are some well-used redwood tanks and a long line of concrete tanks. But even these latter are not what they seem; the interiors have been lined with a glass coat to make them as a clean and neutral as any stainless steel tank.

The Foppianos are a durable presence in the California wine industry. The original Foppiano, John, bought the property in 1896. The first Louis Foppiano took over in 1910. His son, also Louis, re-established the business in 1934, and still directs it with help from his two sons, Louis and Rod.

They began bottling vintage-dated varietals in the late 1960s, after a long career in the bulk and jug wine trades. Production shifted sharply to varietal wines in the 1970s. The roster now includes Chardonnay, Chenin Blanc, Fumé Blanc, Cabernet Sauvignon, Petite Sirah, and Zinfandel.

With the coming of varietals, the winery began to elaborate on its welcome to visitors. A new tasting room and picnic area were under construction in 1979. There was no plan for regular guided tours, but visitors with an appointment may have a look around.

Geyser Peak Winery is one of several Sonoma County wineries that are both old and new.

As an old cellar, it made both bulk wine and wine vinegar under the ownership of the family Bagnani. Veteran drivers of U.S. 101 through Geyserville may recall the stone-and-wood facade of the old winery, which was tucked into a hillside north of town and west of the road. At least they may remember a prominent sign saying that no Geyser Peak wine was for sale because the proprietors drank it all.

As a new cellar, a subsidiary of the Jos. Schlitz Brewing Co., Geyser Peak is slightly less and a great deal more than the old. It is slightly less because the vinegar works is gone. It is a great deal more because the earlier winery now serves only to anchor one wing of a whole complex of new concrete cellars. One holds a vast array of stainless steel fermentors and the processing equipment that goes with them. A second contains an equally vast collection of large stainless steel aging tanks. The old building now contains the wood aging cellar, plus a bottling line. Still more wood cooperage is in a separate cellar east of the highway.

At publication time, tours were essentially limited to groups with appointments. However, all comers are welcome to taste Geyser Peak wines in a handsomely appointed room in the aging cellar—the middle building. The winery also has some picnic tables next to the old cellar building, and some in a grove of trees east of the highway, next to a vineyard. (A pair of hiking trails maintained by Geyser Peak amble through vineyards to the river, and through other vineyards into the hills west of the cellars.)

In summer, Geyser Peak hosts a variety of music troupes in the riverside picnic ground. For information, write Geyser Peak at the address on page 21.

The roster of wines includes Chardonnay, Fumé Blanc, and Gewürztraminer in whites; Cabernet Sauvignon, Pinot Noir, and Zinfandel in reds. A second label, Summit, goes on generic wines.

Hop Kiln Winery occupies the most outrageously dramatic building of any cellar in the whole of Sonoma County. As the name forthrightly states, it was a hop kiln, which is a guarantee of at least one tower, but not necessarily three. Neither is it a guarantee that all three will soar above the general roof line. However, at Hop Kiln, three towers soar almost to the point of improbability.

Hop Kiln belongs to Dr. Martin Griffin (hence the full name, Hop Kiln Winery at Griffin Vineyard), who uses the ground floor as his winery and a sort of mezzanine as the tasting room.

The view out the windows is of vineyards. The view inside is of antique woodworking—cabinets, bar, and more.

The winery itself is very small. A crusher and press are outside the back wall. Inside, there are a few small stainless steel tanks and several racks of oak barrels. To lean on the mezzanine railing is to see the cellars. However, the proprietors will take people downstairs so they can have a look at the old hop drying gear.

The roster of wines includes Gewürztraminer, Johannisberg Riesling, Petite Sirah, and Zinfandel.

Italian Swiss Colony is here, there, and elsewhere about the state, but its public face is at Asti, near the town of Cloverdale.

Andrea Sbarbaro founded Asti in the early 1880s as a communal refuge for Italian Swiss who were out of work and out of money in San Francisco. The communal idea didn't work out, but Sbarbaro reorganized the winery into a private company and persevered. After Prohibition, the winery and label were revived. Over the years since, Italian Swiss has evolved through several forms and now is a subsidiary of the Heublein Corporation.

It must have been hard to get visitors to Asti in Sbarbaro's time. An inveterate practical joker, he rigged the grounds of his mansion with all kinds of gadgets modeled after the ones at Hellbrunn Castle in Austria—which is to say that most of them sprinkled or sprayed their victims with abundant water.

The mansion still is there but defused and, what is more, safely off the tour routes just in case some of the old booby traps escaped demolition. The winery, meanwhile, is one of the prime tourist attractions in all the California wine industry.

(Continued on next page)

... *Continued from page 23*

Italian Swiss (ISC for short) sprawls along U.S. 101 in a little pocket valley just east of the roadway. It is an old winery, exhibiting many souvenirs of its past, but it also has much to show that is new. In sum, it is a good place to see how wine is made on a large scale.

Tours depart from a chalet-style reception building en route to close-up looks at a modern crushing station, an impressive array of big stainless steel fermentors, and an even more impressive collection of big redwood tanks. Included among the latter is the largest one known, an 80,000-gallon piece with enough room inside to sleep a platoon of infantry.

In the tasting room, hosts offer the full wide range of wines, now labeled just "Colony." This winery has explored the production of flavored wines more thoroughly than any other that offers tasting. They include coffee-flavored, citrus-flavored, fruit-flavored, and lightly spiced wines. There are also several each of varietal and generic table, appetizer, and dessert wines of the traditional sorts.

Johnson's Alexander Valley Winery

Johnson's Alexander Valley Winery looks like a good many of the wooden barns that dot the countryside in northern Sonoma County. Vertical wooden siding and a sharply peaked metal roof mark the structure. However, this is another book that is not to be judged by its cover. The crusher and press are modern types, and the fermentors are of temperature-controlled stainless steel.

More suprising, the building is also a sort of unofficial museum and repair shop for pipe organs.

The tasting room is amidships, between the fermentors at one end and the wood aging cellar at the other. In it, visitors may sample Johnson varietal wines daily, the roster including Chenin Blanc, Johannisberg Riesling, Cabernet Sauvignon, Pinot Noir, Zinfandel, and a white wine from pinot noir grapes. Once a month during the cool months, the room doubles as a concert hall for a guest organist. (In the warm months, the monthly concerts move outdoors to a small stage and picnic lawn.) At all times, the room holds a variety of consoles, pipes, and other parts, both of organs that play and organs that are being restored.

The winery and vineyards are owned by three brothers—Jay, Tom, and Will Johnson. Tom makes the wine. Jay is the organ buff.

F. Korbel & Bros.

F. Korbel & Bros. is a famous name, mainly for Champagnes. The winery was founded in 1862 by Francis, Joseph, and Anton Korbel, a trio of diligent brothers from Bohemia. The three of them logged mature redwoods off several hillsides to make room for vineyards. A few of the stumps were too much for them, and these remain today, implacable in the midst of the vine rows. Surviving trees ring the Korbel vineyard blocks near Guerneville.

First the Korbels and then, since 1954, the Heck family have mixed tradition and progress. Much of the basic method used at the winery is little changed from the earliest days of sparkling wine. What has changed has changed only slightly. For example, sediment used to be moved down into the neck of each Champagne bottle by means of hand shaking. Now a machine shakes whole batches of bottles at once, but the result is the same. This is but one of several ingenious devices developed at this winery to retain the old methods in more efficient forms. The tour should be a delight to anyone who has ever taken pleasure in tinkering with machinery, as well as to all who take pleasure in bubbling wine.

During their tenure the Hecks have added table wines to the production at Korbel. Separate cellars hold the barrels and casks in which these wines age.

Crushers and other working gear are at the rear of the winery. Tours stay for the most part inside the brick main building. They start out front at a former Northwestern Pacific Railroad depot, acquired in 1935 for $5 in one of the best deals anyone ever made with a railroad. They end with the tasting of both sparkling and table wines in an elegantly refurbished building that once housed aging brandies.

Lambert Bridge

Lambert Bridge is one of several new California wineries housed in a gracefully proportioned wooden building, but is surely the only one with a huge fireplace at one end of the main aging cellar.

Unstained redwood siding and a shake roof cause the building to blend easily into a site between vines in the foreground and an oak-studded hill in the background. The interior is finished in wood as well, except for the stone fireplace. Overhead illumination is from chandeliers high in the rafters. These cause the cellarmen to curse now and again when they over-fill one of the oak puncheons in the soft shadows, but the effect for visitors is one of fine romance.

Owner Gerard Lambert crushed his first wines in the vintage of 1975. The building was completed in 1976. An expansion is to house the stainless steel fermentors that were in the main cellar with the oak cooperage at the time of publication.

Lambert Bridge, open to visitors only by appointment, concentrates on Chardonnay and Cabernet Sauvignon.

Landmark Vineyards

Landmark Vineyards draws its name from a long double row of old cypress trees that line the entry drive. The winery proper draws its architectural style from the two-story Spanish colonial house at the head of that drive.

The owning William Mabry family launched the business in leased space in 1974, completed the first winery building in 1976, and a second one in 1979. The original building holds stainless steel fermentors and part of the oak cooperage. The newer structure has the rest of the cooperage, a bottling room, and cased goods storage.

Tasting goes on in the old house, which has had its living room turned into a retail sales area and the dining room into a place for tasting. Visitors may also picnic in the old gardens around the house.

Landmark production focuses on Chardonnay, Cabernet Sauvignon, and Pinot Noir. Gewürztraminer and Johannisberg Riesling were to be added to the list.

Lytton Springs Winery

Lytton Springs Winery was founded in 1975 to focus on one wine, Zinfandel, from grapes grown in an old vineyard long-since known as Lytton Springs.

In classic coastal hills north and west of Healdsburg, this cellar is typical in equipment and plain in architecture. For students of Zinfandel, the combination makes for a most appropriate place to visit. An appointment is required since the cellar crew is one man. There are tours in all seasons, and tastings and sales when the small annual production is not sold out.

Mark West Vineyards

Mark West Vineyards perches on the crest of a round knoll, just where the Santa Rosa plain gives way to the westernmost hills of the Coast Ranges. The winery is an L-shaped building with re-sawn redwood siding and a shake roof, appropriate materials for the lightly wooded countryside all around. Vineyards form a skirt around the knoll.

Mark West belongs to airline pilot Bob Ellis and winemaker Joan Ellis, who welcome visitors by appointment.

Stainless steel fermentors, processing gear, and a collection of French oak barrels occupy the longer leg of the structure. An office, lab, bottling line, and retail sales room fill the short leg of the L.

The list of wines includes Gewürztraminer, Johannisberg Riesling, Chardonnay, and Gamay Beaujolais. There is also a proprietary blend, Fondu Blanc.

With time, the new-in-1976 winery will replace some leftover outbuildings from a former dairy ranch with a new fermenting room, a separate storage building for bottled wines, and a more elaborate welcome for visitors.

Martini & Prati

Martini & Prati is a winery of few exterior charms. Wooden and concrete block buildings ramble in all directions across a small knoll planted to grapes. The major physical distinction is a water tower of great height.

Indoors, however, the firm has a vast array of aged redwood tanks, oak oval casks, and all sorts of other cooperage. The effect is pleasant to see.

The winery dates to the 1880s, including a previous ownership, and to 1902 under the Martini side of its present ownership. Its age explains both its external homeliness and its interior attractions.

In Sonoma County this winery was for years second in size only to Italian Swiss Colony, though a very distant second. Recently, newcomers have dropped it several notches down the list, even as it has continued to grow.

Most of the wine made here goes elsewhere in bulk, but wines sold in jug or bottle under the Martini & Prati label cover a range of types. The Zinfandel and Burgundy are much prized by the proprietors. The company also maintains the Fountain Grove label, which came from a once-famous winery in Santa Rosa and which now is reserved for the most prestigious varietals made at Martini & Prati.

Only on weekdays is Martini & Prati open for tasting and for tours of the extensive premises.

Mill Creek Vineyards

Mill Creek Vineyards, just west of Healdsburg, is the property of the Charles Kreck family.

Kreck and his two sons planted their first vineyards in 1965, and began making wine in leased space in 1974. Their own winery saw its first crush in 1976.

The small cellars are open only by appointment because the family is virtually the entire work force, but the Krecks will sell their vintage-dated varietals to casual visitors during business hours on weekdays. The office is on the flat area behind a block of vines at the end of the right-hand fork in the entry road. The winery is built on a bench of the steep hill that looms up behind the vine blocks. Originally built as a hay barn, it is a plain-faced concrete block building. Inside, the cellar is modern and thoughtfully organized. Stainless steel fermentors occupy an upper level, oak barrels a lower one.

The roster of wines includes Chardonnay, a Rosé called Cabernet Blush, Cabernet Sauvignon, Merlot, and Pinot Noir.

Nervo Winery

Nervo Winery is a fine stone barn alongside a frontage road to U.S. 101, near Geyserville. A landmark for years, it lasted two generations as a family business. In 1974, manager Frank Nervo and his family sold the business to the Jos. Schlitz Brewing Co., which earlier had purchased the Geyser Peak Winery a short distance to the north. Since then, Nervo has been maintained as a separate label, and the winery has been kept as an aging cellar and tasting room.

Pastori Winery

Pastori Winery came into being in 1975 as a full-grown business, partly because wine is a tradition in the Pastori family and partly because the proprietor brought with him stocks he had made in earlier vintages as the winemaster of another cellar.

Frank Pastori's father, Constante, launched a winery near Geyserville in 1914. After Prohibition, Frank grew grapes on the family ranch but did not restart the winery. (He did, however, revive the old bond number, 2960, for his new start.) For some years before launching out on his own, he had served as winemaker at the nearby Nervo Winery.

The old Nervo stocks were part of Pastori's initial inventory in his frame and concrete block cellar north of Geyserville.

With both old and new wines at Pastori, the emphasis is on varietal types. Reds, including Cabernet Sauvignon and Zinfandel, lead the list. They are available for tasting in a no-frills tasting and sales room in a front corner of the cellar.

J. Pedroncelli Winery

J. Pedroncelli Winery is a mile into the rolling hills west of Geyserville, on the ridge that separates the Russian River Valley from Dry Creek Valley.

(Continued on next page)

Hop Barn

. . . Continued from page 25

The wood-frame main winery building, behind a finely crafted facade of redwood, dates from 1904, with additions in six separate later years. It is flanked on one side by a masonry building, erected all of a piece, and on the other by another masonry building that arose in three distinct phases.

Because the episodic additions have made the winery a bit difficult to walk through, the Pedroncellis do not mind when visitors forego a tour as a prelude to tasting. People who insist on a tour will find the original wooden building filled mainly with redwood tanks, along with stainless steel fermentors for white wines. The red wine fermentors are outdoors, between the original building and the smaller concrete block one, which holds steel storage tanks. The larger concrete block building holds oak barrels, the bottling room, cased goods, and, not least, the tasting room.

The tasting room is separated from stacked cases of aging wine by a sturdily wrought frame full of French oak barrels. These were brought from Europe in 1967 in time to hold a prized lot of Pinot Noir. Their arrival signaled the Pedroncellis' shift from bulk wines and generics to a focus on vintage-dated varietals.

The Pedroncelli family has owned the property since 1927. They sold grapes until 1934, made wine in that year, and have made it annually since. The founder was John Pedroncelli, Sr. The present proprietors are his sons, John, Jr. and Jim.

Grapes for Pedroncelli wines come primarily from hilly vineyards adjacent to the winery and a mile or so to the west, though the family had to give up one block of vines because they couldn't cultivate it after a particularly sure-footed horse died in 1965. The only livestock on the premises now are dogs that have been reduced to barking at tractors for a living.

The list of Pedroncelli wines includes Chardonnay, Gewürztraminer, and Johannisberg Riesling among whites and Cabernet Sauvignon, Pinot Noir, and Zinfandel among reds. The Pedroncellis also offer wines cheerfully identified as Sonoma White, Sonoma Rosé, and Sonoma Red.

A. Rafanelli Winery comes as close as any spot is likely to get to a perfect vision of the family cellar. A gentle fold in a hillside above West Dry Creek Road cradles a trim red barn. A pasture full of sheep is visible on one side of the barn, a hillside covered in oaks is on the other, and a comfortable white frame house screens out the road on the remaining side. Inside the barn, there is wood panelling in all three of its major rooms—one for fermenting, one for oak aging, and, above stairs, one for bottling and cased goods storage.

Americo Rafanelli built this quiet place for himself and his wife. He makes small lots of Gamay Beaujolais and Zinfandel more to please himself than to be in business, and for this reason sells only in case lots, and only by appointment.

Rege Winery caps a small crest at the Dutcher Creek Road off-ramp from U.S. 101, about halfway between Asti and Cloverdale.

The winery is a squat, gray building surrounded by sheds and odds and ends of winery equipment. It evokes the old era of the country jug winery to perfection. A small crusher and a basket press flank one wall of a cellar which is filled partly with concrete fermentors and partly with redwood tanks. There could be a museum quality about the place except that it obviously is a busy winery.

In any case, the appearances are correct. Rege wines are marketed under the family name, mostly in jugs, and mostly in San Francisco's North Beach, where the Rege business offices are. Such has been the case since the winery's beginning in 1939.

A small frame building next to the cellar houses the tasting and sales room.

Sausal Winery started out purely in the bulk wine business, but, in 1978, began a slow turn toward offering its wines under its own label.

The cellars are housed in an attractive wood-frame building with redwood siding. They contain two long rows of good-sized stainless steel fermentors, similar rows of stainless steel storage tanks, and only a handful of oak tanks and barrels, all in neat order. The ratio of steel to wood is to tighten as planned shifts to bottled wines take place. The first wine released was a Zinfandel. Others, mostly reds, were to follow during 1979. While the pace of change gathers speed, visits are by appointment only.

Although the winery dates only from 1973, the proprietors are long-time grape growers and winery proprietors in the Alexander Valley. Leo Demostene was a partner in the now inactive Soda Rock Winery for years. His two sons and two daughters built Sausal as a tribute to him; they own and operate the winery and family vineyards today.

Simi Winery is yet another Sonoma County cellar that is at once old and new in both its history and its working equipment.

After a long heyday in the era before Prohibition and another one just afterward, the place slid slowly but inexorably downhill through the 1950s and 1960s. At the end of the 1960s, the last of the founding Simi family sold to the Russell Green family. The Greens superintended the new start (having grown grapes in the nearby Alexander Valley as a prelude); they sold the winery in 1974 to Scottish & Newcastle Vintners. In 1976, Schieffelin & Co. of New York purchased the completely refurbished Simi.

The history-conscious Greens had re-equipped the old stone building with a thoughtful mixture of old and new. In the fermenting room, for example, a long row of temperature-controlled stainless steel tanks for white wines lines one wall. Opposite these vessels, open-topped redwood tanks serve as fermentors for the reds, the only new collection of such fermentors in the state in any winery of size. A special deck above them is the most useful place to stand during the harvest season in order to contemplate the real power of yeast. A red wine in full fermentation has a vigor unimagined by anybody who has not had a chance to see how the affair progresses. This is the closest guaranteed vantage.

The rest of an informative tour takes in a modern crusher, two handsome galleries of small oak barrels, and a fine old cellar full of redwood uprights. The oak, for connoisseurs of fine detail, includes both French barrels and air-dried American oak.

Since Simi has the only winery tours in California that cross a fully signaled, grade-level crossing of the Southern Pacific railway, these tours are the only ones

Sherry: variations on the theme

As a word, "Sherry" is not a great deal more precise than, say, "nuts." Both cover a vast ground (and they go well together).

The most noticeable difference from one Sherry to the next is in degree of sweetness. Some relatively dry ones are intended as appetizer drinks. Others, very sweet, come under the dessert category. In California the appetizer Sherries for the most part are labeled "dry" or "cocktail." The dessert types mostly go forth as "Cream Sherry."

Sherry begins being Sherry when the winemaker adds a bit of brandy to a newly fermented dry white wine. The purpose is to stabilize the wine so it will not turn to vinegar when it is exposed to oxidation, the next step.

After this initial step, California winemakers produce their various Sherries in several ways, adding still more distinctions of flavor than sweetness.

Many "bake" it, though the word suggests more heat than they in fact apply. The usual limits are 120° to 140°F/49° to 60°C for 45 to 120 days. Air space is left in the barrel or tank. Heat and air together produce the darkened color and characteristic flavor. Sweeter Sherries are made by blending in a certain amount of Angelica or a similar wine after the base Sherry has been baked. The wine may or may not be aged further after baking.

A variant method is the long aging of partly filled barrels without the unusual warmth. In this instance, oxygen and wood together form the flavor.

A radically different method involves cultivating a specific yeast as a film floating atop aging Sherry in a partially filled barrel or tank. The yeast, "flor," produces a distinctive flavor of its own. The yeast, oxidation, and the wood of the barrels all come together to form the characteristic flavors of this type of Sherry. In the case of flor Sherries, the initial addition of brandy is very slight and is augmented at the end of the aging period.

In California, several wineries use a variant method developed at the University of California. It is called "submerged yeast culture," an unromantic but accurate designation. Instead of a film of yeast being allowed to form and then work very slowly, a yeast is introduced into the wine and episodically agitated so it is present throughout the wine. The method, faster than film flor, produces a characteristic yeast flavor but without the wood flavor associated with film flors.

Whichever of these methods it uses, a winery may establish a "solera." Solera indicates only that a barrel is never emptied of all its wine. Rather, a certain fraction is removed for bottling, then a newer wine is added to the remaining part.

Ol' Sol *can help make Sherry-type wines with its daily warmth on open-air barrels.*

that ever wait for the afternoon freight to roll through. Wait they must, for the tasting room and parking lot are on one side of the track, winery on the other.

Simi's roster of vintage-dated wines includes Chardonnay, Gewürztraminer, and Johannisberg Riesling among whites; Cabernet Sauvignon and Zinfandel among reds; and a Rosé of Cabernet Sauvignon.

In addition to the handsome new tasting room, the winery has installed a kind of country store in an old redwood tank, which had been turned on its side and augmented with conventional rooms in the 1940s to serve as the original tasting room.

The word "Montepulciano" crops up here and there on the premises. It is the name of the home village of the founders, Giuseppe and Pietro Simi, who emigrated from there to Healdsburg in the 1870s.

Sonoma Vineyards is a sort of vinous Topsy, a winery that "just growed."

The company started as a small tasting room and mail-order business under the name of Tiburon Vintners. Headquarters was an old frame house in the Marin County town of Tiburon. A few successful years later, the company acquired an old winery in the Sonoma County town of Windsor, adding the Windsor label to the earlier one. The business was still essentially mail order. In 1973, under the direction of founder Rod Strong, the corporation changed its name to Sonoma Vineyards as it built a substantial new winery and greatly enlarged its vineyard holdings. The Sonoma Vineyards label was added to the earlier two, but this time for regular retail sales.

The headquarters winery, set into one of its vineyards alongside Old Redwood Highway between Windsor and Healdsburg, is a striking combination of a cross and a pyramid, by architect Craig Roland.

The notion was to establish separate work areas radiating from a central processing core. As a result, the fermentors are in one wing, small barrels in another, and so on, around the four arms. Several California wineries are descended from this prototype, which reveals itself to visitors from a dramatic tasting room and view gallery suspended among the great roof beams. There is a tour of this building and an adjacent fermenting and aging cellar of conventional design.

In addition to the tasting room and tour, Sonoma Vineyards has an expansive lawn between two arms of the winery. It can be used for picnicking.

The roster of Sonoma Vineyards wines focuses on vintage-dated varietals, and especially on single vineyard bottlings of Chardonnay, Johannisberg Riesling, Cabernet Sauvignon, and Pinot Noir. The older mail-order labels are available, with emphasis on varietals.

Sotoyome Winery, nestled into a steep slope just south of Healdsburg, is one of the few California cellars that actively defy gravity.

In pre-electric days, most wineries were built so fresh fruit arrived at the high side of a building and bottled wine left by the low side, gravity having done much of the moving in between. The habit persists in most hillside cellars. But here the outdoor crushing and fermenting deck is downhill from the metal building that holds the miscellany of redwood tanks and oak barrels in which proprietor Bill Chaikin's Cabernet Sauvignons, Petite Sirahs, and Zinfandels age.

People interested in small-scale winemaking will find much to engross them in this well-organized and impeccably kept cellar, which dates from 1974. Tours are by appointment only. There is no tasting room for lack of wine to spare.

The name, Sotoyome, comes from a huge Spanish land grant that one-time historian Chaikin is trying to establish as an appellation of origin. His label shows a map of the territory.

Souverain Cellars is patterned on the old hop barns that still dot the north Sonoma countryside. The stark profiles of its twin towers and its sheer size make the building highly visible from U.S. 101 even though it sits deep in a fold in the western hills.

By design this winery lends itself to tours. Elevated walkways run throughout it, allowing clear views of every department from crushers to bottling lines. It is a very substantial winery to see. The stainless steel fermenting tanks outside at the rear of the building are both sizable and numerous. So are the stainless storage tanks inside. However, the most impressive perspectives are from the walkways above long rows of Slovenian oak tanks and both French and American oak barrels.

Tasting goes on in one of several small rooms just above a country inn, incorporated into the winery so visitors can eat at this relatively remote site.

Souverain Cellars has packed a great deal of history into its short existence, an exemplary demonstration of the speed with which life moves in these modern times. The winery was founded in 1972 by Pillsbury Company as a younger sister to Souverain Cellars of the Napa Valley. It was first known as Ville Fontaine. The first crush was at the older Napa winery. By 1973, construction of the Sonoma cellar was advanced enough for wine to be made there, the name having been changed to Chateau Souverain. By the 1974 harvest, the cellar was complete, but shortly after the vintage, Pillsbury again changed the name, this time to Souverain of Alexander Valley. By 1976, the Pillsbury Company had sold both wineries. There is no Souverain at all in the Napa Valley now, and the Sonoma winery has taken the original name under its new owners, a cooperative of grape growers banded together as North Coast Cellars, Inc.

Throughout all of the name changes, the focus at Souverain has remained on vintage-dated varietal wines, especially including Chardonnay, Colombard, Johannisberg Riesling, Cabernet Sauvignon, Petite Sirah, and Zinfandel. The company has released one port-type, made from cabernet sauvignon.

This is another of the wineries that hosts art shows, musical and theatrical events, and even holiday fairs. For information, write the winery at the address shown on page 21.

Trentadue Winery nestles in the middle of its vineyards at the end of a half-mile lane leading east from U.S. 101 between Healdsburg and Geyserville.

Owner Leo Trentadue crushed his first vintage in 1969 and has been expanding slowly since then. By 1972, he had gained enough size to open a tasting room in the upper floor of the concrete building that houses his main aging cellars. Here visitors are welcome to taste Semillon, French Colombard, Sauvignon Vert,

Carignane, Petite Sirah, and other table wines while studying the methods of production visible in the cellars below.

Trentadue sells most of his wine on the spot. He makes only a tiny volume each year, all of it in a time-honored fashion that leans hardly at all on fancy machinery or other sophistications of our technological age.

More wineries. It is a boom time for vineyards and wineries in northern Sonoma County. In addition to wineries listed above, nearly a score more are in the Russian River watershed. Some are bulk producers; some are old-timers in the midst of revitalizing. But most are too new or too small (or both) to welcome visitors on any regular basis. The following roster will help wine buffs who wish to work hard at their studies.

In the plain west of Santa Rosa: Dehlinger Winery is a small cellar dating from 1976. The winery, at the intersection of Guerneville Road and Vine Hill Road, specializes in vintage-dated varietals. Fenton Acres, on West Side Road near Hop Kiln/Griffin, released its first wine, a Chardonnay, in 1978. River Road Winery is on the road of that name near the community of Mirabel Park. It was founded in 1978, with a plan to sell mostly at the winery door. Samperton Winery is on West Side Road; construction was in progress early in 1979, with a first crush planned for the same year. Joseph Swan, near the intersection of Laguna Road with River Road, is the old-timer in the lot. Swan sells all of a very limited production via a mailing list. Such has been the case since the cellar was founded in the late 1960s.

Around Healdsburg: Clos du Bois and River Oaks are the labels of Western Eleven Cellars, a company with substantial vineyards in the region, but only a very small winery west of Healdsburg. The main cellar is to be built, beginning in 1979, just north of town. In the meantime, company headquarters is at 403 D Street in San Rafael; interested students of grapes and wine can make appointments for vineyard tours there. An architecturally impressive addition to the region is a winery called Jordan. Its large cellar, patterned very closely on a great chateau of Bordeaux, is at the crest of a hill above the Russian River just north of Healdsburg. A producer only of Cabernet Sauvignon, Jordan has no visitor facilities at present. Preston Cellars began operations in 1976, in a very small winery west of Healdsburg. The winery produces vintage-dated varietals in tiny lots. The Robert Stemmler Winery, just across Lambert Bridge Road from Dry Creek, is, if anything, a shade smaller than Preston. The first wine, a Chardonnay, appeared on the market in 1978.

At Asti-Cloverdale: Bandiera Winery is being revitalized by members of the founding family after a long period of relative inactivity. The proprietors do sell at retail, although there are no formal hours at the old building near Cloverdale. Jade Mountain, the property of a physician named Douglass Cartwright, was planning to sell its first small lots of wine in 1979. The Mazzoni Winery near Asti has been around since the repeal of Prohibition; its proprietor will sell his jug wines when he has some in stock. As in the case of Bandiera, there are no set hours. Seghesio Winery, a near neighbor to Mazzoni on Chianti Road, is an old-line, family-owned bulk winery in the district. Its

Mendocino County

Cresta Blanca. From U.S. 101 in Ukiah, N. State St. exit, N ½ mi. to winery. (2399 N. State St., Ukiah, CA 95482) Tel (707) 462-0565. Daily 10-5. GT/Ta

Edmeades Vineyards. 3½ mi. N of Philo on State 128. (5500 State 128, Philo, CA 95466) Tel (707) 895-3232. Daily 10-6. /Ta

Fetzer Vineyards. Tasting room on U.S. 101 at Hopland. Daily 9-5. Winery: From U.S. 101 8 mi. N of Ukiah, exit W on Uva, 1 mi. on Uva, then W ½ mi. on Bel Arbres Rd. to winery. (1150 Bel Arbres Rd., Redwood Valley, CA 95470) Tel (707) 485-8998. By appt. only.

Husch Vineyards. 5 mi. N of Philo on State 128. (PO Box 144, Philo, CA 95466) Tel (707) 895-3216. Daily 9-5.

Milano Winery. On U.S. 101 1 mi. S of Hopland. (14594 S. Hwy. 101, Hopland, CA 95449) Tel (707) 744-1360. /Ta

Navarro Vineyards. (PO Box 47, Philo, CA 95466) Tel (707) 895-3686. By appt. only.

Parducci Winery. From U.S. 101, Lake Mendocino exit E to N. State St., N ½ mi. to Parducci Rd., W to winery. (501 Parducci Rd., Ukiah, CA 95482) Tel (707) 462-3828. Daily 9-6 summer, 9-5 winter. GT/Ta

Weibel. 6 mi. N of Ukiah, E side of U.S. 101 near intersection with State 20. (7051 N. State St., Redwood Valley, CA 95470.) Tel (707) 485-0321. Daily 9-6. /Ta

KEY: GT (guided tour); IT (informal tour); Ta (tasting).

Two sides *of the Russian River Valley reveal themselves in these photos. Lambert Bridge Winery (left) is serene in its isolated setting on West Dry Creek Road, while the wine festival held on Healdsburg's town plaza (below) one weekend each May draws crowds of tasters in carnival mood.*

buildings are plainly visible from the freeway. The Seghesios are working toward bottling wine under their own label. Another winery on the same short road is Viña Vista, which has been growing steadily since the late 1960s as a mail-order winery. The business offices are at 2680 Bayshore Frontage Road, Mountain View, CA 94040. Production is principally of vintage-dated varietals.

In addition to these wineries with wines available or soon to be available, Sonoma County still has a few producers who deal only in bulk, and do not permit visits. Some are prominent enough in the landscape to attract attention. These include the Chris Fredson Winery, on Dry Creek Road west of Healdsburg, and the Sonoma Cooperative, at the village of West Windsor. The Frei Brothers Winery is less obvious but no less private than the others. Situated on Dry Creek Road west of Healdsburg, it belongs to E & J Gallo. Two apparent wineries—Sonoma County Cellars in Healdsburg and Soda Rock Winery on Alexander Valley Road—are presently inactive.

Other Than Wineries

The Russian River, in its endless tacking back and forth, is a diverse source of entertainment when wine has had its turn, and certainly the dominant one in an area not rich in parks.

In winter, the Russian River is a big and muddy, fast-flowing stream, its banks populated by steelhead fishermen. In dry summers, it becomes a miles-long series of pools, connected only by the merest of trickles. Between these extremes of its cycle, the river is popular with canoeists and other paddle boaters. For people who do not own boats, two rental firms operate at Healdsburg.

A municipal park, near the bridge south of town, has swimming beaches and picnic sites.

The only other picnic park in the region is on Santa Rosa Avenue, a few blocks south of the city center in Santa Rosa, across the street from a public garden at Luther Burbank's old home. (Though Burbank was a teetotaler, he helped local growers improve grapevines.)

The town of Healdsburg pays wine a direct tribute each year on a weekend in the first half of May. At that time, the town square comes alive with a friendly, low-key wine festival at which tasting of local wines is the main event, though supplemented with music, food, and other celebrations.

Santa Rosa is the commercial hub of the region, offering the widest range of accommodations and restaurants, but both Healdsburg and Cloverdale have modest motels. They and Geyserville add restaurants to the roster of possibilities. For lists, write the Cloverdale Chamber of Commerce, P.O. Box 476, Cloverdale, CA 95425; Healdsburg Chamber of Commerce, 217 Healdsburg Ave., Healdsburg, CA 95448; or Santa Rosa Chamber of Commerce, 637-1st St., Santa Rosa, CA 95404.

Plotting a Route

U.S. 101 is the nearly inevitable means of heading into the Russian River basin from either north or south,

and it is an efficient route through the wine district. However, confirmed shun-pikers can find local routes leading into the region.

State Highway 128 is a particularly engaging road from end to end. It starts at a junction with State Highway 1 on the Mendocino coast at Albion and reaches the freeway, U.S. 101, at Cloverdale. After a short run in company with the freeway, it branches east at Geyserville, looping through the Alexander Valley on its way to Calistoga in the Napa Valley. (It runs east out of the Napa Valley to a terminus at Davis.)

State Highway 12 is another road that passes through several wine districts. For immediate purposes, it connects the town of Sonoma, in the Valley of the Moon, with Santa Rosa, at the edge of the Russian River wine districts. Like State 128, State 12 extends west to connect with State 1 at the mouth of the Russian River and east into the great Central Valley, through Lodi.

Both State 128 and State 12 are two-lane roads, fairly straight and fast most of the time, but sometimes hilly and winding.

Within the district, a whole network of local roads ambles around the west side. Some of the most useful and scenic of these are, from north to south: Dutcher Creek, Dry Creek, West Dry Creek, West Side, and River roads. Each of these meanders, sometimes amid vines, sometimes amid orchards, not infrequently in oak-dotted hill country, but always where there is something to see.

Mendocino County

For years, Mendocino County vineyards struggled along in anonymity as a sort of appendage to Sonoma County's wine industry. Only the Parducci winery retained any local identity, until the beginning of the 1970s brought large acreages of new vines and several new wineries.

Now Mendocino has not only its own identity, but also two districts within it that are recognized independently of each other. The larger, older district is the Ukiah Valley, where Parducci, Cresta Blanca, Fetzer, Milano, and Weibel are active producing cellars. The smaller, newer region is the Anderson Valley, from Boonville west to the coast, where Edmeades, Husch, and Navarro were making wine at publication time.

Because the two districts are almost an hour's drive apart, their wineries are grouped separately.

Ukiah Wineries

Ukiah's wineries are the largest and longest established ones in the county, though two of the five have immigrated to the region only in recent years.

Cresta Blanca Winery holds forth these days in two solid, square-cut buildings just east of U.S. 101.

The buildings, having been designed for humbler purposes (as part of a local growers' cooperative), lack any architectural frills. The equipment, though, is right up to the minute: temperature-controlled stainless steel fermentors, a trailer-mounted centrifuge, and other kindred gear. There is also a traditional cellarful of American oak barrels for aging the reds.

(Continued on next page)

. . . Continued from page 31

In the masonry tasting room building out front, visitors will find a complete range of table, sparkling, and dessert wines. The essentially home-grown ones include French Colombard, Gewürztraminer, Gamay, Petite Sirah, and Zinfandel. Tours, as well as tasting, start here.

Readers of old books about wine may wonder how Cresta Blanca comes to be at the north edge of Ukiah. As a name, Cresta Blanca dates to the late 1800s, when Charles Wetmore founded a winery and made famous wines in the Livermore Valley. After Prohibition, his property was bought by Schenley, which later caused Cresta Blanca to wander all over the state until it ended up as one corner of the Roma wineries in Fresno. When Guild Wineries and Distilleries acquired Roma, it re-established Cresta Blanca as a separate label in this northerly home.

Fetzer Vineyards maintains its public face in an agreeable tasting room and gift shop on the west side of U.S. 101 in downtown Hopland.

Here visitors are welcome daily to taste the longish list of Fetzer varietals, several of them identified as single-vineyard wines. The list includes Chardonnay, Sauvignon Blanc, Semillon, Cabernet Sauvignon, Carignane, Petite Sirah, Pinot Noir, and Zinfandel.

Because the winery is small and is also the home of owner Bernard Fetzer, it is open for tours only by appointment. The cellars were founded in 1968 by one-time lumberman Fetzer, whose background in the forest products business led to a handsome set of wooden winery buildings in an attractive corner of Mendocino County known as Redwood Valley.

The Fetzers maintain 120 acres of vineyards in the favorable parts of a two-mile stretch of canyon leading from the winery westward. The grapes from these vineyards provide many of Fetzer's varietal wines, but the family also buys from other growers in Mendocino and Sonoma Counties. The Fetzer vines go back to 1958.

Milano Winery occupies one of the most picturesque of several old kilns left from the days when the nearby village of Hopland was earning its name by growing and curing hops.

Local growers James Milone and Gregory Graziano had founded their winery in 1977. The weathered wood structure had been refitted completely on one side of a central partition by 1979. Beneath the old kiln tower, the second side was in the process of being remodeled at publication time.

The already-refitted side holds a combined fermenting and aging cellar at ground level and a tasting room, lab, and cased goods storage agea on the upper level.

When the tower side of the building is remodeled, it will hold the barrel aging cellar. The fermentors will move to a deck at the rear. What is now the all-purpose aging cellar will become the bottling room.

In the meantime, the tasting room—a quiet nook with unstained redwood walls—is an agreeable place to taste Milano.

Parducci Wine Cellars, just on the north side of Ukiah, is the patriarch winery in Mendocino County. Founder Adolph Parducci came to Ukiah in 1931, having launched his first winery in Cloverdale, Sonoma County, in 1916.

Three generations of the Parducci family have had a hand in the steady evolution from country winery to the present one, which concerns itself mostly with varietal wines.

The progress can be measured by the steady expansions of family vineyard holdings. In the early 1960s, they owned about 100 acres. In the mid-1960s they doubled that. In 1972 they acquired another 100 acres, give or take a few. The new plantings are principally of chardonnay, chenin blanc, johannisberg riesling, and pinot noir. Their wines join a traditional roster of varietal wines dominated by Cabernet Sauvignon, Petite Sirah, and Zinfandel.

A white masonry building of graceful proportions first comes into view for visitors to Parducci. Built in 1974, it is the bottling and cased wine storage cellar. The older producing winery nestles into a narrow draw 100 yards or so farther up the hill. This is one of the few small wineries in California that insists on aging wines in large redwood or oak tanks, completely excluding small cooperage. The fermentors in the spick-and-span cellar all are stainless steel.

After an informative tour of all departments, visitors are offered the resulting wines for tasting in a romantically traditional tasting room flanking the bottling and storage cellar.

Weibel Vineyards, the long-time producer of sparkling and other wines at Mission San Jose in Alameda County, established a new producing winery and an attractive tasting room north of Ukiah in 1973.

In time the Weibels plan to add barrel-aging cellars to the several banks of steel fermentors. At that point the Mendocino winery will make all Weibel table wines.

Sparkling wines will continue to be made at Mission San Jose. The Ukiah tasting room will be a reminder of them: it resembles a Champagne coupe turned upside-down.

Anderson Valley Wineries

In this old-line apple-growing district, vines and wineries are beginning to be as important as orchards. In 1979, all three of the region's wineries were small, family-owned and operated businesses, all of them flanking State Highway 128 north of the wee village of Philo.

Edmeades Vineyards dates from 1971 as a winery, although its vines were among the first planted in Anderson Valley, in 1963.

The property of Deron Edmeades, the winery proper is housed in a pair of wood-frame buildings—when it is not in the open air. The original structure houses some of the aging cooperage. It perches on stilts on a steep bank just above the highway. A newer oak aging cellar is up on the crest of the same hillock. Between the two are the crusher-stemmer, a Howard basket press, and several jacketed stainless steel fermentors, all protected by a towering redwood and lesser trees.

The tasting room is at the rear corner of the proprietor's residence. It is open daily. Tours of the winery require an appointment, the staff being too small to drop its work without advance notice.

The roster of Edmeades wines includes Chardonnay, Gewürztraminer, and Cabernet Sauvignon. From time to time, it also has a rarity, an Ice Wine from french colombard grapes. (The model is from Germany, where Eiswein—wine from Botrytised grapes harvested at sub-freezing temperatures—is an ancient tradition. For an explanation of Botrytis, see the Chateau St. Jean description on page 12.)

Husch Vineyards was bonded by Tony and Gretchen Husch in 1971, when they made wine on the patio behind their house. By 1974, the business had grown enough for them to build a sturdy winery building just downslope from the house. With one subsequent expansion, it holds a shade more than 10,000 gallons of wine in upright oak tanks and both European and American oak barrels.

The sales room is directly adjacent to the winery, in a one-time granary, its wood still unpainted on the outside, but much remodeled inside. One corner of the building is given over to paintings and drawings by Gretchen Husch. The rest is filled with stacked cases.

There are neither tours nor tasting, but the Husches have two picnic tables available, first-come, first-served. One of them is beneath an improbably lush grape vine trained onto an arbor.

The roster of wines includes Chardonnay, Gewürztraminer, and Pinot Noir from the rolling home vineyard, and Johannisberg Riesling and Cabernet Sauvignon from grapes purchased from nearby growers.

Navarro Vineyards joined the roster of Anderson Valley wineries in 1975. Visitors were to be welcomed daily in a tasting room and retail shop alongside State Highway 128 by mid-summer, 1979, if construction proceeded on schedule.

Looking around the winery requires an appointment. Proprietor Ted Bennett built his small cellars—unpainted wood siding on a wood frame—to match the appearance of an adjacent old barn he had converted earlier into his family residence. The winery also was built to spare some old oaks. The net effect is a visual pleasure—a cluster of tree-shaded, weathered barns on a soft knoll, all impeccably orderly but not groomed.

The sense of order extends into the winery, in which one cellar is devoted to reds (Cabernet Sauvignon and a bit of Pinot Noir), the other to whites (Gewürztraminer, Johannisberg Riesling, and a bit of Chardonnay). The cooperage is European oak divided about equally between puncheons and barrels. Stainless steel fermentors, a Howard basket press, and other modern processing equipment are on a deck at the rear.

Other Than Wineries

Most of the diversions in Mendocino County, other than wineries, are outdoorsy and, above all, watery.

In the Ukiah region, manmade Lake Mendocino fills a sizable bowl in the hills northeast of town. The lake has three recreation areas, two accessible from State Highway 20, the road to Lake County, and the third by way of Lake Mendocino Drive from U.S. Highway 101. The lake offers fishing, boating, and swimming. Its shoreside parks offer an abundance of picnic sites.

In the town of Ukiah, a fine municipal park just west of the main business district amplifies the potential for picnics. Scott Street leads to it from the main business route.

For a list of accommodations and restaurants in the Ukiah area write the Chamber of Commerce, 495 E. Perkins, Ukiah, CA 95482.

The most famous miles of the Mendocino coast begin only a few miles west of the Anderson Valley, running north from the junction of State Highway 128 with State Highway 1. In the other direction along State 128 is Boonville, home of a first-rate county fair each September.

Close to Philo is a small, little-known county picnic park. It is just off State 128, just east of town. The name of the park is Indian Creek. It is clearly signed.

Plotting a Route

The highway network serving Mendocino's winegrowing regions is straightforward, even inexorable.

U.S. Highway 101 burrows straight and fast through the Ukiah Valley, the upstream end of the Russian River watershed. The highway passes close by each of the wineries in the Ukiah region, and also gives close approach to Lake Mendocino. No other direct route leads into the region from either north or south.

State Highway 128 runs the length of the Anderson Valley. It connects with U.S. 101 at Cloverdale in Sonoma County, and with State Highway 1 on the coast near Albion.

Only two other roads come into play. State Highway 253 runs a high, curving course across the Coast Ranges from Ukiah to Boonville. It is the shortest route between the two wine districts of Mendocino County, but its twists and turns forbid speed, and its scenery discourages haste.

State Highway 20 is a winding way to get into the Ukiah Valley from the Sacramento Valley. In spring, it has a glorious profusion of redbud to recommend it.

Lake County

In 1979, Lake County was just getting going as a modern home to wineries. Vineyards have been a part of the landscape around Clear Lake since the nineteenth century. The region once had the famous actress Lily Langtry as a winery owner. However, most of the grapes went elsewhere to be made into wine before Prohibition, and all have done so in recent years. Only with the vintage of 1978 did part of the crop stay at home.

The Lower Lake Winery of Harry and Marjorie Stuermer began operations a mile south of Lower Lake in time for the harvest of 1978. In the spring of 1979, theirs was still the only cellar in the county. It is visitable by appointment only (write PO Box 950, Lower Lake, CA 95457).

Plans called for two more wineries to join Lower Lake in the county within two years. Konocti Cellars, the property of a grower group called Lake County Vintners, was scheduled to build a winery on State Highway 29, a mile north of Kelseyville, during 1979. A second winery was in the planning stage for the Guenoc Ranch in Butts Canyon, probably for 1980. The latter property, incidentally, is Lily Langtry's old vineyard and winery, and the notion is to restore her old house as the visitor facility.

The Napa Valley

A small place synonymous with Wine Country

The "Napa Valley" often is used interchangeably with "The Wine Country," and not without reason. A few more than 60 wineries, most of them handsomely traditional but some handsomely contemporary, are spaced at close intervals all the way from Yountville to Calistoga. Many of their names reach far back into the nineteenth century, and most are entered more often in the cellar books of knowledgeable wine hobbyists than almost any in other parts of California. Further, the cellars in this valley are surrounded by seas of vines, some 24,000 acres of them.

The vineyarded reaches of the Napa Valley may have an occasional peer for beauty in California, but they have no superior. Though the floor of the valley is level and easily negotiable, it never becomes wide enough to lose the imminent sense of tall and consistently rugged hills on either side. Local roads burrow into the heart of the vineyards on both flat and mountainside alike, offering visitors a whole gamut of views to admire.

The near end of the valley is just an hour from San Francisco; the far end is not quite two hours away if one hurries, non-stop. However, it is of the essence *not* to hurry.

The Wineries

An old rule of thumb among veteran visitors to California wineries is this: three cellars a day, no more. If there is any district in California that tempts people to stretch the rule, the Napa Valley is it, because distances between wineries are so short. In spite of the temptation, it is wise to resist.

It is worth noting that most of the many new wineries in the valley are very small indeed, no few of them staffed by a single full-time man. Though the larger cellars are able to offer highly developed tour and tasting programs, the small cellars do not have enough hands to do that. More to the point, they cannot always give an appointment when someone calls for one, simply because the lone hand may have to spend the day delivering wine, or chasing after a replacement part for something that broke, or—the crux of it all—working on the winemaking itself.

There are no internal divisions within Napa in this book because the cellars are so regularly spaced.

Alatera Vineyards is one of the smallest of the new wave of Napa Valley vineyards, and one of the more plain, pending construction of its permanent building.

The original winery is a modular metal structure tucked behind a cottage at one side of a venerable vineyard near the city of Napa.

Visits are by appointment only. The equipment is typical: a small crusher-stemmer, an equally small basket press, steel fermentors, and oak cooperage.

The property of winemaker Bruce Newlan and partners, Alatera was founded in 1977. The first wine released was a Blanc de Pinot Noir.

Beaulieu Vineyard in Rutherford is one of the Napa Valley's more telling demonstrations of the state of international winemaking in modern times.

The crusher-stemmers are Garolla-types, made in Fresno after an Italian design. The presses are Willmes, from Germany. The filters are both Italian and American. The cooperage includes American stainless steel for fermenting, while California redwood and both American and French oak are used for aging.

Touring Beaulieu (pronounced bowl-you, more or less) requires some sense of direction. The oldest part of the building dates (under another name) to 1885. Occasional expansion since then has not imposed any rigid order on the whereabouts of walls or equipment. Still, guides tack back and forth with expert ease and cover all departments from crushing station through small barrel aging to bottling.

Beaulieu was founded as a company in 1900 by a newly arrived Frenchman named Georges deLatour. The winery was continued first by his widow, then by his daughter, who married the eminently Gallic Marquis dePins. The dePins' daughter took a brief part in the management, but in 1969 mother and daughter elected to sell the winery to the Heublein Corporation.

The buildings give some indication of growth. All of the parts painted a cream color date from the 1855 original or the dePins years. The parts left unpainted are additions since Heublein acquired the winery.

Though the whole physical plant is right in downtown Rutherford, Beaulieu spreads its vines over much of the valley.

The resulting wines include Chardonnay, Johannisberg Riesling, Sauvignon Blanc, Cabernet Sauvignon, Gamay Beaujolais, and Pinot Noir. All are vintage dated, as are BV sparkling wines.

They are available for tasting, as selected by the proprietors, in a handsome building at one side of the winery. BV also has a retail outlet in the same building, from which all tours are launched.

Beringer/Los Hermanos Winery dates from a modest migration of Germans into the Napa Valley in the mid-nineteenth century. Architecturally it is German, but not modest.

The winery is fronted by the Rhine House, built by Frederick Beringer as a replica of the Rhenish home he and brother Jacob left behind when they emigrated.

Uphill from the stone and half-timbered house, about level with its steep slate roof, Beringer's aging cellars include a thousand feet of tunnels. The founding brothers employed Chinese laborers to dig the tunnels, start-

By dawn's early light, *pickers in Napa Valley race to take advantage of cool morning air.*

ing in 1876, the winery's inaugural year. In some sections, pick marks still show plainly through a veil of dusty black lichen. Most of the overhead ceiling looks newer. After the caves developed a slight tendency to drop chunks of stone on workers, the proprietors reinforced the weak spots and coated them with gray gunite.

The tunnels are filled with long lines of oak puncheons for aging particular lots of Beringer wines.

The stone building that fronts the tunnels holds a sizable collection of big, upright redwood tanks and several old casks carved by German masters.

Tours take in both tunnels and the lower level of the stone building. They do not go onto the second story of the building, which only holds more puncheons, but, to give proper credit to the craftsmen who built the structure, observe that the upper floor was deck-laid so watertight that it still could be flooded for washing after nearly a century of service.

The enterprise has long since outgrown the tunnels and the old stone building. The third generation of Beringers had expanded the business considerably in the final decades before they sold it in 1969. The current owners—the Nestle corporation and a French family named LaBruyere hold separate segments—have added still more. All crushing and fermenting and some aging now are done across State Highway 29 from the old winery and Rhine House, in a facility dating from 1975. Although the stainless steel fermentors are readily visible, the tour does not encompass that part of the winery. Instead, a film in the visitor center explains the newer facility's role with close-up views.

In the Rhine House, visitors taste selected wines from a list that includes Chardonnay, Fumé Blanc, and Johannisberg Riesling among whites; and Cabernet Sauvignon, Pinot Noir, and Zinfandel among reds. Beringer also offers sherry and port types, and a Malvasia Bianca. There is a second label, Los Hermanos.

Burgess Cellars is well up in the hills east of the Napa Valley floor, in one of the few classic stone and wood-frame wineries still in operation in the county.

When such wineries were built into hillsides in the 1880s, the wooden upper story held the fermentors and other processing gear, while the cooler stone lower levels held the aging cooperage. The idea was that the wine would not be cool during fermentation anyhow.

Matters still are arranged somewhat along the original lines, although the winery has been much modernized in recent years. The fermentors are stainless steel so that the wine can be kept cool if the proprietor wishes, and Burgess has a centrifuge in place of settling tanks or old-style filters. Also, the grapes arrive at the lower level, and must be pumped up to the fermentors, rather than starting at the top.

In addition to the old cellar there are two newer buildings. One dates from the era when Lee Stewart operated the property as Souverain Cellars. The other was built by Burgess after he acquired the property.

A retail sales room is open daily, but there is not enough wine to allow regular tasting, and not enough staff to give tours except by appointment.

Picnic tables beneath trees at one edge of the vineyard are available for use; reserve well ahead.

Cakebread Cellars is being built in the architectural style of a residence at Sea Ranch on the Sonoma Coast: unpainted wood laid vertically over a wood frame, with steeply pitched shake roofing as the cap.

The phrase, "is being built," reflects the not infrequent story of a small, family-owned winery. In this case, the Jack Cakebread family finished one section of its cellars in time for the harvest of 1974. Other sections followed in the next 3 years, then attention turned to a second building, which, in 1979, remained some distance from completion.

The original is now a fermenting and aging cellar devoted exclusively to Chardonnay. It rests on the bank of a 15-foot-deep irrigation pond. Visitors on a sunny afternoon sit on a deck in the shade of the cellar walls and watch ducks paddle about or gaze on Mt. St. Helena while they talk wine (or photography or automobile mechanics, the other two occupations of the multifaceted proprietor). Visitors on wet or windy days can retreat indoors to a comfortable office with the same view. Taking a look at the vineyard requires going outdoors on the opposite, west side of the winery.

The second building, several hundred feet closer to State Highway 29, houses the stainless steel fermentors and French oak barrels for other wines on the roster, Sauvignon Blanc, Cabernet Sauvignon, and Zinfandel being the principals among them. This building also houses the bottling line.

There is no formal tasting at Cakebread Cellars. Visits are by appointment only.

Carneros Creek, founded in 1973, snugs into a hidden fold of the Carneros district south of Napa city, in a small, pleasantly understated structure built in two phases—one wing at a time.

Stainless steel fermentors occupy a roofed shed at the rear; two barrel aging cellars take up the majority of floor space inside the masonry block walls. Visitors are welcomed within a small office and laboratory just inside the main entry.

When work does not demand undivided attention, someone—probably winemaker Francis Mahoney or one of the other owning partners—gladly will stop to talk shop with casual visitors. An appointment assures time to go into detail about the source vineyards or the style of the wines. There is no tasting, for lack of size, but the short list of wines—Chardonnay, Cabernet Sauvignon, Pinot Noir, and Zinfandel—is available for retail sale. Usually there are two of each variety (and sometimes three), because individual vineyards or regions are bottled separately.

Caymus Vineyards straddles Conn Creek, east of Rutherford and more or less at the heart of the huge nineteenth century Spanish land grant from which it draws its name.

Proprietor Charles Wagner is an old hand in the Napa Valley, the second generation of his family to grow grapes on the property. He is also not a man for frills. As a result of both facts, he and his son Chuck have assembled their winery in a trio of plain buildings and equipped it in part with gear that goes back almost as far as the family does. For example, the crusher-stemmer dates from 1909, which makes new parts hard to come by. Similarly, the presses are a pair of baskets with the same kind of hydraulic lifts used for automobile hoists (a device once common, but seldom seen in wineries these days).

(Continued on page 39)

California Wine Chart

Table wines

Varietals
Named for the grapes from which they are made.

White wines
Light, freshly fruity flavors. Most bottlings slightly sweet. Meant for early drinking.
Chenin Blanc
Emerald Riesling
French Colombard
Gewürztraminer
Green Hungarian
Grey Riesling
Sylvaner
White Riesling
   (Johannisberg Riesling)

Full-bodied, flavorful enough to withstand aging in oak. Dry. Many made to age well in bottle.
Chardonnay
   (Pinot Chardonnay)
Dry Chenin Blanc
Pinot Blanc
Dry Semillon
Sauvignon Blanc
   (Fumé Blanc)

Richly fruity. Sweet enough to serve with dessert rather than dinner.
Malvasia Bianca
Muscat of Alexandria
Moscato Canelli
Sweet Semillon
Late Harvest White Riesling

White wines from black grapes. Sometimes dry. Should be white to salmon color but usually pink, slightly sweet, more akin to rosé than to white.
Pinot Noir Blanc
Zinfandel Blanc
Cabernet Sauvignon Blanc
White Barbera

Rosé wines
Light, freshly fruity. Sometimes dry, more often slightly sweet. Meant for early drinking.
Rosé of Cabernet Sauvignon
Gamay Rosé
Grenache Rosé
Grignolino Rosé
Rosé of Pinot Noir
Zinfandel Rosé

Red wines
Fresh, fruity. Dry or just off-dry. Light-bodied, meant for early drinking.

Carnelian
Gamay
Gamay Beaujolais
Grignolino
Pinot St. George
Ruby Cabernet

Full-bodied, with distinctive flavors. Sturdy enough to require oak aging. Aging in bottle improves them.
Barbera
Cabernet Sauvignon
Charbono
Merlot
Petite Sirah
Pinot Noir
Zinfandel

Generics
Named—usually after European wine districts—to hint at style.

White wines
Light, relatively dry. Meant for early drinking.
Chablis
Dry Sauterne
Mountain White

Light, noticeably sweet, but suitable with meals.
Rhine

Medium-sweet to very sweet, meant for dessert rather than dinner.
Haut Sauterne
Light Muscat
Sweet Sauterne
Chateau _____
   (winery name)

Rosé wines
Fruity, slightly sweet to sweet.
Vin Rosé
Rosé

Red wines
Dry or just off-dry. Versatile with meals. Meant for early drinking.
Burgundy
Chianti
Claret
Mountain Red

Full-bodied, noticeably sweet, but suitable with meals.
Barberone
Vino Rosso

Appetizer wines
Made with higher alcohol content than table wines (17 to 20 percent compared to 12 to 13 percent), usually with deliberate oxidized flavors or with added herbal flavors.
Sherry (Cocktail, Dry, Medium-dry)
Vermouth (Dry, Sweet)

Special natural wines: These are appetizer wines flavored with fruit juices or natural essences. Citrus is especially popular as a flavoring. Also used: mint, coffee, chocolate, several herbs. Most carry proprietary names.

Dessert wines
Made with higher alcohol content than table wines, as in the case of appetizer wines, but markedly sweeter.
Angelica
Cream Sherry
Madeira
Marsala
Muscatel
Port (Ruby, Tawny, White)
Tokay

Sparkling wines
Made in a variety of styles, with a range of colors. Meant as versatile accompaniments to appetizers, entrées, desserts.

Champagne (white sparkling wine; subtitled by degree of sweetness)
   Natural—very dry
   Brut—dry
   Extra Dry—hint of sweetness
   Sec—noticeably sweet
   Demi-Sec—very sweet

Blanc de Noir (White champagne from black grapes, usually styled as Brut)

Cremant (Fewer bubbles than regular Champagne, usually sweet)

Sparkling Muscat, Sparkling Malvasia (From muscat grapes, usually sweet)

Pink Champagne (usually sweet)

Sparkling Burgundy, Champagne Rouge (Red sparkling wine, usually off-dry)

PROPRIETARIES: Some wines of each major type are labeled with special names coined by the proprietors of wineries. These proprietary names frequently echo generic place names; the wines parallel generics in range and use.

Napa Valley's *wineries offer a wide variety of architectural styles ranging from Sterling's Moorish look (above) to the romantic appearance of Chateau Chevalier (right).*

. . . Continued from page 36

This is not to say the Wagners turn a blind eye to the present. The four fermentors are made of jacketed and insulated stainless steel. Two of the buildings house thoughtful collections of European and American oak in the forms of barrels, oval casks, and upright tanks. The third structure houses a modern bottling line.

Visits are by appointment only. When wines are available for tasting, it is at an upturned barrel in one of the cellars. (This may change; a small office building was under construction in 1979, with some idea that it would house tastings as well as an office. But the Wagners may cling to their original set-up because they like the informality of it.)

As a winery, Caymus dates from 1972. It was one of the earliest to produce an *Oeil de Perdrix* ("partridge eye" in French) from pinot noir. That wine continues as part of the list along with Chardonnay, Johannisberg Riesling, Sauvignon Blanc, Cabernet Sauvignon, Pinot Noir, and Zinfandel.

Chateau Chevalier revives one of the Napa Valley's more flamboyant bits of nineteenth century winery architecture.

An aggressive businessman named F. Chevalier had erected the towered and turreted stone building on its steep hillside in 1891. He called the place and its wines Chateau Chevalier.

After a long hiatus, the old building became a winery once again in 1973, though on a smaller scale than originally. The upper stories had been transformed into a residence during the property's nonvinous days and now are occupied by the family of owner Greg Bisonnette. Only the lowest cellar holds wine.

The vineyard land was cleared in 1969 and replanted in 1970. Chardonnay, cabernet sauvignon, and johannisberg riesling grapes from these vines are labeled Chateau Chevalier. Wines labeled Mountainside Vineyards are from grapes purchased from independent growers.

Even with the added grapes from other vineyards, production is so small that tasting is at the proprietor's discretion. All who wish to visit, however, are welcome to do so if they call or write ahead for an appointment.

Chateau Montelena is both a new winery and an old one in the Napa Valley.

The finely crafted stone building dates back to the 1800s, when Alfred A. Tubbs had it built on its hilly site north of Calistoga, just where the road to Lake County starts over one shoulder of Mt. St. Helena.

In its present form, dating from 1969, the winery borrows one of the label names from the pre-Prohibition Tubbs days, but otherwise is a modern, efficient example of a small, estatelike property. Within the old stone walls, one half of the main cellar holds stainless steel fermentors; the other half is devoted to row upon row of oak barrels from all over Europe, and one row of ovals from Germany. A flanking room contains the bottling line and bottled wines.

During the long interval between Tubbs's proprietorship and the current one, one owner, named Yort Frank, began to make the property into a showcase Chinese garden. His legacy—a lake with tea houses on islands—makes a serene setting for picnics. It is available only to wine-oriented clubs, which may reserve the grounds for weekend dates. Individual visitors must make appointments to come on weekdays and be content with a strolling tour of winery and grounds. The picnic areas are not open then.

Chateau Montelena has but four wines on its list: Chardonnay and Johannisberg Riesling in whites, and Cabernet Sauvignon and Zinfandel in reds. They can be purchased on the premises, but the supply is too short for regular tasting.

The Christian Brothers began their California winemaking in Martinez shortly before the turn of the century. A bas-relief in the winery office at Mont LaSalle shows one of the brothers at Martinez crushing grapes in a horse trough with a wooden club.

By the time the Christian Brothers packed up to come to the Napa Valley in 1930, the equipment they barged across San Francisco Bay was much improved over the trough and club. Now their winery operations are the largest in Napa, far-flung, and a dazzling mixture of the traditional and the technically advanced.

Headquarters is at Mont LaSalle, west of Napa city and just below the Mayacamas Mountains' ridge tops. In the midst of 200 acres of rolling vineyard, a winery and a novitiate stand side by side against a backdrop of thickly wooded hills. The winery is the older building. A traditional stone barn, it was built in 1903 by Theodore Gier, whose pre-Prohibition Giersberger Rhine was a critical success in its time. The original home of the Brothers in Napa, this winery now serves only as an aging cellar, its two stories filled with both old and new oak. The old uprights on the ground floor were Gier's fermenting tanks at the turn of the century.

The other aging cellar in the valley is a good deal larger than the Gier place. It is the monumental Greystone Cellars at the northern edge of St. Helena. Greystone dates from 1888, when William Bowers Bourn used a small part of his great fortune to build the vast stone building. The Christian Brothers bought the property in 1950 when their stock of aging wines grew too great for Mont LaSalle to hold.

Crushing, fermenting, and bottling are all done at the workaday South St. Helena Winery, its big, ultramodern fermenting installation visible from State Highway 29 but not open to visitors.

There are tours of both Greystone and Mont LaSalle and tasting at both cellars. Greystone has, as a bonus attraction, some of Brother Timothy's seemingly limitless corkscrew collection.

At the two tasting rooms, nearly all of The Christian Brothers' long list of wines is available for sampling. The list includes several estate bottlings from selected vineyards. Of special pride are the Pineau de la Loire and Napa Fumé among whites, and the Pinot St. George among reds. A specialty is a light, sweet Muscat called Chateau LaSalle.

Clos du Val, an altogether new winery at its founding in 1972, comes by its French name honestly, for both the principal owner and winemaker-manager Bernard Portet are French.

The winery building, elegantly proportioned and handsome in an understated, almost plain-faced way, occupies a square cut into one corner of the Chimney Rock Golf Course on the Silverado Trail.

At present it is not organized for visitors beyond retail sales of its only two wines: Cabernet Sauvignon and Zinfandel. A walk through would show two rows of stainless steel fermentors, a double row of small tanks of French oak, and several ranks of European oak barrels, all arranged exactly as a Bordelais winemaker would do it.

Cuvaison houses itself in a deft architectural tribute to the Spanish colonial heritage of California wine, its white-walled, red-tile-roofed cellars distinguished by a long row of graceful arches facing onto the Silverado Trail not far south of the town of Calistoga.

The winery has grown steadily since its founding in 1971, when a since-departed partnership opened it in a building that looked suspiciously like a depression-era hunting camp. The original building—remodeled by later owners to match the main cellar—is now the tasting room.

Visitors are welcome to taste wine four days a week. Cuvaison makes only three wines: Chardonnay, Cabernet Sauvignon, and Zinfandel. Visitors are also welcome to use tree-shaded picnic tables just outside the tasting room.

To tour the winery requires first a group, then an appointment. A walk through will reveal stainless steel fermentors and other modern processing gear in a separate structure to the rear of the Spanish-style building. The latter holds lofty racks of French oak barrels and a modern bottling line.

The name, incidentally, is French for the practice of fermenting red wines with their grape skins.

Domaine Chandon, of all the new wineries in the Napa Valley, is the one that looks newest. It is the first (and so far only) one in the current era of heroic architecture to follow a purely modern style. Barrel vault roofs cover stone, concrete, and glass-walled buildings. The complex flows across one slope of a gentle hill just west of Yountville.

Within the buildings, the story is somewhat different, for this winery was built to make sparkling wines only according to the ancient verities of the *methode champenoise*. There is no arguing the technical truths of the matter. Domaine Chandon is owned by Moët-Hennessey, the French proprietors of Moët et Chandon, and the winemaster in the Napa Valley is the same one as in Epernay. As a result, to see Domaine Chandon is to see sparkling wine made on a scale that the French tend to think of as right, using equipment and techniques favored there.

The main winemaking building has, on its curving upper story, twin rows of horizontal stainless steel fermentors, and on the underground lower story, row upon row upon row of old-fashioned riddling racks. A glass-walled wing of this building holds the yeast culturing room, and all of the bottling and disgorging equipment.

As a counterpoint to the working winery, the parent firm has loaned ancient equipment which is placed here and there about the premises, but mainly in the separate building that houses the visitor center and an elegant French restaurant. The old gear includes pickers' baskets, vineyard cultivation tools, bottles, and more. The single most impressive piece is on the walk leading to the fermenting cellar. It is an ancient wooden press: a horizontal basket with remarkable similarities to modern ones such as Vaslins or Howards.

Well-conducted tours take in all of these details. There is a fee for tasting Domaine Chandon Napa Valley Brut, or Napa Valley Blanc de Noirs.

The restaurant is popular enough that advance reservations are required for lunch or dinner.

Franciscan Vineyards is of a size that makes it highly informative to see. It is small enough that all of its departments fit together into a clear pattern, from freshly arrived grapes to finished wine. But it is big enough so that much of the equipment is kindred to gear at much larger wineries, where patterns of production may not be so clear to see.

In addition, the tour is sign-guided, so visitors may pursue learning at their individual paces. Hosts in the spacious tasting room will amplify on any subjects the signs do not explain to satisfaction.

The main building is a concrete-walled rectangle. Franciscan's substantial collection of stainless steel fermentors stands outside the north wall, in the company of crushers and presses. Stainless steel storage tanks run along the inside of the same wall. Oak cooperage of varying sizes runs through the center of the building, and a substantial bottling line parallels the south side. In other words, grapes come in one side and wine goes out the other.

A redwood building covers the front wall of the cellar. In it, twin tasting bars face each other across a central court. The roster of Franciscan wines focuses on Chardonnay, Johannisberg Riesling, Cabernet Sauvignon, and Zinfandel. It also includes Carnelian Nouveau, a red wine from a hybrid variety developed at the University of California at Davis.

Franciscan is the property of Ray Duncan and winemaker Justin Meyer, who acquired the cellar in 1975. The winery was built in 1973, and changed hands several times before its present proprietors bought it for vineyards they had developed earlier.

Duncan and Meyer also own another cellar, SilverOak, which produces only Cabernet Sauvignon. It is not open to visitors, but the wine is available at Franciscan.

Freemark Abbey, when the firm was founded in 1967, revived an old label and older winery building.

The original label dated from 1939 and endured into the early 1960s. (There was no particular religious affiliation. The name derived from the Free in Charles Freeman, the Mark in Mark Foster, and the Abbey which was a nickname of Albert Ahern—this trio was the original partnership.) Seeing no way to improve on the original name, the partnership of seven new owners applied it to a new generation of wines that includes Chardonnay, Johannisberg Riesling, Cabernet Sauvignon, Pinot Noir, and Petite Sirah. Edelwein is made when conditions are right.

The current owners have been required to improve upon the building in which they launched their winery. After the demise of the original Freemark Abbey, the fine old stone cellars built in the 1880s as the Lombarda Winery had been turned into specialty shops.

The new Freemark Abbey had to crowd itself into the lower story, less than half the original space. In 1973, weary of going everywhere sideways, the partners built a new structure alongside the old one to house the bottling and cased wine storage.

Tours begin in the new building in a room furnished to break an antique collector's heart. They lead first into the original cellars (where stainless steel fermentors and oak barrels are so closely packed that visitors must go single file) and then back to the bottling room in the new building.

There is no tasting of Freemark Abbey wines on the premises, only retail sales.

Grgich-Hills Winery, new in 1977, is yet another of the small California cellars that demonstrate the internationality of winemaking.

Its proprietors are Miljenko Grgich and Austin Hills. Grgich studied formal enology at the University of Zagreb in Yugoslavia before emigrating to the United States to begin a long career in the Napa Valley. (He worked for several wineries before launching his own.) Partner Austin Hill is pure Yankee, a vineyard owner for some years before joining forces with Grgich.

The architecture of their trim building nods to the Spanish colonial heritage of California with white plaster walls, red tile roof, and arched entryway. The equipment includes, among other things, American stainless steel fermentors and French oak barrels.

There are no formal tours at Grgich-Hills. A walk across the parking lot reveals the fermentors and other processing gear under an overhanging roof at the rear. A talk with the host at the sales room in one front corner of the aging cellar reveals whatever else a visitor might care to know.

Production is dominated by Chardonnay and Johannisberg Riesling. Zinfandel rounds out the roster.

Heitz Cellars comes in two parts. The original winery building now is the tasting room and a supplementary aging cellar. It is a small, redwood-faced structure on the St. Helena Highway just south of town. The present producing winery is tucked away east of St. Helena and the Silverado Trail in a small pocket called Spring Valley.

The Heitz family bought the Spring Valley property in 1964, having outgrown the original winery in 3 years. When the Heitzes acquired the second ranch it had not changed a great deal since 1898, when a man named Anton Rossi finished building a stone cellar as the capstone of his development of the place. Happily for the new owners, capable caretakers had occupied the buildings between 1914, when Rossi quit making wine, and the 1964 purchase.

Except for replanting abandoned vineyards and re-equipping the cellar with stainless steel fermentors and a veritable library of oak casks and barrels, the new owners did not change the appearance of the place they bought until 1972, when progress dictated more space for the making and aging of wine.

There are several ways to go about expanding a winery. An old building can be enlarged or torn down for replacement or abandoned for a new site. The Heitzes elected to keep the fine old stone cellar intact and erect a whole new structure near it. The new building is an octagon of textured block, scheduled in due time to be the cellar for red wine, while the original holds whites.

The replanted vineyard, stretching away south to the end of the little valley, is devoted almost entirely to Grignolino, used for red and rosé.

Other Heitz varietal table wines come from selected vineyards throughout the Napa Valley. The roster includes Cabernet Sauvignon, Pinot Noir, and Zinfandel among reds, and Johannisberg Riesling and Pinot Chardonnay among whites.

Regular tasting goes on only at the original winery on St. Helena Highway South, where all of the wines also are available for retail sale. Because the Spring Valley winery buildings are behind the family home, visitors there must acquire an invitation beforehand.

Inglenook Vineyards is located in several buildings but for visitors, all of the action is in the stately original cellar at Rutherford.

Built in the 1880s, the stone-walled building looks very much the way romanticists think wineries should. The front wall has a long row of arched doors and another of arched windows. Several cupolas and other frills serve as relief from the ordinariness of mere roof. Boston ivy, which turns flame red in the fall, covers the blank spots.

Inside, six parallel tunnels contain row upon row of 1,000-gallon oak oval casks. Most of the casks came from the Spesart Mountains in Germany in the last decades of the 19th century and show very nearly flawless craftsmanship. Ordinary cask heads begin to buckle after a certain time; these still follow the curves formed by their German coopers. The wood has blackened with age but not bowed.

The tasting room offers a broad sampling of selected wines each day. It is inside the main door of the original building. Tours also start here.

In its early days all of Inglenook was under the one roof. Now a new aging cellar big enough to house a dirigible faces the original across a courtyard; it is filled with towering racks of oak barrels. Fermenting and some aging takes place in two other buildings at the intersection of State 29 and Oakville Cross.

The Inglenook label covers three separate lines of wine. The Napa Valley varietals are presented under the premier label, and include Chardonnay, Johannisberg Riesling, Gewürztraminer, Cabernet Sauvignon, Pinot Noir, and Zinfandel. A secondary line of North Coast varietal and generic table wines appears under the Inglenook Vintage label. The Inglenook Navalle wines come mainly from San Joaquin Valley sources.

The evolutions have come in stages. The founding family revived Inglenook after Prohibition under the proprietorship of John Daniel. Daniel ran Inglenook in the original manner until he sold it in 1964, when United Vintners bought it and launched some expansion. Heublein acquired control of United Vintners in 1969, and has made even more substantial additions to the original property.

Robert Keenan Winery is a spanking new cellar within a set of old stone walls. The walls were put there in 1904, according to a keystone over one arched doorway. According to the keystone over the other arch, their builder was Pietro Conradi.

Robert Keenan bought the long-idle property in 1974, and set about transforming it from a standard stone barn into an architecturally elegant modern winery. The revamped building has a centrally supported red tile roof and some redwood gables as its most visible new elements. Several compatible touches are to be seen within.

The equipment is typical of contemporary small cellars in this part of the world: a Howard basket press, stainless steel fermentors, and, for aging the wines, French oak barrels.

All of this tucks into a serene fold on one flank of Spring Mountain. There are but two wines, Chardonnay and Cabernet Sauvignon.

There is no tasting and sales are by the case only. The one-man staff requires an appointment for tours.

Hanns Kornell Champagne Cellars on Lark-mead Lane at the north end of the Napa Valley is devoted almost entirely to sparkling wines.

The old two-story, tree-shaded building started as Larkmead winery early in Napa's vinous history. Other buildings in the complex were added by interim owners, including United Vintners. Hanns Kornell bought the property in 1958. With only a tiny head start from 6 years in a leased winery in Sonoma, Kornell in the next decade built an inventory of a million and a half bottles of aging Champagne. Since 1968, he has augmented that total only slightly.

His is a remarkable one-man achievement. Kornell fled Germany in 1939 and followed a path set by earlier German liberals and political exiles (including winemaker Charles Krug several decades before). Kornell landed in New York broke, worked his way west, in time got work as a maker of sparkling wine, and finally started producing his own Champagne in 1952.

The Larkmead property provides a textbook picture of Champagne-making. A guide (sometimes the owner himself, sometimes one of his children) starts visitors out with the new cuvée wine and goes step by step from there. The visitor can peer at the yeast deposit in a still-fermenting bottle, jostle wine in riddling racks, and in general stay within arm's reach of the evolution of a traditional, bottle-fermented sparkling wine.

There is a tasting room in the small frame office building to the rear of the winery. Visitors are always welcome to taste some of Kornell's authentically bottle-fermented sparkling wines. The types include Sehr Trocken, Brut, Extra Dry, Demi-Sec, Rosé, Champagne Rouge, and sparkling Muscat Alexandria.

Charles Krug, in a shady grove of tall oaks, presents a classic picture of an old Napa estate winery.

Charles Krug, the man, founded his winery in 1861. He built one massive stone building to keep his wines and another to keep his horses—both at 59°F/15°C.

Krug died in 1892, leaving two daughters to carry on. They continued, with help from a cousin, until Prohibition, when the winery closed. It remained in the hands of a caretaker-owner until Cesare Mondavi bought the property in 1943. Since his death in 1959, the winery has remained in his family's hands. His son, Peter, is now president.

Various aspects of the Krug ranch have changed over the years, but the two stone buildings remain and are the core of the present winery. The old winery building continues in its original role. The one-time coach house at present holds small cooperage for aging select wines. In addition, the Mondavis have erected a pair of large buildings to hold more oak barrels and the bottling part of the operation. Small frame buildings house the winemaker's lab, the offices, and, most important to visitors, the tasting room.

A spacious lawn outside the coach house serves a variety of uses. Favorite customers and friends are invited to a series of tastings on the lawn on summer Sundays. The August Moon Concerts combine first-rate chamber music with wine tasting (see page 71).

No matter how busy the day, Krug never requires reservations for its ably led and unusually complete winery tour. During the harvest the fermentors are out of bounds. Otherwise, visitors get to see every department, in which a fine balance exists between old and new. The red wine fermentors, for example, are upright, open-topped redwood tanks. Very few are left in California. They contrast with long rows of glass-lined steel tanks in which Krug wines wait from the time they have had enough wood aging until their turn comes up on the bottling schedule.

The redwood fermentors are scheduled to disappear one day in favor of stainless steel. In the meantime, they are a picturesque reminder of what was the norm.

The tasting room offers a selection of three or four wines on any one day; they come from a complete range of varietal table wines. The list includes Chenin Blanc, Gewürztraminer, Chardonnay, Johannisberg Riesling, Zinfandel, Cabernet Sauvignon, and Pinot Noir. Most are vintage dated. There are among the reds some special selections (not opened for tasting) with extra age. Krug also has generic table wines and Sherries and Port under the main label. The Mondavis also offer table wines under their secondary label, CK.

Markham Winery is another of Napa's new starts in an old place. In this case, the new start is by advertising executive Bruce Markham, who bought the first of his three vineyards in the valley in 1976.

Then, in 1978, Markham bought a winery to have a home for his grapes. The old place was known locally as The Little Co-op. Regular visitors to the valley may remember it as a plain building hidden by four large steel tanks at State 29 and Deer Park Lane.

Markham's first moves included removal of those four tanks to the rear of the cellars, which showed the 1876 stone-front building to be less plain than one might have thought.

In the early years of his ownership, Markham is using only half of the winery for his own production. Oddly, the building is divided into four long, narrow segments, and the new winery is using the first for its stainless steel fermentors and the third for its French oak cellar and a new bottling room. (The second and fourth contain large redwood tanks leased to other wineries for bulk storage.)

A tasting room was in the planning stages in 1979. Pending its completion, touring is by appointment. The first Markham wines were scheduled for release in mid-1979. The roster includes Chenin Blanc, Johannisberg Riesling, Muscat de Frontignan, Gamay Beaujolais, and Merlot.

Louis M. Martini dates only from 1934 as a winery and yet is honored as one of the old-school labels in the Napa Valley. Family continuity is the key.

The founder, the late Louis M. Martini, began his career as a California winemaker in 1906 in Guasti and

(Continued on page 47)

Different lessons *come at different places. Domaine Chandon (above) is a source of information about fermented-in-the-bottle sparkling wines, while Beaulieu Vineyard (left and below) offers a look at its famed Cabernet Sauvignon and other reds.*

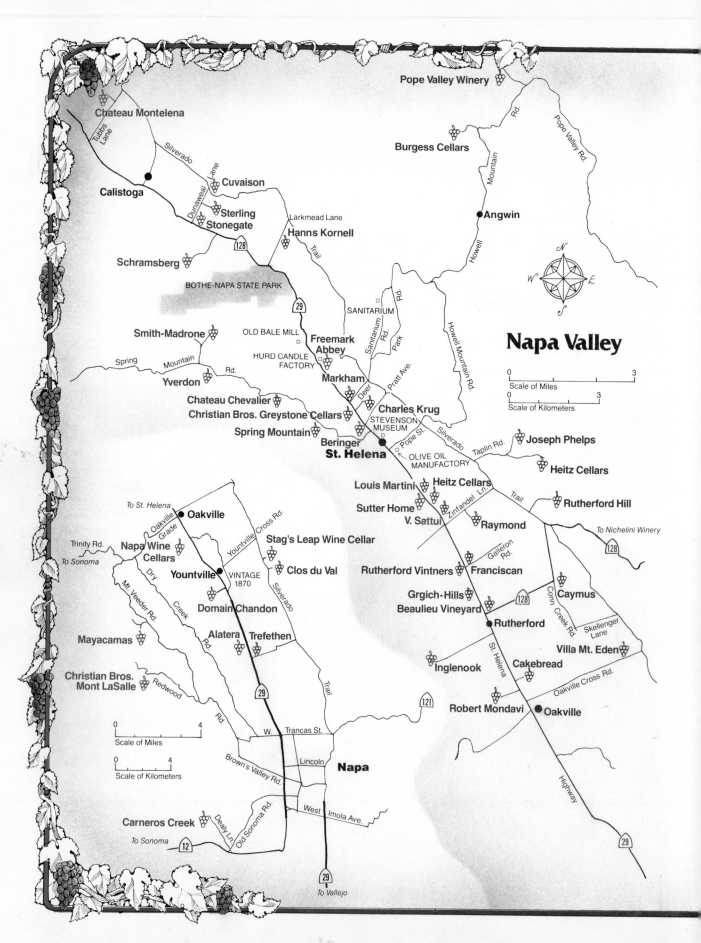

Napa Valley

Pope Valley Winery

Chateau Montelena

Burgess Cellars

Cuvaison

Calistoga

Angwin

Sterling
Stonegate

Larkmead Lane

Hanns Kornell

Schramsberg

BOTHE-NAPA STATE PARK

SANITARIUM

Smith-Madrone

OLD BALE MILL

Freemark
Abbey

HURD CANDLE
FACTORY

Yverdon

Markham

Spring   Mountain   Rd.

Chateau Chevalier

Charles Krug

Christian Bros. Greystone Cellars

STEVENSON
MUSEUM

Joseph Phelps

Spring Mountain

Beringer

Heitz Cellars

St. Helena

OLIVE OIL
MANUFACTORY

Louis Martini

Heitz Cellars

Rutherford Hill

Sutter Home

V. Sattui

Raymond

To Nichelini Winery

To St. Helena

Oakville

Rutherford Vintners

Franciscan

Caymus

Stag's Leap Wine Cellar

Trinity Rd.

Napa Wine
Cellars

Grgich-Hills

To Sonoma

Clos du Val

Beaulieu Vineyard

Rutherford

Yountville

VINTAGE
1870

Villa Mt. Eden

Mayacamas

Domain Chandon

Cakebread

Alatera

Trefethen

Inglenook

Christian Bros.
Mont LaSalle

Robert Mondavi

Oakville

Carneros Creek

To Sonoma

W.   Trancas St.

Lincoln

Napa

Brown's Valley Rd.

West   Imola Ave.

To Vallejo

Scale of Miles

Scale of Kilometers

Alatera Vineyards. On State 29 frontage road at Darms Lane 3½ mi. N of Napa. (5527 Hwy 29, Napa, CA 94558) Tel (707) 944-2914. By appt.

Beaulieu Vineyard. E side State 29 at Rutherford. (Rutherford, CA 94573) Tel (707) 963-2411. Daily 10-4. GT/Ta

Beringer/Los Hermanos. W side State 29, N limit of St. Helena. (2000 Main St., St. Helena, CA 94574) Tel (707) 963-7115. Daily 9-4:45 (last tour 3:45). Groups by appt. GT/Ta

Burgess Cellars. From State 29, 1½ mi. N of St. Helena, E 3 mi. on Deer Park Rd. Private drive on N side of rd. (PO Box 282, St. Helena, CA 94574) Tel (707) 963-4766. Sales daily 10-4. GT by appt.

Cakebread Cellars. Midway between Oakville and Rutherford on State 29. (PO Box 216, Rutherford, CA 95473) Tel (707) 963-9182. By appt.

Carneros Creek. From State 12/21 S of Napa, W on Old Sonoma Rd. to Dealy Lane, W 1 mi. (1285 Dealy Ln., Napa, CA 94558) Tel (707) 226-3279. Tours by appt.

Caymus Vineyards. 1½ mi. E of Rutherford at junction of State 128, Conn Creek Rd. (8700 Conn Creek Rd., Rutherford, CA 94573) Tel (707) 963-4204. Sales M-F 10-4. GT/Ta by appt.

Chateau Chevalier. From State 29 on N side of St. Helena, W 3 blocks on Madrone Ave., W 2 mi. on Spring Mtn. Rd. to winery on S side of road. (3101 Spring Mtn. Rd., St. Helena, CA 94574) Tel (707) 963-2342. Tours by appt.

Chateau Montelena. N of Calistoga, take Tubbs Lane to private drive, ¼ mi. to winery. (1429 Tubbs Ln., Calistoga, CA 94515) Tel (707) 942-5105. Sales daily 10-4. Tours by appt.

The Christian Brothers. Mont LaSalle: From State 29 at Napa, W on Redwood Rd. 7 mi. (PO Box 420, Napa, CA 94558) Tel (707) 226-5566. Daily 10:30-4, GT/Ta. Greystone Cellar: W side of State 29, N limit of St. Helena. Tel (707) 963-2719. Daily 10:30-4. GT/Ta

Clos du Val. From Yountville Cross Rd., S on Silverado Trail 3 mi., E on private rd. (5330 Silverado Trail, Napa, CA 94558) Tel (707) 252-6711. Tours by appt.

Cuvaison. Just S of Dunaweal Lane, E side of Silverado Trail. (4550 Silverado Trail, Calistoga, CA 94515) Tel (707) 942-6266. Ltd. picnic. Th-M 10-4. Tours by appt./Ta

Domaine Chandon. Exit State 29 at Yountville, W on California Dr. to winery drive. (PO Box 2470, Yountville, CA 94599) Tel (707) 944-8844. W-Su 11-6 (last tour 5:30). GT/fee Ta

Franciscan Vineyards. E side State 29, 1½ mi. S of St. Helena at Galleron Rd. (PO Box 407, Rutherford, CA 94573) Tel (707) 963-7111. Daily 10-5. IT/Ta

Freemark Abbey. E side State 29, 2 mi. N of St. Helena. (PO Box 410, St. Helena, CA 94574) Tel (707) 963-7106. Daily 11-5. GT (M-F, 11 & 2; Sa, Su, 1:30 and 3:30)

Grgich-Hills. ½ mi. N of Rutherford on State 29. (PO Box 450, Rutherford, CA 94573) Tel (707) 963-2784. Sales daily 10-4. IT.

Heitz Cellars. Tasting room E side State 29, ½ mi. S of St. Helena. (436 St. Helena Hwy. S., St. Helena, CA 94574) Daily 11-4:30. /Ta. Winery: 500 Taplin Rd., St. Helena, CA 94574. By appt.

Inglenook. W side State 29 at Rutherford (on private lane). (Rutherford, CA 94573) Tel (707) 963-7184. Daily 10-5. Ltd. picnic by res. GT/Ta

Hanns Kornell. From State 29, 5.9 mi. N of St. Helena, E ¼ mi. on Larkmead Ln. (PO Box 249, St. Helena, CA 94574) Tel (707) 963-2334. Daily 10-4. GT/Ta

Charles Krug. E side of State 29, N limit of St. Helena. (PO Box 191, St. Helena, CA 94574) Tel (707) 963-2761. Daily 10-4. GT/Ta

Markham Winery. On State 29 at intersection with Deer Park Rd. 1 mi. N of St. Helena. (2812 St. Helena Hwy. No., St. Helena, CA 94574) Tel (707) 963-9577. GT by appt.

Louis M. Martini. E side State 29, ½ mi. S of St. Helena. (PO Box 112, St. Helena, CA 94574) Tel (707) 963-2736. Daily 10-4, GT/Ta

Mayacamas. From State 29 at Napa, W on Redwood Rd.-Mt. Veeder Rd. 8 mi. to Lokoya Rd., W to pvt. winery rd. (1155 Lokoya Rd., Napa, CA 94558) Tel (707) 224-4030. Tours by appt.

Robert Mondavi. W side State 29 at N limit of Oakville. (7801 St. Helena Hwy., Oakville, CA 94562) Tel (707) 963-9611. Daily 10-4:30. GT/Ta

Napa Wine Cellars. 2 mi. N of Yountville on State 29. (7481 St. Helena Hwy., Oakville, CA 94562) No telephone. Daily 11-5. IT/Ta

Nichelini. From State 29 at Rutherford, E 11 mi. on State 128. (2349 Lower Chiles Rd., St. Helena, CA 94574) Tel (707) 963-3357. Ltd. picnic. Sa, Su, holidays 10-6. /Ta (Outside map.)

Joseph Phelps. From Silverado Trail ½ mi. N of Zinfandel Ln., E on Taplin Rd. ½ mi., then N on private rd. (200 Taplin Rd., St. Helena, CA 94574) Tel (707) 963-2745. GT by appt. M-Sa.

Pope Valley. From State 29, E 11 mi. on Deer Pk.-Howell Mt. Rd., left 2 mi. on Pope Valley Rd. (6613 Pope Valley Rd., Pope Valley, CA 94567) Tel (707) 965-2192. Picnic. M-F 12-5; Sa, Su 9-6. /Ta

Raymond Vineyard and Cellar. From State 29 2 mi. S of St. Helena, E on Zinfandel Ln. ½ mi. to winery drive. (849 Zinfandel Ln., St. Helena, CA 94574) Tel (707) 963-3141. Tours by appt. M-Sa.

Rutherford Hill. From intersection of State 128 and Silverado Trail, N ¼ mi. on trail to Souverain Rd., E to winery. (PO Box 410, St. Helena, CA 94574) Tel (707) 963-9674. GT/Ta second Saturday of each month.

Rutherford Vintners. On State 29 1 mi. N of Rutherford. (PO Box 238, Rutherford, CA 94573) Tel (707) 963-4117. Daily 10-4:30. GT by appt./Ta

V. Sattui. E side of State 29, 1½ mi. S of St. Helena at White Lane. (St. Helena Hwy. S., St. Helena, CA 94574) Tel (707) 963-7774. Picnic. June-Oct. Daily 10-6; Nov.-May W-M, 10-5:30. /Ta

Schramsberg. From State 29, 6 mi. N of St. Helena, W off hwy. on pvt. rd. (Calistoga, CA 94515) Tel (707) 942-4558. Tours by appt. M-Sa.

Smith-Madrone Vineyards. From St. Helena, W via Spring Mountain Rd. to Sonoma Cty. line; N on private road. (4022 Spring Mountain Rd., St. Helena, CA 94574) Tel (707) 963-2283. Tours by appt.

Spring Mountain Vineyards. From State 29 on N side of St. Helena, W 3 blocks on Madrone Ave., N ½ mi. to pvt. rd. (2805 Spring Mtn. Rd., St. Helena, CA 94574) Tel (707) 963-4341. Tours by appt.

Stag's Leap Wine Cellars. From Yountville Cross Rd. S on Silverado Trail 2.2 mi. E side of hwy. (5766 Silverado Trail, Napa, CA 94558) Tel (707) 944-2020. Tours by appt.

Sterling Vineyards. From State 29, 7 mi. N of St. Helena, E ½ mi. on Dunaweal, S to parking lot. (1111 Dunaweal Ln., Calistoga, CA 94515) Tel (707) 942-5151. Daily 10:30-4:30 (except closed M-T Nov. 1-Apr. 30). IT/Ta

Stonegate. From State 29, 7 mi. N of St. Helena, E ⅛ mi. on Dunaweal, S side of rd. (1183 Dunaweal Ln., Calistoga, CA 94515) Tel (707) 942-6500.

Sutter Home. W side State 29 ½ mi. S of St. Helena. (PO Box 248, St. Helena, CA 94574) Tel (707) 963-3104. Daily 9:30-5. /Ta

Trefethen Vineyards. From Napa, N 3 mi. on State 29 to Oak Knoll Ave., E .4 mi. to winery drive. (1160 Oak Knoll Dr., Napa, CA 94558) Tel (707) 255-7700. Tours by appt.

Villa Mt. Eden. N side Oakville Cross Rd. near Silverado Trail. (Mt. Eden Ranch, Oakville, CA 94562) Tel (707) 944-8431. Weekdays by appt.

Yverdon Vineyards. From St. Helena, W 4 mi. on Spring Mountain Rd. to winery drive. (3787 Spring Mountain Rd., St. Helena, CA 94574) Tel (707) 963-4270. Sales M-F 8-3:30. Tours by appt.

(Winery listings continued on page 46)

KEY: GT (guided tour); IT (informal tour); Ta (tasting).

. . . Continued from page 45

Wineries Not on Napa Map—Restricted Visitor Facilities

Beckett Cellars. 1055 Atlas Peak Rd., Napa, CA 94558. Tel (707) 224-2022.

Buehler Vineyards. 820 Greenfield Rd., St. Helena, CA 94574.

Cassayre-Forni. 531 Jefferson St., Napa, CA 94558. Tel (707) 255-0909.

Chappellet Winery. 1581 Sage Canyon Rd., St. Helena, CA 94574. Tel (707) 963-7136.

Conn Creek Vineyard. PO Box 987, St. Helena, CA 94574. Tel (707) 963-9100.

Diamond Creek. 1500 Diamond Mountain Rd., Calistoga, CA 94515. Tel (707) 942-6926.

J. Heminway (Green & Red Vineyard). 3208 Chiles-Pope Valley Rd., St. Helena, CA 94574. Tel (707) 965-2346.

William Hill Winery. PO Box 3989, Napa, CA 94558. Tel (707) 226-8800.

Robert Keenan Winery. 3660 Spring Mountain Rd., St. Helena, CA 94574. Tel (707) 963-9177.

Long Vineyard. PO Box 589, Angwin, CA 94508.

Mt. Veeder Winery. 1999 Mt. Veeder Rd., Napa, CA 94558. Tel (707) 224-4039.

Robert Pecota Winery. PO Box 571, Calistoga, CA 94515. Tel (707) 942-6625.

Ritchie Creek. 4029 Spring Mountain Rd., St. Helena, CA 94574. Tel (707) 963-4661.

St. Helena Wine Co. 3027 Silverado Trail, St. Helena, CA 94574. Tel (707) 963-7108.

Stags' Leap Vintners. 6150 Silverado Trail, Napa, CA 94558.

St. Clement Vineyards. PO Box 261, St. Helena, CA 94574. Tel (707) 963-7221.

Stony Hill Vineyards. PO Box 308, St. Helena, CA 94574. Tel (707) 963-2636.

Tulocay Winery. 1426 Coombsville Rd., Napa, CA 94558. Tel (707) 255-4699.

Z-D Winery. 8383 Silverado Trail, St. Helena, CA 94574.

Survivors *of the past, Charles Krug (right) and Inglenook (upper right) date from the 1880s.*

. . . Continued from page 42

owned his first winery as early as 1922. Those facts, along with his immediate post-Prohibition start in the Napa Valley, earned him a secure reign as dean of California winemakers. His son and successor, Louis P., continues the family ownership in the traditional vein and in the original cellars.

Hosts at Martini do not insist on touring visitors through the buildings. They often skip that whole segment of the proceedings. Persuade them, if necessary, for the Martini cellars are instructive in several ways. The original Louis built his winery without costly adornments, but he built it to last.

Most of the Martini fermentors, for example, are now of stainless steel. Yet, for a couple of years at least, the original open concrete fermentors for reds will be around and in use. (The proprietor recalls how well they were constructed, and he shudders at the prospect of demolishing the things.) Then, too, the Martinis fermented white wines cold before refrigerated steel tanks came into use; the huge, refrigerated room full of redwood tanks remains in the winery and in use because it does a couple of jobs very well.

The main aging cellar holds a diverse lot of redwood and oak cooperage, as well as the bottling line, to round out a complete look at all phases of winemaking. (The tour does not go to a pair of flanking buildings that contain the majority of Martini's small oak cooperage, nor does it go down into a cellar that runs most of the main building's length beneath the central part of the main floor. In this latter room are the oak casks and bins of bottles full of specially aged Martini Private Reserve and particularly prized Special Selection wines, purchased more easily at the winery than elsewhere.)

In the tasting room, a new-in-1973 structure adjoining the main cellar, the complete roster of Martini wines is available for appraisal. The roster includes vintage-dated Folle Blanche, Gewürztraminer, Johannisberg Riesling, and a dry Chenin Blanc in whites, and Barbera, Cabernet Sauvignon, Gamay Beaujolais, Merlot, Pinot Noir, and Zinfandel in reds. The supporting cast includes generic table wines and Sherries.

Mayacamas Vineyards clings to the topmost ridges of the Mayacamas Mountains. Just getting to the winery taxes the suspension systems of most automobiles of ordinary manufacture. The road from the winery up to the highest vineyards is even more adventurous.

The owners are Bob and Nonie Travers, who acquired the site in 1968 from another family ownership.

The property centers upon an old stone winery erected by a man named J.H. Fisher in 1889 and operated as Mt. Veeder vineyards until 1910 or so. Restoration proceedings began in 1941 when a couple named Jack and Mary Taylor bought the property and named it Mayacamas. They got the cellers back in condition in 1947 and ran the estate until the Traverses bought it.

Mayacamas is cupped in the rocky rib of a long-extinct volcano, Mt. Veeder, and surrounded by several blocks of vineyard, mostly Cabernet Sauvignon. In a couple of places, sheer rock walls stick up out of the earth to set firm limits on vineyard size. Several hundred feet higher than the winery, ridge-top terraces carry the Chardonnay vineyards.

The owners will run guided tours of the winery by appointment. In addition to being a good example of traditional stonework, it provides a clear picture of how a small winery might be arranged. The modern crusher and press are in a small building on the uphill side of the main structure. The primary cellar is full of a diverse mixture of cooperage ranging in size from 1,500-gallon capacity down to 60-gallon oak.

The primary wines of Mayacamas are Chardonnay and Cabernet Sauvignon, both vintage dated.

Robert Mondavi Winery in Oakville crushed its first wine in 1966 while the carpenters still were struggling to get the roof on the building.

It does not look that new, mainly because founder Robert Mondavi commissioned designer Cliff May to pay architectural tribute to the role Franciscan missions had in developing California as a wine district.

On the other hand, most of the building is newer than 1966. Steady growth required Mondavi to expand 3 times in 10 years.

A faintly churchlike tower serves as the anchor point for two wings, one straight and one bent.

The south wing houses the tasting and sales rooms, as well as other rooms designed for use in celebrations of large and small events. The sales room is furnished with early California pieces of interest. Also, one wall has a demonstration for serious wine collectors. It is a stacked mass of agricultural tiles used as wine racks—light-proof, excellent insulators, and sized exactly to hold wine bottles. Further, the design is imposing.

To the north, the bent wing holds the offices and then a whole series of fermenting and aging cellars. Robert Mondavi, the man, is a ceaseless experimenter. As a result, his winery is an ever-changing one, full of wizard equipment for visitors to gaze upon and learn from.

Up in the roof rafters of the fermenting room, for example, are several horizontal tanks powered so they can rotate continuously. The original purpose was to keep red wines mixing throughout fermentation for maximum color extraction. At this task, the tanks were failures, but the ingenious Mondavis experimented until they learned that the mixing action was ideal for white winemaking. French continuous presses and German centrifuges are other pieces of equipment for which the guides at Mondavi have able explanations.

A spacious open arch separates the two wings of the winery, framing a view across long rows of vines to the steep flanks of the Mayacamas Mountains beyond. A plush lawn between the wings is the site of summer concerts, art shows, and frequent special tastings.

The wine list at Mondavi includes Chenin Blanc, Johannisberg Riesling, Chardonnay, and Fumé Blanc; a Gamay Rosé; and the reds Cabernet Sauvignon, Pinot Noir, and Zinfandel. All are vintage dated.

Mt. Veeder Winery is another of the recent crop of small mountainside wineries. Dating from 1973, the property of Michael and Arlene Bernstein specializes in Cabernet Sauvignon and Chardonnay.

Housed in a trim wood-framed building, Mt. Veeder can be visited only by appointment. For wine buffs, the major fascination is a vineyard growing all of the classic blending grapes for Cabernet Sauvignon—Malbec and Petit Verdot included.

Napa Wine Cellars has a playful architectural appeal from the outside. The front section of the building bears some resemblance to an igloo while, at the rear, another section has walls that taper inward.

Within, the playfulness gives way to a serene beauty. The igloo is in fact a slightly modified geodesic dome, much of it finished in stained wood. A skylight of stained glass casts a churchly kind of light on five upright oak tanks clustered under the dome. Barrels line the walls, save for one occupied by the tasting table.

The tapered rear section allows for lofty stacks of European and American oak barrels in which proprietor Charles Wood ages his Chardonnay, Cabernet Sauvignon, and Zinfandel.

Since the winery's opening in 1975, visiting hours have been irregular. However, in 1979, the cellar is scheduled to be open daily the year around.

Nichelini Vineyard

Nichelini Vineyard is way up in the east hills. East of Conn Dam and a reservoir, State 128 curls along bare shoulders of hills forming one side of a large canyon. Just at the head of the canyon, the road slips into a grove of oaks. There amid the trees and set into the downslope is Nichelini.

Steps descend the slope between an age-enfeebled barn and a solid frame house. The wine aspects of the place do not reveal themselves forcibly until the foot of the stairs, where it turns out that within the rock foundations of the house, there is a substantial cellar full of redwood and oak cooperage.

Tasting goes on, under clear skies or cloudy, on a terrace just outside the cellar door and within the immense framework of one of the last Roman presses in this hemisphere. It worked until the early 1950s. Though it still could be used, the Nichelinis would rather have it serve only ornamental purposes. (There is scarcely a slower, more laborious way to press grapes.)

Nichelini, founded in the late 19th century and now in the hands of the third generation, makes a number of varietal table wines. Sauvignon Vert is the specialty in the whites; Cabernet Sauvignon, Zinfandel, and Gamay are among the reds.

There are no formal tours, but poking around is encouraged. The family winery is open weekends and holidays only, when 12 visitors at a time can make use of a tree-shaded picnic table.

Joseph Phelps Winery

Joseph Phelps Winery, set against a vine-covered slope in the first row of hills on the east side of the Napa Valley, was built in 1974. Its contractor-proprietor came to wine as a builder of other wineries and was so attracted that he stayed to build his own.

The wood building is in effect two pavilions joined by a closed bridge that holds offices and labs. On the uphill side, a reconstructed trestle from another construction site has been turned into a Brobdingnagian arbor (due, in time, to be covered by wisteria).

One pavilion holds the fermentors—steel ones in an otherwise woody environment—along with a considerable number of oak oval casks from Germany and a smaller number of upright oak tanks.

The other pavilion holds lofty racks full of oak barrels from both French and American forests. The bottling room adjoins the barrel racks.

For the most part, the walls at Joseph Phelps are of large-dimensioned, rough-sawn redwood. But in the offices and reception rooms, walls and ceilings are of fine paneling with richly detailed decorative trims.

Tours are by appointment daily except Sunday. There is no regular tasting of the wines. The list includes Chardonnay, Fumé Blanc, Gewürztraminer, Cabernet Sauvignon, Pinot Noir, and Zinfandel. Some bottlings come from identified single vineyards. The specialty of the house is Johannisberg Riesling, made in a variety of styles, ranging from early-picked to late harvest. Some late-harvest bottlings are comparable in sweetness to a German Trockenbeerenauslese. (For an explanation of Noble Mold, the source of such sweetness, see the Chateau St. Jean entry on page 12.)

Pope Valley Winery

Pope Valley Winery is located in the valley of the same name parallel to and east of the Napa Valley.

The weathered, old-fashioned wood barn exterior of the three-story winery fits comfortably into its hillside setting, as it has since 1909. From then until 1959 it was operated as the Sam Haus Winery by Sam himself and his sister.

In 1972, James and Arlene Devitt and their two sons bought the property and reequipped and restored the workings of the winery to modern standards.

Chardonnay, Chenin Blanc, Semillon, White Riesling, Gamay, Cabernet Sauvignon, Zinfandel, and Zinfandel Rosé are made from Napa and Lake County grapes. Most are vintage dated.

It is a longish drive over a winding two-lane mountain road from the Napa Valley to the winery, so visitors should phone ahead to be sure the gate is open.

Raymond Vineyards

Raymond Vineyards belongs to an old-line Napa Valley winemaking family. Roy Raymond and sons Roy, Jr., and Walter established their own vineyard in 1971, and made their first wines from the harvest of 1974 after careers with other firms.

In spring of 1979, the permanent Raymond winery was under construction on the family vineyard just south of St. Helena. The cellars are to have wood-frame, wood-sided walls atop masonry lower walls, after the fashion of a good many early-day wineries in Napa.

While that building moves toward completion, a modular metal building continues full to the rafters with barrels of aging wine.

Full-fledged visitor facilities are still in the future, but the Raymonds will conduct tours of their premises and also have wines for sale by appointment.

The list of wines from vines surrounding the winery includes Chardonnay, Chenin Blanc, Johannisberg Riesling (regular and late harvest), Cabernet Sauvignon, and Zinfandel.

Ritchie Creek Vineyard

Ritchie Creek Vineyard is the small, single-minded winery of Richard Minor. The lone wine from his steep vineyard on Spring Mountain is Cabernet Sauvignon.

The entry drive ends at the proprietor's house, at the top side of the forest-girt vineyard. The winery tunnels into the slope just downhill from the bottom row of vines, the proprietor reasoning that it is easier to get downhill with boxes full of grapes than it is to get up.

Taking a look into the L-shaped tunnel with its double racks of oak barrels requires an appointment. Tasting is at the discretion of the owner because production is so limited that a single bottle matters in the statistics.

Rutherford Hill Winery

Rutherford Hill Winery is open for tours and tasting only on the second Saturday of each month.

This retiring pose is not taken out of shyness, but rather because the owners are essentially the same partnership that owns Freemark Abbey, so all of the business and sales departments are concentrated there.

In spite of the short schedule, Rutherford Hill is worth seeking out for one major and one minor reason. The major reason is that this cellar is architecturally distinctive and efficient. The shake-roofed, wood-sided structure echoes old Napa hay barns in form, though it is a great deal bigger than any barn that might have inspired it.

The reception and tasting hall is just inside a pair of towering doors at the lower level.

Wines available for tasting or purchase include Gewürztraminer, Johannisberg Riesling, a white wine from pinot noir, Cabernet Sauvignon, Merlot, and Zinfandel. All are vintage dated.

The minor reason for visiting Rutherford Hill is that this is California's capital of *pétanque,* the ancient Mediterranean game of bowls. All comers may play on the court, but betting against one of the cellar staff is a serious mistake.

Rutherford Vintners has a tasting room open daily in a white, wood-frame cottage next to State Highway 29, between Rutherford and St. Helena.

To have a look at the workings of the trim winery in its grove of towering eucalyptus trees, an appointment is required, since proprietor Bernard Skoda is the only tour guide as well as the winemaster.

Skoda has wedged a remarkable amount and variety of oak cooperage into his rectangular masonry block building. The back wall has German ovals for the Johannisberg Riesling. Both side walls have Slavonian oak ovals for the mid-term aging of his Cabernet Sauvignons and Pinot Noirs. In the middle are a row of American oak upright tanks for the initial aging, and separate racks of American and French oak barrels for the final aging of the two reds. In addition to all of this, Skoda has somehow worked in an automatic bottling line, engineered to have the shortest track and tightest curves on record, and a stainless steel tank for a specialty Muscat of Alexandria sold only at the winery.

The Willmes press and fermentors are under an overhanging roof at the rear of the aging cellar.

St. Clement Vineyards occupies a fine old Victorian house near St. Helena. The winery is composed of a fermenting and processing area just behind the house, and a cellar full of fat Burgundian barrels. Because the building is the residence of proprietor Dr. William Casey, and because production is so limited, no visitors are allowed except those who make appointments to purchase St. Clement wines in case lots. Produced here are Chardonnay and Cabernet Sauvignon.

V. Sattui Winery, just south of St. Helena, opened its tasting room in 1976 and was quickly discovered by wine country visitors.

In addition to the winery and tasting room, the attractive building houses a gift, cheese, and deli shop. Flanking the white stucco, mission-style structure are many large, tree-shaded picnic tables for use by winery and cheese shop customers.

The label dates not from 1976 but from 1885, when Vittorio Sattui established it for his own wines. It dis-

appeared during Prohibition, but has been revived in a new building by Vittorio's great-grandson, Daryl, and a limited partnership.

The initial offering of Sattui wines was purchased from other Napa Valley sources, but the Sattui label now goes onto varietals made on the premises.

Schramsberg Vineyards, having been founded by Jacob Schram in 1862, won quick immortality in the writings of Robert Louis Stevenson after the great British novelist's visit to the winery in 1880.

For a long time the immortality was more literary than practical. Stevenson's *The Silverado Squatters* has gone on and on, but the winery began to fade as soon as Schram died. It closed altogether in 1921, experienced two ephemeral revivals in 1940 and 1951, and then closed again.

Jack Davies launched Schramsberg anew in August, 1965, this time as a sparkling wine cellar. (Schram had made only still wines.) The old property has lived up to Stevenson's notions since then.

It's a romantic place to visit. Stevenson's original description of the trail up from the main road remains fairly accurate, though the surface is a good deal better.

The original winery building still stands at the top of a large clearing next to the old Schram home. Two tunnels going back into the hill from the winery have been turned into modern fermenting rooms for production of the wines that become Champagne a few hundred yards away.

A short lane leads to the Champagne cellar itself. The wood-faced building encloses a set of three more tunnels that hold the aging Champagne in bottles, thousands of them piled row on row in the *methode champenoise* fashion.

Supplies of Schramsberg Champagnes are limited. The four styles include Blanc de Blancs from white grapes, Blanc de Noir from pinot noir grapes, Cuvée de Gamay—dry wines all finished Brut—and a dessert cremant Champagne finished Demi-Sec.

Davies conducts tours of the winery, past and present, when he has a spare moment.

Smith-Madrone Vineyards belongs to the brothers Stuart and Charles Smith and to Stuart's wife Susan, the three having built what may be the ultimate image of a California cellar to house their wines.

The lower half is masonry, the upper half wood-frame and wood-walled, after a model common to the 1880s. But this one has some contemporary turns. The roof of the fermenting and main aging cellar is sod-covered for energy-efficient insulation. The residence and offices above that have steep roofs and off-set walls that bring to mind contemporary housing at coastal developments.

The building is set on a shelf at the mid-point of a long, steeply sloping vineyard on Spring Mountain.

As for the working winery, stainless steel fermentors occupy one end of the main level. French oak barrels occupy the other end, and fill an underground cellar.

Wines made here are Chardonnay, Johannisberg Riesling, Cabernet Sauvignon, and Pinot Noir. The first vintage was 1977, from vines planted in 1972. There is no tasting. Tours are by appointment only.

Spring Mountain Vineyards evokes both of the great eras of building in the Napa Valley about as well as any single property can.

(Continued on next page)

. . . Continued from page 49

The first great era, the 1880s, gave rise to a splendid Victorian house, a less imposing but still fine barn, and a hand-hewn tunnel for storing wines in the cool earth. The original builder was Tiburcio Parrott, an enthusiastic participant in everything that made the late nineteenth century a golden age for most of man's tangible possessions.

In 1976, Michael and Shirley Robbins bought the old property to house the winery they had founded in 1968 on another site. Parrott's legacy had fallen into considerable disrepair, so the new owners set about restoring it before adding to the current era of fine architecture in the Napa Valley.

By 1979, they had the old buildings tuned up, and were well advanced on their own new construction. The new winery is being built out from the face of the steep slope Parrott chose for his tunnel.

There is as much romance in the new structure as in the old. For example, stained glass windows on the new front wall cast soft light onto the European oak barrels used for aging Spring Mountain Cabernet Sauvignon. The windows were set so they could be seen from the depths of the old tunnel. However, since the tunnel was to be used for aging Chardonnay and Sauvignon Blanc, the Robbinses wanted it cooler. The solution was glass doors to separate it from the red wine aging cellar without separating it from the view.

There is no tasting. Nor is there always wine for sale from the limited production. Tours are limited owing to on-going construction.

Stag's Leap Wine Cellars

Stag's Leap Wine Cellars tucks neatly into its hillside amid a grove of oaks. The original 1972 building fit in so well that it was nearly invisible from the Silverado Trail, no more than a hundred yards away. A second white-walled building added in 1976 sits out in fuller view.

The original building contains the wood aging cellar—two rows of upright oak tanks, a row of fine old oak oval casks, and several tall stacks of barrels. Outside, on the uphill side, two rows of stainless steel fermentors run the length of the building.

The newer building houses stainless steel storage tanks, the bottling line, and newly bottled wines. Stag's Leap is so thoughtfully designed that it offers a virtual textbook example of how to put together a small, specialized winery. One example: both crusher and press straddle a single channel cut into the concrete work pad. Stems, pomace, and wash water all course downhill, out of the way until the work is done and they can be disposed of at leisure.

Production at Stag's Leap is not great enough to permit tasting, but proprietor Warren Winiarski will explain to all who call ahead for an appointment how the winery works and how he makes his short list of wines: Chardonnay, Johannisberg Riesling, Cabernet Sauvignon, Gamay Beaujolais, and Merlot.

There is another Stags Leap, called Stags' Leap Vintners (see "More wineries," on page 55).

Sterling Vineyards

Sterling Vineyards looks from the outside like a fair approximation of the sort of church Crusaders left on similarly craggy hilltops on Greek isles.

From the inside it looks like the modern winery it is. The main cellar runs downhill from the crusher, Willmes-type air bag press, and jacketed stainless steel fermentors, through a series of oak aging cellars, the lowest one of which is given entirely to barrels. The purpose is to allow gravity rather than pumps to move the wine as much as possible. A separate two-story cellar at the crest of the knoll above the main building holds two years' worth of reserve wines, one vintage on each story.

However, Sterling is more than just a winery. The whole establishment also is set up to provide an ongoing show for visitors. The showmanship begins at the beginning. Visitors travel from the car park up to the winery on an aerial tramway (at a fee of $2.50 per head). The tour from there on is self-operated. A long elevated walkway threads through the main building with visual displays at every stop to explain what takes place within view.

The bells of St. Dunstans—an audible extra—ring at random intervals to entertain whomever is on hand.

In a separate building, between the main winery and the reserve cellar, is the tasting room, an elegantly airy place with awesome views down the valley. In it, the proprietors offer for tasting wines selected from a list dominated by Chardonnay, Sauvignon Blanc, Cabernet Sauvignon, and Merlot.

The present proprietors are The Coca Cola Co., which bought Sterling in 1978 from a trio of partners which had founded the winery in 1969.

Stonegate Winery

Stonegate Winery opened in 1973. It squeezes itself into a one-time tractor shed on Dunaweal Lane, just a few yards from the lane's intersection with State 29.

The proprietors have left the exterior of the place unornamented but have turned the interior into an attractive, neatly organized, small winery. Three oak tanks fill one room. Approximately 200 close-stacked barrels, most of them from Europe, make an even tighter fit in the second room. A battery of stainless steel fermentors sits outside.

Though the winery is too small to provide tasting, an affable staff—which is to say one of the owning Spaulding family—will stop to talk shop whenever the work is not too pressing. The list of wines on hand for sale includes Chardonnay, Sauvignon Blanc, Cabernet Sauvignon, and Pinot Noir.

Stony Hill Vineyards

Stony Hill Vineyards does not fit easily into a day of casual touring. An appointment is required to visit it, but that is only half the story. Stony Hill is at the top of a long, winding road, high in the westside hills. The drive up takes as long as a thorough look.

The cellar dates from 1951, when the late Fred McCrea and his wife Eleanor built it as a place to keep busy in retirement. The building, part stone, part plaster, nestles into a grove of trees at the foot of a sloping block of white riesling vines. A pair of handsome doors carved by the founder leads into a cellar full of European oak puncheons and barrels, and containing one of the last classic binning systems for bottled wines in California.

Stony Hill, under the direction of Eleanor McCrea and winemaker Mike Chelini, makes three vintage-dated wines, all white. They are Chardonnay, Gewürztraminer, and White Riesling. They ferment in the puncheons, the CO_2 dispelled through bubbler hoses with their noses stuck into water-filled wine bottles. Then the wines age in either the puncheons or barrels.

(Continued on page 52)

Hectic pace *of a vintage can be seen, almost felt. Pickers work a roadside vineyard near St. Helena (above). At wineries, the grapes go into crushers (right) tons at a time.*

... *Continued from page 50*

A visit is pretty much in the way of a pilgrimage. Once a year the winery dispatches a letter to its mailing list, and all the wine sells out within a few weeks. Thus, there are neither tastings nor sales, only an opportunity to see a cellar that is legendary to its followers.

Sutter Home Winery, straight across State 29 from Louis M. Martini, offers various contrasts to its neighbor.

The winery is housed in a handsomely proportioned board-and-batten structure originally built to house the cellars of J. Thomann, one of the major forces in the early history of Napa wine. The building proves the durability of properly assembled, good wood.

Sutter Home belongs, these days, to the Trinchero family. Theirs since 1946, it comes by its name honestly. John Sutter and son Albert built their first winery in the east hills of the valley in 1890. Sutter's son-in-law transferred the winery—lock, stock, and barrels—to its present site in 1906–07 and operated it until 1930.

The Trincheros operate their historic winery, with its historic name, as a small and highly specialized cellar. Nearly all of the production is Zinfandel from Amador County grapes. Most of the wine is red, but some of the annual production is White Zinfandel. The other wine in the roster is a small annual lot of Moscato Amabile.

This specialization is relatively recent. Through the 1960s, the Trincheros offered a full range of wines.

There are no tours, but the three specialties (along with a handful of residual stocks from earlier times) are on hand to be tasted daily.

Trefethen Vineyards looks as if a good deal of history should surround it, and a good deal does. However, until the winery became Trefethen in 1968, that history was surprisingly quiet.

The vast three-story wooden building is the only survivor of its type in the valley. It is doubtful if it ever had a peer among wooden buildings in Napa. The designer and builder was Captain Hamden McIntyre, who also designed Inglenook's original building and Greystone Cellars, now the property of The Christian Brothers. But, while the other two cellars have had more or less famous labels attached to them down through the years, the Trefethen building was, until bought by the current owners, mainly a bulk winery, or leased to a winery with its headquarters elsewhere. The current owners have paid tribute to one of their winery's earlier careers with wines labeled Eshcol Red and Eshcol White, but there was rarely an Eshcol label when the winery went by that name.

Be all that as it may, the winery has a name now, and is a most agreeable and informative cellar to visit. Under the ownership of the Gene Trefethen family, the vineyards are harvested mechanically, so their presses and other processing gear are set up to accommodate field-crushed must. Within the winery building, the fermentors are stainless steel and the wood aging cellars are full of European oak.

Villa Mt. Eden began as a vineyard in 1881 and endured as both vineyard and winery property through numerous ownerships. The best known of its earlier proprietors was Nick Fagiani, who used the place to make sherry type wines just before Prohibition.

The property now belongs to James and Anne McWilliams, who bought it in 1970 and installed sophisticated new equipment for a comeback as a table wine cellar in 1974.

Grapes are field-crushed into rolling stainless steel tanks—a German system called the Mörtl—then fermented in stainless steel before aging in either American or French oak barrels.

The one-story, white stucco winery is one of several similar buildings grouped around an open courtyard in the classic fashion of a Mediterranean country villa. Vineyards surround the cluster of buildings.

Current wine production is small, and plans are to keep it that way. All wines are varietals, and focus on Chenin Blanc, Chardonnay, Napa Gamay, Pinot Noir, and Cabernet Sauvignon.

Winemaker-vineyard manager Nils Venge can accommodate visitors by appointment on weekdays only. He requests patience from phone callers; it is a long sprint from cellar to office telephone.

Yverdon Vineyards is a virtuoso one-man show of the building arts. Owner Fred Aves designed and built not only his two-story stone winery, but almost everything in it. He gathered and split local stone for the walls, designed and cast the flaring pillars that hold up the upper floor and gently sloping roof, designed and executed a series of quatre-foil stained glass windows, designed a Gaudi-esque metal spiral staircase with its motif of grapes, and even designed and cast concrete cradles for the oak casks he coopered himself.

About the only gear in the place which Aves did not build are the stainless steel fermentors, the Italian press, and some Swiss pumps and filters.

Tours are by appointment only. There is no tasting, but Yverdon Chenin Blanc, Johannisberg Riesling, Cabernet Sauvignon, and Napa Gamay are on sale weekdays. Finding the entry is not easy. It is marked only by a plaque bearing the numbers 3787. The plaque is nailed to a tree next to a pipe and wire gate.

The name, Yverdon, is taken from the ancient Swiss town on Lake Neuchatel. It is the ancestral home of the family Aves.

More wineries. The Napa Valley has a substantial number of wineries with extremely restricted ability to welcome visitors, or no ability at all. They are noted here to aid serious students of California wine, who may have seen wines under their labels, and to explain their presence in the landscape.

Beckett Cellars is a new face in an old place, proprietor John Beckett having refurbished an 1885 stone cellar and tunnel in time for the harvest of 1975. The winery, high up Atlas Peak Road east of Napa, has no visitor facility at present.

Buehler Vineyards bottles wines under the family label of John Buehler, but one cannot visit the tiny cellar in Conn Valley for tours, or even purchases. The road leading to both winery and residence will not bear more traffic than residents already impose.

Cassayre-Forni Winery began operations with the harvest of 1977, using a small red barn as an interim cellar. The permanent winery was under construction in 1979 on the site near Rutherford. There will be very limited visitor facilities until that structure is up.

Champagne: how the bubbles get there

Sparkling wine dates from the time of Dom Perignon, a Benedictine monk who made wine for l'Abbaye d'Hautvillers in the late 1600s. In a sense, effervescing wine had long since invented itself, and Perignon only invented bottles and stoppers suitable for keeping the bubbles in.

His original method was chancy. It involved starting a secondary fermentation in the tightly corked bottle and hoping that the total accumulation of CO_2 would not explode the glass. (One scholar has it that the odds ran no better than 60–40 on any bottle in those pioneer years.) Fermentation is the conversion of sugar by yeast into roughly equal parts of CO_2 and alcohol; like Perignon, the early cellarkeepers took a relaxed view of the interrelationship between sugar and eventual gas pressure.

Now, with refined measurements, the same technique is still used and called *la methode champenoise*. The Champagne master assembles a cuvée—a blend of still wines—to his taste, bottles it, and adds a mixture of sugar and yeast before capping each bottle. This mixture produces the secondary fermentation. After it has finished its work, the mixture falls as sediment and is worked into the neck of the bottle. Next, the neck is frozen in brine or another solution so that the sediment can pop out as a plug of ice (aided by an average gas pressure of 100 pounds per square inch). Next is added "dosage," a syrup that governs the sweetness of the finished wine. The final cork is wired into place. After a period of rest, the wine

Latterly, science has added some variations. One is the German method called "Carstens transfer process." It starts out in the same way as the *methode champenoise*. But when the time comes to remove the sediment, the bottles are emptied under pressure into a holding tank, the wine is filtered, and then is returned to bottles with the desired dosage. Another method, French in origin, is called "Charmat" or "Bulk Process." In this case, the wine undergoes its secondary fermentation in a glass-lined tank, rather than in bottles. Then, as in the transfer process method, it is filtered on its way to the bottles.

A great many California wineries make sparkling wines; most have tours. Among the clearest demonstrations: Domaine Chandon, Hanns Kornell, Schramsberg, Korbel, and Mirassou for *methode champenoise*; Paul Masson for the transfer process; Weibel and Guild for Charmat.

Chappellet Vineyard, east of Rutherford, is such an imposing hillside property that owner Donn Chappellet could afford to underplay the winery he had built in 1969. In the shape of a pyramid, it nestles into its slope at the bottom corner of a vineyard block. The sloping walls are of earth-tone oxidized metal sheathing. Earth mounds up against their bases as a gesture toward integration into the site. Within, however, the cathedral-like dimensions of the building assert themselves. The roof soars to its peak above three triangular work areas—stainless steel fermentors on one side, small barrels on the second, and bottled wines on the third. There are no visitor facilities here, and alas, for this is one of the most dramatic of California wine estates.

Conn Creek Vineyards will welcome visitors in time, but in 1979, it was in transition. The winery, belonging to William Collins and William Beaver, began operations in 1974 in a leased cellar near Freemark Abbey. In 1979, the proprietors began construction of their permanent cellar buildings on the Silverado Trail, near its intersection with Conn Creek Road.

Diamond Creek Vineyards does not have a tourable winery at present. Proprietor Al Brounstein's wines are in leased space away from the vineyard. But he does welcome groups of wine buffs for tastings and picnics around a little lake at the high side of his Calistoga property during weekends in June, July, and August. Groups can petition for reservations at the address with map listings on page 46. The only wines are Cabernet Sauvignon, separately bottled from three different blocks of his vineyard.

The Jay Heminway winery, more formally known as Green & Red Vineyard, is located on the Chiles Valley-Pope Valley Road in Pope Valley. Founded in 1977, it remains so small that the proprietor has no program for visitors, as of publication time.

William Hill Vineyards is on the way to becoming a substantial winery. The owner, after whom the winery is named, planted the first of three sizable vineyards on Mt. Veeder in the early 1970s, and made his first Cabernet Sauvignon from the vintage of 1976. That debut wine is to go on sale in 1980, but the winery construction will not advance enough to permit visitors even then. The cellars are temporarily in a leased industrial building in the city of Napa.

Long Vineyards is another small winery from the class of 1978. It is the property of vineyardist Bob Long and winemaker Zelma Long, who founded their cellar on a remote corner of Pritchard Hill to make Cabernet Sauvignon and Chardonnay. Zelma Long worked for another Napa winery for some years before she and her husband established their own label, due to appear in 1979. Size and use-permit restrictions severely limit the Longs' ability to welcome visitors.

Robert Pecota Winery, north of Calistoga, crushed its first wines in 1978. The mainstays of the house are to be Sauvignon Blanc and Petite Sirah, with Flora as a specialty. (Flora is a grape variety with kinships to

Able guides *lead tour groups at all of Napa's sizable wineries. The scene here is Robert Mondavi, one of the most modernly equipped cellars in the state, in contrast to an architectural style harking back to mission days.*

Gewürztraminer, developed at the University of California at Davis.) Because the winery is very small, and adjacent to the family home, it is not open to visitors.

St. Helena Wine Co. was established in time to crush Merlot and Cabernet Sauvignon from the vintage of 1978, but will not be open for visitors before the wines are ready themselves, sometime in 1980. It is a cliché that wine starts with the vineyard. St. Helena Wine Co., the property of the Daniel Duckhorn family, goes the cliché one better: the winery on Silverado Trail near Lodi Lane occupies a one-time grape nursery.

The firm called Stags' Leap Vintners, owned by Carl Doumani and partners, dates from 1972. Its vineyards are at the old Stags Leap Manor property in the southeastern quarter of the Napa Valley, but the cellars planned for that site are not yet complete. While the winemaking goes on in leased space, there are no facilities to host visitors. (This is not Stag's Leap Wine Cellars, another company. For a description of that winery, see page 50.)

Tulocay Winery is a tiny winery adjacent to the home of its owners, William and Barbara Cadman, in the hills east of Napa city. The wines are Cabernet Sauvignon, Pinot Noir, and Zinfandel. There are neither tours, tastings, nor retail sales at the winery, which was founded in 1975.

Z-D is a well-established winery, but in transition as of 1979. Gino Zepponi and Norman de Leuze founded Z-D in 1969 as a small cellar near the town of Sonoma. At publication time, they had just begun construction of a new, larger winery on the Silverado Trail east of Rutherford. The Sonoma cellar was to close before the vintage of 1979, as soon as the Napa building was complete. Z-D focuses on Chardonnay and Pinot Noir. It also produces White Riesling and Gewürztraminer. Visits were to be by appointment only.

Finally, there are a scattered few bulk wineries in the Napa Valley. The Napa Valley Cooperative is the most prominent, on State Highway 29 just south of St. Helena. It sells all of its wine to E & J Gallo. Also on the south side of St. Helena is the old Sunny St. Helena winery, now leased for storage by The Christian Brothers. At Oakville, two side-by-side wineries next to State 29 belong to United Vintners, which uses them for fermenting and some aging of Inglenook wines.

Other Than Wineries

The happy town of St. Helena is the hub of the Napa Valley, but attractions for visitors range from Yountville north beyond Calistoga.

A citizen's action committee called the Napa Valley Wine Library Association some years ago founded a specialized wine library. Much of the collection came from the bookshelves of local winemakers. The rest was (and continues to be) purchased with membership fees.

The St. Helena Public Library, where the collection is housed, is open weekdays and half-days Saturday.

Another special possibility is offered in the library. The Silverado Museum, a practical monument to Robert Louis Stevenson, occupies a wing of the new-in-1979 library structure.

The museum, full of Stevenson materials and memorabilia, is located in the Napa Valley partly because founder Norman Strouse likes the region but primarily

because Stevenson lived and worked here in 1880–81. The collection has been praised widely as the finest private one in the world.

Bothe-Napa Valley State Park is the biggest and most varied of several parks in the county. The gates are 4 miles north of St. Helena on State Highway 29. The park proper ranges well back into the west hills. Picnic and camping facilities, hiking trails, and a swimming pool are its prime attractions.

An adjunct, a few hundred yards to the south, is the Old Bale Mill. Built by pioneer Dr. Edward Bale, the mill with its towering overshot waterwheel has been rebuilt from a stage of advanced decay so that it looks workable.

Conn Dam Recreation Area, up off the valley floor in the east hills, has cooling water and some picnic tables. The turnoff from the Silverado Trail is marked State Highway 128-Conn Dam.

On another level altogether, the Napa Valley's hills offer the right kind of air to glider pilots. The little airport at Calistoga is headquarters for a sizable contingent of silent fliers, whose takeoffs and landings are one of the two best shows in the valley for winery-weary small fry.

The other attention-getter for children is the Calistoga Steam Railroad, on the Silverado Trail just a short way south of its intersection with Calistoga's main street. The tiny, elegantly machined locomotive that hauled fair-goers around the Panama-Pacific Exposition in San Francisco in 1915 now huffs and puffs its way around a meadow and up a steep hill for a modest ticket price.

The Napa Valley has a number of restaurants, inns, and motels, but few enough that reservations are required in all seasons.

Plotting a Route

Napa County sandwiches neatly between U.S. 101 to the west and Interstate Highway 80 to the east. State Highways 12, 29, 37, and 128 connect it variously with the major highways.

Of the possible combinations of access routes from San Francisco or Oakland, I-80, then State 29 from Vallejo to Napa is the most direct, the flattest, and the least scenic. From Sacramento, the combination is I-80, State 12, then State 29.

Another route from San Francisco that is slower, hillier, and prettier goes across the Golden Gate, then north on U.S. 101, State 37, and State 12-29. From the north, U.S. 101 and State 128 combine easily.

The Napa Valley, being long and narrow, has two major roads of its own. They parallel each other on a north-south axis.

State 29, the westerly one, has almost all the wineries on it. It cuts a straight swath a few hundred yards from the feet of the westerly hills. Its border is mostly vineyards, partly towns.

The eastern parallel route is the Silverado Trail, which loops along a leisurely and almost purely uncommercial way. It runs right at the foot of the east hills, elevated just enough to give fine vineyard panoramas.

Several crossroads tie the two together, making it easy to swap back and forth.

Still other roads poke up into the hills on either side of the valley. Nearly all offer pleasant panoramas.

The Central Coast

A ranging district of great vinous variety

Mission Santa Barbara

The Central Coast counties of California are in a curiously unbalanced state at present. Although most of the vines grow in Monterey and others of the more southerly counties, most of the visitable wineries are in Santa Clara and others of the more northerly counties.

The urban pressures that began to be inexorable on Santa Clara vineyards early in the 1960s will, no doubt, weigh ever more heavily on wineries through the 1980s. In the meantime, students who wish to see both vine and wine at the source have an enormous territory to consider when they go looking at Almaden, Paul Masson, Mirassou, and their like in this divided region.

The north side of Santa Clara County, where commercial winegrowing got its start south of San Francisco Bay, has been heavily urbanized since the late 1950s. Though vines almost have disappeared, this area—coupled with neighboring Santa Cruz—remains a focal point for wineries.

The more rural south half of Santa Clara also has a considerable number of wineries. Many of them have at least some of their vines at or near the winery.

Monterey County now supports a tremendous majority of the Central Coast's vineyards, but is just beginning to show wineries to go with the grapes. Farther south, San Luis Obispo and Santa Barbara counties have substantial new vineyards and a number of wineries to use their crops.

U.S. Highway 101 slices straight down the length of the region, from San Jose at the north to Santa Barbara at the south, a distance of more than 250 miles. In every part of the region, wineries welcome visitors. A serious student would require at least a week to cover all the ground. More time would be better. Those with the advantage of living on the spot can divide the territory into several engaging weekend loops.

Santa Clara Valley

To remember the Santa Clara Valley as a beautiful bowl of cherries, plums, and grapes is almost impossible, even though it was dominated by orchards and vineyards well into the 1950s.

Now it is known as Silicon Valley after its prosperous electronics and space industries, and the roadsides are lined by manufacturing plants, warehouses, car dealers, and just plain houses.

Driving through the region to see its wineries is hardly a pastoral experience. Still, for all the gritty aspects of getting around, there are some pleasing moments to savor and some agreeable lessons to learn. Most surprising, the number of wineries is increasing.

The Wineries

Eight wineries open their doors to visitors here and there about the teeming floor of the Santa Clara Valley. The larger five are easy to visit; the small and tiny ones tend to require appointments even though they are open only one or two days a week.

Almaden Vineyards dates back to 1852, counting all the ancestors, and has spread out mightily in its time without ever losing its original home.

The founders were two Frenchmen named Etienne Thée and Charles Lefranc, who planted vines on the site of the present Almaden home winery in San Jose. (Lefranc, having married a Thée daughter, watched history recycle a few years later when his own daughter married his junior partner, Paul Masson.) The property eventually passed out of Lefranc's hands, fell idle during Prohibition, then was restored by Louis Benoist. Benoist in time sold to the present owners, National Distillers.

While all of this was going on, San Jose grew to surround the original property. And, while the suburbs were surrounding the home place, Almaden was growing in several new directions. The original property is now a sparkling wine cellar and bottling arena. The two producing Almaden wineries are some miles south of Hollister in San Benito County. The company also has a storage cellar in Kingsburg (which, history students should know, was Louis M. Martini's first winery). Finally, there is a warehouse for cased goods on the southern fringes of San Jose.

Almaden welcomes visitors at the original cellar in San Jose and tasters at the tasting room on the Pacheco Pass Highway.

The old home property on Blossom Hill Road holds one of the largest and fastest bottling operations in the California wine industry. It is open to view. In the same building is a historical museum, recording the company's growth from early times onward. The company has kept enough vines on the site to retain a handsome setting.

To taste the wines, one must go to the northern edge of Hollister, where Almaden has installed a pleasant tasting room. Its two nearby producing wineries are not open for tours, but a drive past gives a fair impression of the company's scope, as well as some superb vineyard panoramas (see page 78).

The list of Almaden wines encompasses every type. Vintage-dated varietals head the table wine roster under both the Almaden label and the more expensive (and much more limited) Charles Lefranc label. Almaden also offers dessert and sparkling wines.

Gemello Winery, hidden away behind a bowling alley on El Camino Real in Mountain View, dates from 1934, when the neighborhood consisted of orchards.

Founder John Gemello worked for the original Mon-tebello Wine Company in Cupertino at the time and started his own winery as a hobby. It has proven more durable than the long-defunct Montebello. John Gemello's son Mario assumed control in the early 1940s and found the enterprise so active that he was required to add a good deal to the existing supply of cooperage. Mario is the winemaker still, and still adding to his wood aging capacity.

In spite of the winery's much-augmented collection of redwood tanks and European oak barrels, it remains small enough that visitors on the Saturday afternoon tours can almost see the whole works from one spot. Tasting, too, is limited to Saturday afternoons.

Although the focus is on red varietals (Cabernet Sauvignon, Zinfandel, Petite Sirah, Pinot Noir, and Barbera), white wines are to be found on the list as well. The adjoining retail store once was the only place in the world to buy Gemello wines, but they are currently distributed across the country.

Paul Masson Vineyards spreads across much of the state, as do many of California's sizable wineries. For visitors, though, things are centralized at a complex of buildings on the valley floor just east of Saratoga's business district.

The Paul Masson Champagne and Wine Cellars depart completely from traditional winery architecture. Out front, a free-form metal sculpture sets the tone. The cellars themselves show a wavy roofline, not quite so sharply arched as barrel vaults, but close.

However the outside may strike the eye, the inside is an efficient aging cellar and has much to recommend it to visitors. A raised walkway permits bird's-eye views of an expanse of handsome cooperage (glass-lined steel, oak ovals, and redwood uprights all nestled together in harmony), five model bottling lines, and all the steps in making sparkling wine.

Masson, in fact, offers one of the few chances to study what is called "the transfer process" in the making of sparkling wine. The lesson is presented clearly at listening station 8 on Masson's electronically guided tour, the first such system in a California winery. On the tour, each visitor is given a one-station radio receiver to carry along, allowing each to pace himself, listening to a taped presentation at each station. Hosts are posted along the way to answer any questions the tapes do not.

The Champagne and Wine Cellars were completed in 1959, then expanded in 1967 and again in 1971, long after Masson's owners had decided to move the main body of their vineyards south into Monterey County. No crushing or fermenting goes on at this older site. That part of the work takes place at the Pinnacles Vineyard near Soledad, where a big producing winery was completed only a few days before the harvest of 1966 began, and at the Paul Masson Sherry Cellars in Madera, built in 1974.

But Saratoga is where all Masson wine comes for final aging, bottling, and packaging, and this is where it is at hand for sampling in a spacious and comfortably appointed tasting hall. Masson makes a great many wines: nearly all of the familiar varietal and generic table types, several sparkling wines, and a variety of appetizer and dessert types. Some of the firm's best-known wines are proprietary labels such as Emerald Dry and Baroque. In 1977, vintage-dated, estate-bottled varietals appeared for the first time. These Pinnacles Selections include Pinot Chardonnay and a sparkling Johannisberg Riesling.

Saratoga is where Paul Masson began, but the Champagne and Wine Cellars are not. The flesh-and-blood Paul Masson had a stone winery built in the hills high above Saratoga in 1880, after some years as a partner of Charles Lefranc, the founder of Almaden. Nestled into a hillside, so that gravity could do most of the work before pumps were harnessed to motors, the old cellar had some literal ups and downs. It had to be rebuilt after the earthquake of 1906, at which time it acquired its churchly front from a ruined chapel in San Jose. And it had to be rebuilt a second time after a gutting fire in 1941. (The old man did not have to deal with the fire. He had died a year earlier, after 58 years of winemaking in California and 4 years of retirement.)

The old cellar still holds small lots of dessert wines, but its main interest for visitors is musical. "Music at the Vineyards" offers chamber music on selected summer weekends. A second summer series called "Vintage Sounds" presents jazz and folk music. There is also a chess tournament here in July, and the AAU-recognized Champagne Marathon finishes on the property. Tickets and information about these events can be obtained by writing to the winery.

Mirassou Vineyards, coming now into the hands of its owning family's fifth generation, has one of the oldest names in Santa Clara winemaking, though the label is a relative newcomer in retail stores.

A French vineyardist, Pierre Pellier, established the dynasty in 1854 in what is now downtown San Jose. (Following an earlier exploratory visit in 1848, he had returned to France to gather a wife and thousands of vine cuttings.) Subsequently another Frenchman, Pierre Mirassou, met and married a Pellier daughter. That was in 1881. The Mirassou family has figured in California vintages since.

An old photo on the tasting room wall shows wooden tank trucks loading Mirassou bulk wines into railroad cars for the long voyage east in the era before World War I. After the enforced respite of Prohibition, the third and fourth generations resumed winemaking, again anonymously. This time, though, the Mirassous embarked on the unique course of making varietal wines for sale in bulk to other California wineries.

As late as 1968, it still took a bit of a pilgrimage to find wine under the Mirassou label. It was sold only at the winery, located after a long string of stoplights on U.S. Highway 101, south of San Jose.

Now, with the fifth generation firmly embarked on a path of family identity with family vintages, it is possible to find Mirassou wines at retail shops all across the country. But the winery remains a good place to go looking for them. In fact, the journey is a good deal easier than it used to be, owing to U.S. 101's upgrading to freeway status.

The main winery building, with a richly appointed tasting room in one front corner, is a squarely built, solid masonry structure, nestled into the beginnings of a steep slope southeast of San Jose. Once, not so many years ago, it was the whole winery. Now it holds only a small proportion of the aging cooperage and a bottling line.

A second building just uphill holds the sparkling wine cellar and bottled wines. A third building at the rear stores only bottled wines. (A fourth building, a couple of miles away, holds much of the large wooden cooperage and all the oak barrels.)

Outdoors, at the rear of the original cellar, is a complex assemblage of processing equipment. The usual stainless steel fermentors, a crusher, and two big Willmes-type presses are there. So are some specialized hoppers and dejuicers for handling the must of field-crushed grapes. (Most Mirassou grapevines are in the Salinas Valley of Monterey County, which led the family to pioneer in mechanical harvesting and field-crushing of quality grapes for varietal wines.)

As a result, this is one of Santa Clara's most instructive wineries to visit during the October-November harvest season. The main works are far enough out in the open for sidewalk superintending to be possible.

Mirassou also is a most instructive cellar in which to see traditional *methode champenoise* techniques for making sparkling wine.

The still wines can be tasted in relaxed comfort. The roster includes Chenin Blanc, Gewürztraminer, Johannisberg Riesling, and Monterey Riesling among whites, and Cabernet Sauvignon, Petite Sirah, Pinot Noir, and Zinfandel among reds.

The Novitiate of Los Gatos has few peers for handsome setting. The winery building cuts into a narrow shelf halfway up a hill of some size. Approaching Los Gatos, drivers westbound on State Highway 17 or southbound on Monte Sereno Road can see the white winery and, on the crest above it, some old vineyards.

Within the winery building, amid observable outlines of still older buildings, dim tunnels lead off in several directions. There is no telling the age of some of the oak casks that line the tunnels. The Novitiate has been making sacramental wines since 1888 and has acquired cooperage whenever possible. Some casks came without pedigree papers at the end of Prohibition.

But not all is cobwebby romance. The Jesuit fathers who run the winery are an experimental lot. They have an early-model continuous press on hand that is satisfactory for making the beginnings of brandy but not much else. A since-reassigned winemaker-priest designed and installed a battery of highly efficient stainless steel fermenting tanks after having studied the subject at the University of California at Davis. Both presses and fermentors are on the uphill side of the building.

Down in one of the deeper regions stands a stainless steel tank shaped somewhat after the fashion of a Mercury space capsule and equipped with a porthole. On view inside is the flor culture used in the Novitiate Dry Sherry. (Other flor cultures crop up throughout the winery in a wild variety of bottles, flagons, and demijohns. The winemaker waits patiently to see if variant strains might develop.)

Getting around to see all of this involves a considerable amount of climbing spidery iron stairways, since the office building is at the lowest level and the start of the tour is at the highest, and there is no alternate route. At the end of the tour, the tasting room is in one of the cellars, offering table, appetizer, and dessert wines for leisurely consideration.

(Continued on page 60)

Wide-spaced rows, *trained onto trellises, typify new plantings; these are at Paul Masson near Soledad.*

How to read a California wine label

Both California and federal laws control what a wine label must say.

Estate bottled. This once meant grapes from a single vineyard. Now it can cover the scattered holdings of large corporations.

1974. A vintage date can appear only if 95 percent or more of the grapes were harvested and crushed in the year stated. The margin allows for topping up casks of aging wines.

Napa Valley. Some statement of geographical origin is required. To be labeled "California," all of the wine must be from grapes grown in the state. More specific designations require 75 percent or more from the stated area.

Cabernet Sauvignon. Varietal labeling requires that 51 percent of the wine be from the grape named and that the wine get its predominant taste, aroma, and characteristics from that grape. Other labeling practices are generic (to describe a style of wine inspired by wine from a certain district, such as Burgundy or Sherry) and proprietary, a name coined by the vintner. See the chart on page 37 for a comprehensive list of California wines.

Produced and bottled by. This means the bottler made at least 75 percent of the wine by crushing, aging, and finishing.

Made and bottled by means the bottler was similarly responsible for 10 percent or more (in practice usually close to 50 percent). Terms like **Cellared and bottled by, Perfected and bottled by,** or **Prepared and bottled by** indicate only that the bottler performed some finishing procedures. Federal law requires as a minimum **Bottled by,** with the bottler's name and place of business.

Alcohol 12½ percent by volume. Table wines, 10 to 14 percent alcohol, may carry either a statement of alcohol content with a 1½ percent tolerance, or a statement such as "table wine" or "light wine." A statement of alcohol content is required on all dessert wines, with a tolerance range of 1 percent to the legal maximum of 21 percent.

The federal government has established new and stricter regulations covering what may be said on a label, however these will not take effect until 1983.

...Continued from page 58

The winery is closed to visitors on Sundays and on legal and church holidays.

La Purisima Winery, of all the oddly located urban cellars in California, must be one of the oddest. It shares space with an art supply store in what started out to be a shopping center supermarket in Sunnyvale.

However peculiar the location seems to outsiders, it pleases proprietor Douglas Watson a good deal, partly because supermarkets are well-insulated in general, but mainly because it gave him a huge walk-in refrigerator in which he can conduct cold fermentations in barrels for his white wines.

Because potential walk-in traffic exceeds the possible supply, the winery is open to the public only on Saturdays (visits can be arranged by appointment). Visitors can have a look around at the stainless steel and oak cooperage in the main room as well as the oak barrels in the cold box, then finish up with a tasting of current wines.

The roster includes Chardonnay, Chenin Blanc, Gewürztraminer,White Riesling, a white wine from Barbera, and among reds: Barbera, Cabernet Sauvignon, Petite Sirah, and Zinfandel. LaPurisima began operations in 1976.

Sommelier Winery occupies one bay in one of those multiple space-for-rent warehouses that have sprung up by the dozens in recent years. This one is just off Old Middlefield Road, not far from San Antonio Road in deepest Mountain View. Behind one part of its concrete block front is a full-fledged producing winery, with everything from crusher to bottling line.

Founded in 1976 by the Dick Keezer and Richard Burnham families, Sommelier is open only by appointment, and only on weekends. The short list of varietal wines may be tasted when stocks are not sold out.

Turgeon & Lohr has its brick-front winery on a side street just off The Alameda in San Jose, and its vine-

(Continued on page 63)

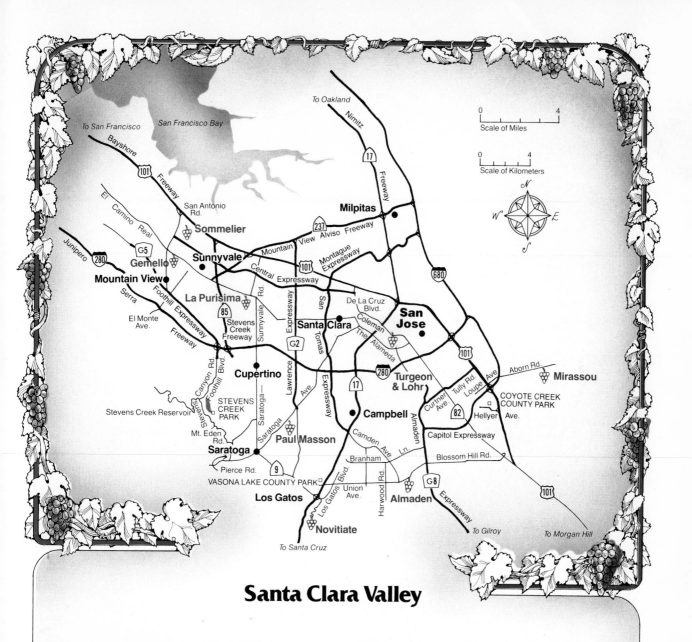

Santa Clara Valley

Almaden. Southbound: on U.S. 101 or I-280 take Santa Cruz-Los Gatos exit at State 17 to Camden Rd. exit. SE 4 mi. to Blossom Hill Rd., E ½ mi. Northbound: on U.S. 101 take State 82 ½ mi. to Blossom Hill Rd. exit, W 4 mi. (1530 Blossom Hill Rd., San Jose, CA 95118) Tel (408) 269-1312. M-F 10-4. GT

Gemello Winery. W off El Camino Real, .8 mi. S of San Antonio Rd. (2003 El Camino Real, Mountain View, CA 94040) Tel (415) 948-7723. Retail store: M-Sa 9-9, Su 9-8.

Paul Masson (Champagne & Wine Cellars). From Saratoga, NE 3¼ mi. on Saratoga Ave.; from I-280, Saratoga Ave. exit, SW 4 mi.; from U.S. 101, Lawrence Expwy. exit, S 7 mi. to Saratoga Ave., W 1 mi. (13150 Saratoga Ave., Saratoga, CA 95070) Tel (408) 257-7800. Daily 10-4. GT/Ta

Mirassou. From U.S. 101, Capitol Expwy. exit, E to Aborn Rd. then E 2 mi. on Aborn to winery. (3000 Aborn Rd., San Jose, CA 95121) Tel (408) 274-4000. M-Sa 10-5, Su 12-4. GT/Ta

Novitiate of Los Gatos. From Main St. in Los Gatos, S on College Ave. to Prospect, W (up hill) on Prospect to winery dr. (PO Box 128, Los Gatos, CA 95030) Tel (408) 354-6471. M-Sa 9-4. Tours M-F: 1:30 & 2:30, Sa: 10 & 11. GT/Ta

La Purisima Winery. From State 85, 2 mi. SE on El Camino Real to Sunnyvale-Saratoga Rd.—SW corner. (725 Sunnyvale-Saratoga Rd., Sunnyvale, CA 94087) Tel (408) 738-1011. Weekends by appt./Ta

Sommelier Winery. From U.S. 101, San Antonio exit W to Middlefield, S on Old Middlefield 2 blocks to Independence, E 1 block to Wyandotte, N 1 block. (2560 Wyandotte Ave., Sec. C, Mountain View, CA 94043) Tel (415) 969-2442. Weekends by appt. GT/Ta

Turgeon & Lohr. From Hwy. 17 in San Jose, SE on The Alameda to Lenzen Ave., N 1 blk. (1000 Lenzen Ave., San Jose, CA 95126) Tel (408) 288-5057. Daily 12-5. GT/Ta

Key: GT (guided tour); IT (informal tour); Ta (tasting).

The old ways *survive in various forms. At the Novitiate Winery in Los Gatos (above), dim, cool cellars are lined with ancient oak oval casks where wines sleep. At Soledad (right), footpower crushes a bit of ceremonial wine each October. It is auctioned to support a charity.*

... Continued from page 60

yards in the Salinas Valley of Monterey County.

The winery, housed in what once was the shop building of a brewery, gives the impression of being several buildings within a building. A cool, redwood-paneled, spacious tasting room is just inside the front door. The tour begins just outside one end of this room, in an open structure housing the temperature-controlled stainless steel fermentors and other modern processing equipment, then dives into an insulated sub-structure filled with almost 2,000 oak barrels of aging wine.

Owned by Bernard Turgeon, Jerry Lohr, and winemaker Peter Stern, the winery opened to the public in 1975 when its first wines were ready for release. The roster includes, among whites: Chardonnay, Chenin Blanc, Pinot Blanc, and the proprietary wine called Jade. The reds are Cabernet Sauvignon, Petite Sirah, and Zinfandel. Also, there is a Rosé of Cabernet Sauvignon. The label in all cases is J. Lohr.

Other Than Wineries

Urban distractions abound in the neighborhood. These notes cover only two with historic ties to wine, and some potential picnic sites.

Leland Stanford in his day ranked as one of the state's most enthusiastic winegrowers, although the histories suggest his skills did not come anywhere near to matching his hopes. Skilled or not, he established three major wineries, one of them on the north side of the present Stanford University campus. The handsome brick building still stands between the Stanford Shopping Center and the university's hospital. Shops and restaurants now fill it.

Farther south, the Mission Santa Clara has similarly dim ties to the vine. Santa Clara is something of a curiosity piece because vines did not prosper there during the mission era. The failure mystified the mission fathers but has been cleared up since. Santa Clara is too cool for the mission variety of grape to ripen properly. This was one of the earliest hints at the complexity of microclimate zones in the northern coast counties.

The mission adjoins the campus of Santa Clara University, on The Alameda.

For picnickers, Stevens Creek Park, a long strip along a narrow and shaded creek, offers picnic sites aplenty in March or April. But as spring wears into summer, the park begins to be crowded. The shallow creek is a fine playground for children, which accounts for a good part of the traffic. The sheltered and wooded nature of the place contributes the rest of the allure.

The park is west of Cupertino on the same road that leads to Ridge Vineyards.

Vasona Lake County Park straddles a creek and reservoir directly alongside State Highway 17 at Los Gatos. It has abundant picnic and recreation facilities on well-kept lawns.

Just west of Los Gatos, where the Coast Ranges begin to climb, Lexington Reservoir's shoreline is a developed picnic and water sports park—but a less manicured one than Vasona.

Picnickers who prefer to be on the east side of the valley will find a county park alongside U.S. Highway 101, not far south of Mirassou. It is Coyote County Park and it has a small lake as well as shaded picnic sites.

Full descriptions of the Santa Clara Valley region are to be found in the *Sunset Travel Guide to Northern California*.

Plotting a Route

Getting around the Santa Clara Valley in the modern era is mainly a matter of picking the most efficient sequence of freeways and expressways.

U.S. Highway 101 (the Bayshore Freeway) steams straight and fast from San Francisco into San Jose. Interstate Highway 280 connects the same two cities and is almost as fast, in spite of its scenic route through coast hill country. On the east side of the bay, State Highway 17 (Nimitz Freeway) is a counterpart to U.S. 101, and Interstate Highway 680 is the easterly equivalent to I-280.

State 17 curves west across the foot of San Francisco Bay, intersects with U.S. 101 and I-280 in quick succession, then continues through Los Gatos all the way to the Pacific shore at Santa Cruz. I-680 ends in a gloriously complicated intersection with U.S. 101 and I-280, just south of San Jose's business area. Visitors coming from the south will find U.S. 101 the only quick approach.

The choice of expressways and major arterials within the region is almost limitless. The map on page 61 shows the most efficient ones for getting to wineries.

Accommodations and restaurants are as plentiful as the large population would indicate. The quietest location is Los Gatos. For lists of visitor facilities, write to the San Jose Chamber of Commerce, 1 Paseo de San Antonio, San Jose, CA 95113; the Saratoga Chamber of Commerce, P.O. Box 161, Sarotoga, CA 95070; or the Los Gatos Chamber of Commerce, P.O. Box 1820, Los Gatos, CA 95930.

The Santa Cruz Mountains

The Santa Cruz Mountains offer almost the perfect fantasy of specialized, hand-crafted winemaking.

Tumultous slopes make every vineyard a scenic wonder, and at the same time keep every vineyard small. Only here and there is the soil deep enough and the sun reliable enough for grapes to mature. So specialist wineries fit themselves—one here, one there—into forests or onto mountaintops, or both at once.

This makes touring a demanding business. The distances are considerable, on winding, narrow roads. The wineries are almost sure to be too small to have daily tastings and tours. But the rewards are singular for wine buffs who wish wine to be an enchanted product from enchanted places.

Even without wine these mountains are enchanted. Thick forests of redwood give way without warning to grassy meadows, which in turn give way to forests again. The enchantment is not undiscovered. The whole region is a vacationland for people who think rustic is better.

The Wineries

At the time of publication, roughly a score of wineries were in operation in the Santa Cruz Mountains from

Half Moon Bay down to Soquel. An exact census is always hard to get in this region because many of the cellars are tiny, part-time businesses which can be—and sometimes are—started with little fanfare, and ended with less.

Of the 20 or so on the rolls in spring, 1979, seven opened their doors to visitors on a consistent schedule. By an accident of alphabet, the only one of these wineries not actually in the mountains leads the list. It is also the largest and oldest winery in the district.

Bargetto Winery is located in the town of Soquel, just inland from the main business intersection. It is housed in a trimly painted red barn that looks just as solid as it is.

The second generation of Bargettos owns it now. John Bargetto and a brother founded it in 1933, and John had a firm hand in the business until his death in 1964. His son Lawrence continues the operation.

There are tours of the premises, starting at the crusher out front and ending at the tasting room on the west end of the building.

In the tasting room, Bargetto offers a substantial number of varietal table wines (Cabernet Sauvignon, Zinfandel, Chardonnay, Johannisberg Riesling, Pinot Blanc, Moscate Amabile), generic table wines, and some fairly ancient dessert wines. The winery uses Santa Cruz Cellars as a second label for generic table and dessert wines.

In addition to being handy to the resort town of Santa Cruz, Soquel is only a moment's detour off State Highway 1. Beach-bound picnickers and anybody en route to Monterey can dip into town with ease. (A second tasting room is on Cannery Row in Monterey.)

David Bruce is up in the hills a couple of miles southwest of Los Gatos on Bear Creek Road. The building is plain, but some distinctive touches in the equipment make this an unusual winery to visit.

Outside are displayed a new style of French crusher-stemmer and a new style of Willmes membrane press, both of which could be explained at textbook length, but are more believable if seen. Inside, the original collection of oak barrels hangs from the walls on cantilevered racks designed by the proprietor and still unique 15 years later. The original barrels have been augmented by many more, stacked conventionally on the floor, and by a modern stainless steel fermenting room.

The other singular touch at David Bruce is a series of solar collectors on the roof of the fermenting room, used to supply hot water to the winery.

Bruce launched his winery in 1964, completed the sizable concrete block aging cellar in 1968, and added the steel fermenting building in 1975.

A physician by profession and a winegrower by avocation, he makes Chardonnay, White Riesling, Cabernet Sauvignon, Petite Sirah, and Zinfandel as his principal wines, most of them from his own steep vineyards around the winery. Tours and tastings are by appointment on Saturdays only.

Congress Springs Winery, new in 1971, is, in spite of the present winery's youth, an old property and one dedicated to preserving old vineyards and an old cellar.

Now the property of the Dan Gehrs and Vic Erickson families, Congress Springs was a winery as early as 1910 under the ownership of a Frenchman named Pierre Pourroy. Now—as then—the working winery is housed on the lower level of a sturdy stucco building while the upper level is home to the winemaker. And, as in the past, the principal vineyard sweeps east from the winery, down a rolling slope. (There are some new vines in the lot, but some go back to Pourroy's day.) The view from the vineyard out across Saratoga is worth the trip all by itself.

The current proprietors also lease other old mountain vineyards in the region, and buy small lots of grapes from local growers. The roster of Congress Springs wines includes Pinot Blanc, Semillon, Sauvignon Blanc, Cabernet Sauvignon, Pinot Noir, and Zinfandel. A Chardonnay is to come.

Tastings are held twice a year, in spring and fall, but visitors may have a look around the tidily kept cellar full of oak barrels on any Saturday, after they have acquired an appointment.

Felton-Empire Vineyards somehow gives an impression of being away from it all, even though the winery and vineyard tuck in behind a row of houses just above the main business street in Felton.

This is a winery property with some history. It was the famous Hallcrest Winery, belonging to San Francisco lawyer Chaffee Hall before his death in the 1960s. (One legacy remains, in the form of a band of awesome wine labels around the tasting room walls, a silent tribute to Hall's expert taste.)

In Hall's day, the winemaking was organic, even primitive in some respects. It is no such thing now. Owners John Pollard and James Beauregard brought in a microbiologist named Leo McCloskey as their winemaker and partner. He has transformed the place into as technically impeccable a place as imagination can conjure.

On the upper level, along with a roomful of stainless steel fermentors and the tasting room, is a laboratory equipped to measure things and creatures only dimly known outside academic halls. Just outside, the crusher-stemmer is an ultra-modern French type which looks like a collection of cockle shells whirling on edge, and the press is a German design, the Willmes membrane type, new in California in 1978. On the lower level of a building cut into a hillside, there are some oak barrels for aging the small production of red wines, and a tiny—but scientific—sterile bottling room. (Medical folks will recognize the air filter from hospital and laboratory applications.)

The production of this winery focuses on sweet white wines, especially Johannisberg Riesling. There are also dry Johannisberg and Gewürztraminer, and very limited amounts of Cabernet Sauvignon and Pinot Noir. One other product of the house is an unfermented varietal grape juice.

Obester Winery was just getting underway as a visitable cellar at publication time, in the unlikely environs of Half Moon Bay.

There is some instant history. Sandy Obester is the granddaughter of John Gemello, founder of the Gemello winery in Mountain View (see page 57), and John

(Continued on page 67)

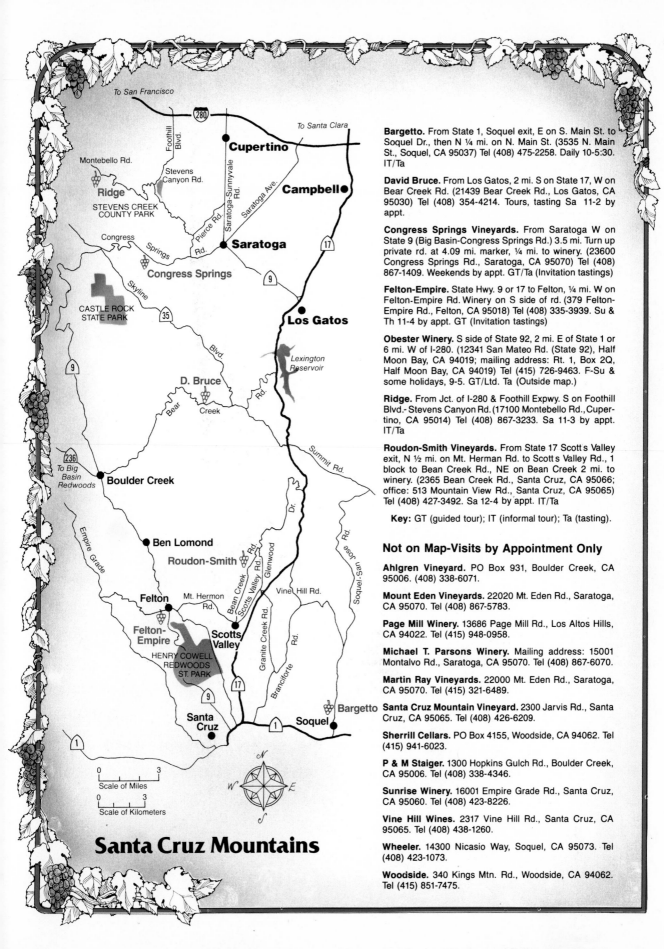

Bargetto. From State 1, Soquel exit, E on S. Main St. to Soquel Dr., then N ¼ mi. on N. Main St. (3535 N. Main St., Soquel, CA 95037) Tel (408) 475-2258. Daily 10-5:30. IT/Ta

David Bruce. From Los Gatos, 2 mi. S on State 17, W on Bear Creek Rd. (21439 Bear Creek Rd., Los Gatos, CA 95030) Tel (408) 354-4214. Tours, tasting Sa 11-2 by appt.

Congress Springs Vineyards. From Saratoga W on State 9 (Big Basin-Congress Springs Rd.) 3.5 mi. Turn up private rd. at 4.09 mi. marker, ¼ mi. to winery. (23600 Congress Springs Rd., Saratoga, CA 95070) Tel (408) 867-1409. Weekends by appt. GT/Ta (Invitation tastings)

Felton-Empire. State Hwy. 9 or 17 to Felton, ¼ mi. W on Felton-Empire Rd. Winery on S side of rd. (379 Felton-Empire Rd., Felton, CA 95018) Tel (408) 335-3939. Su & Th 11-4 by appt. GT (Invitation tastings)

Obester Winery. S side of State 92, 2 mi. E of State 1 or 6 mi. W of I-280. (12341 San Mateo Rd. (State 92), Half Moon Bay, CA 94019; mailing address: Rt. 1, Box 2Q, Half Moon Bay, CA 94019) Tel (415) 726-9463. F-Su & some holidays, 9-5. GT/Ltd. Ta (Outside map.)

Ridge. From Jct. of I-280 & Foothill Expwy. S on Foothill Blvd.-Stevens Canyon Rd. (17100 Montebello Rd., Cupertino, CA 95014) Tel (408) 867-3233. Sa 11-3 by appt. IT/Ta

Roudon-Smith Vineyards. From State 17 Scotts Valley exit, N ½ mi. on Mt. Herman Rd. to Scotts Valley Rd., 1 block to Bean Creek Rd., NE on Bean Creek 2 mi. to winery. (2365 Bean Creek Rd., Santa Cruz, CA 95066; office: 513 Mountain View Rd., Santa Cruz, CA 95065) Tel (408) 427-3492. Sa 12-4 by appt. IT/Ta

Key: GT (guided tour); IT (informal tour); Ta (tasting).

Not on Map-Visits by Appointment Only

Ahlgren Vineyard. PO Box 931, Boulder Creek, CA 95006. (408) 338-6071.

Mount Eden Vineyards. 22020 Mt. Eden Rd., Saratoga, CA 95070. Tel (408) 867-5783.

Page Mill Winery. 13686 Page Mill Rd., Los Altos Hills, CA 94022. Tel (415) 948-0958.

Michael T. Parsons Winery. Mailing address: 15001 Montalvo Rd., Saratoga, CA 95070. Tel (408) 867-6070.

Martin Ray Vineyards. 22000 Mt. Eden Rd., Saratoga, CA 95070. Tel (415) 321-6489.

Santa Cruz Mountain Vineyard. 2300 Jarvis Rd., Santa Cruz, CA 95065. Tel (408) 426-6209.

Sherrill Cellars. PO Box 4155, Woodside, CA 94062. Tel (415) 941-6023.

P & M Staiger. 1300 Hopkins Gulch Rd., Boulder Creek, CA 95006. Tel (408) 338-4346.

Sunrise Winery. 16001 Empire Grade Rd., Santa Cruz, CA 95060. Tel (408) 423-8226.

Vine Hill Wines. 2317 Vine Hill Rd., Santa Cruz, CA 95065. Tel (408) 438-1260.

Wheeler. 14300 Nicasio Way, Soquel, CA 95073. Tel (408) 423-1073.

Woodside. 340 Kings Mtn. Rd., Woodside, CA 94062. Tel (415) 851-7475.

Santa Cruz Mountains

Irrigation *is a way of life in the rain-shy counties from Monterey south (above), but old vines in Santa Clara County are farmed dry. The pickers (right) are at Thomas Kruse's vineyard at Gilroy.*

. . . Continued from page 64

was not only the inspiration, but, at 95, the overseer of the construction and equipping of a winery that was, thus, three generations old at its birth.

The first crush was in 1977. The roster of wines is to include Cabernet Sauvignon, Petite Sirah, and Zinfandel, from grapes grown in warmer climes than Half Moon Bay.

Ridge Vineyards

Ridge Vineyards started in 1959 as a weekend hobby. It has long since grown past that stage, and become one of the largest of the Santa Cruz Mountain wineries. At this point there is enough Ridge to fill the original cellar and a much larger second building. Or, as its proprietors put it, Ridge is about the size of a large chateau in Bordeaux.

Ridge's two locations, almost a mile apart, are both spectacular. The name comes from the fact that the winery does indeed sit on a ridge due west of Cupertino. The topmost vineyard yields views out to the Pacific Ocean and down into a vast portion of San Francisco Bay. The rest of the premises does not lag far off that scenic pace.

Visitors with reservations are welcomed on Saturdays at the rustic original winery, now a bottling and case storage building. It is hidden in a little fold 100 yards or so off Montebello Ridge Road. (Drivers need to watch mailbox numbers carefully for the cue to angle left into a dirt drive that, from the road, appears to have no purpose.)

When the weather is reasonably good, tasting and talking go on outdoors, at one edge of a small patch of vines, but there is indoor space for gloomy days.

From time to time the hosts are moved to cart visitors up to the producing winery, a handsome old frame building that covers a sizable cellar dug into the stone hillside. The equipment is modern, but the building goes back to before the turn of the century, when it housed the Montebello Winery.

The labels on Ridge wines are probably the most explicit of any in California. The list of labels is dominated by Cabernet Sauvignon and Zinfandel, but also includes Chardonnay and White Riesling.

Roudon-Smith Vineyards

Roudon-Smith Vineyards moved into a new building in 1978, in the Scotts Valley district of Santa Cruz County.

The wood-sided structure is best described as prim. Indeed, it would look at home somewhere in New England. But it is cut into a side slope above a fine meadow, and is hedged all about by tall conifer forests, so leaves no doubt about its California location.

Like several other wineries of its era, Roudon-Smith started in 1972 as a cross between a hobby and a business, and quickly grew into a full-sized business. The proprietors are Robert Roudon and James Smith, whose basic thought is to make Chardonnay, Cabernet Sauvignon, and Zinfandel every year, plus a fourth wine of whichever variety seems right for the time — a sort of elective subject. Petite Sirah and Pinot Blanc have been two choices to date.

The well-equipped and tidily kept winery has stainless steel fermentors and other processing gear outside, barrels for fermenting and aging on the lower level, and an upper story for storage of cased goods and relaxed Saturday tastings.

Since Bean Creek Road was under-designed even for the Model T, the atmosphere is almost certain to be tranquil for those who write or call for appointments to visit.

More wineries

More wineries. Connoisseurs of California wine will recognize some prestigious names on this long list, along with some new ones. They are grouped here for a variety of reasons that make each almost as hard to get into as Harvard. In most cases, the reason is a lack of size. For diligent students of wine, the addresses are noted with the map for this region.

A man named Martin Ray managed, from 1943 onward, to create vast interest in one such small winery high in the hills west of Saratoga. Ray died in 1975 shortly after his property had been divided into two parts.

A new owner now operates the Ray winery, with Ray's son, Peter Martin Ray, as winemaker. A second winery, Mount Eden, is operated by a consortium of vineyard owners who used to sell their grapes to Ray.

The property was never large enough to allow casual visits. Now neither of the two wineries is large enough to accept any visitors other than well-established friends.

In addition to continuing on their own, the properties' successes under Ray inspired a whole school of similar enterprises.

Ahlgren is a tiny, family-owned winery located under the home of the Dexter Ahlgren family. The aim is to explore microclimates at Boulder Creek and learn which grape varieties will fare best there. Page Mill Winery is in Los Altos Hills, again beneath the home of its owners, the Richard Stark family. The Michael Parsons Winery in Soquel is as small as these others, though in its own separate building. Santa Cruz Mountain Vineyard was founded in Santa Cruz so that its proprietor, Ken Burnap, could explore Pinot Noir and naught else.

Sherrill Cellars, yet another husband-wife partnership, was in the process of acquiring a new home in 1979, after a spell under the post office at Woodside. As the new property matures, it may become at least as visitable as Congress Springs.

P. and M. Staiger, another family winery housed under its owners' residence, is both tiny and inaccessible. Sunrise Winery, the propriety of Keith Hohlfeldt and R. EuGene Lokey, suffered a fire in 1978 in its aging cellars, and was proceeding at half speed in 1979. Its premises are the old Vincent Locatelli winery in Boulder Creek.

Vine Hill, in the hills east of Santa Cruz town, belongs to Richard Smothers, whose name goes on the label of limited-production varietal wines from the home and other vineyards. Wines by Wheeler are made by Dan Wheeler at his Nicasio Cellars. The winery is a twin-bore cave, hand-dug into sandstone, downslope from the proprietor's residence.

Finally, in this alphabetic listing, comes Woodside, the property of Bob and Polly Mullen, who use their small winery to make— among other wines—a Cabernet Sauvignon from the last few vines of the legendary LaQuesta estate of Dr. E. H. Rixford. LaQuesta Cabernet Sauvignons were much treasured in pre-Prohibition California.

Other Than Wineries

Entirely in keeping with the wooded nature of this part of the world are two fine redwood parks with both picnic and camping facilities.

Big Basin Redwoods State Park is the larger of the two. On a loop road off State Highway 9, it is slightly more distant from the wineries than its running mate, but not enough to disqualify it as a respite, or a refuge.

The other is Henry Cowell Redwoods State Park, which straddles State 9 near Felton. It has several fine picnic grounds accessible from the highway. Its campground is reached via Graham Hill Road from Felton.

In addition to the parks, one other important diversion is the Roaring Camp & Big Trees Steam Railroad, a narrow-gauge line that was built for loggers but now serves to amuse small fry (and, not incidentally, to impress their elders with some superior wooded scenery).

From Boulder Creek down to Felton, State 9 is fairly regularly lined with visitor accommodations ranging from rustic cabins to fancy motels. For lists, write to the Santa Cruz Convention and Visitors Bureau, P.O. Box 921, Santa Cruz, CA 95061.

Wineries away from this core area can suggest parks and accommodations near them.

Plotting a Route

State Highway 9 forms a snaking loop into the heart of the Santa Cruz Mountains from the freeway, State Highway 17. One end of the loop is at Los Gatos, the other at Santa Cruz. With modest help from local roads, it leads into the neighborhoods of four of the region's seven wineries welcoming visitors on a regular basis.

Thus, the main question is how to get to State 9. The efficient way is via freeways. U.S. Highway 101 and Interstate Highway 280 intersect with State 17 not far from Los Gatos.

However, the main thing in winery touring is to get in tune with the subject. In this woodsy part of the world, getting in tune calls more for curving excursions through back country than flat-trajectory flights on freeways. To get a day in the Santa Cruz Mountains off to a proper start, use State Highway 1 to Santa Cruz, from north or south, then shift to State 9 or Scotts Valley Road from that town.

From San Francisco, it is better to follow the Skyline Boulevard (State Highway 35) to its junction with State 9 in the hills above Saratoga. The Skyline does what its name suggests: runs along the top of the immediate world—the backbone of the mountains. A good, lightly trafficked, two-lane road, it provides a whole series of sweeping views east over San Francisco Bay and the Santa Clara Valley. On the west side the sweeping views are fewer, but include a few distant seascapes. Sometimes the hills are open and grassy, sometimes tightly furred with conifer forests.

South Santa Clara

Time was when South Santa Clara was all of a piece, vinously speaking. Its wineries offered good, sound jug wines, and almost nothing else. That day is gone.

Increasing urbanization, a wine boom that placed strong emphasis on varietal wines, vintage dates, bottles with corks, and new blood in the region's community of winemakers all combined to broaden the spectrum of wines from Gilroy and Morgan Hill until it included high-priced varietals along with solid values in jugs.

In a quiet way, this is appealing country for winery visitors to seek out. U.S. Highway 101 cuts a straight swath through it, giving a hint of the countryside, but the nature of the region reveals itself more truly from byways close to the hills.

West of U.S. 101, the district called Hecker Pass is made of vine-filled bottomlands, grassy hills, oak knolls, cactus farms, wandering creeks and reservoirs, the beginnings of conifer forests just below the namesake pass, and a nest of small wineries.

Gilroy, the major center, has revitalized its downtown district since being bypassed by the new stretch of the freeway, U.S. 101. What used to be a tedious stretch of stop-lighted highway now has become a stylish shopping street. The landmark building remains unchanged. It is the old city hall, built a year before the great earthquake of 1906. Having survived the quake, the structure has provided continuous wonderment to students of architecture ever since.

In season, a heavy, sweet aroma of drying fruit hangs in the still air, even in the middle of town. This is prune and apricot as much as grape country, and the dehydrators perfume the district for week after warm summer week.

The Wineries

Most of the south county's 16 wineries are west of U.S. 101, especially in the Hecker Pass district. However, the quartet ranged along U.S. 101 from Morgan Hill down to Gilroy includes the largest and most visitable cellars in the district.

Bertero Winery, set well back from State 152 behind a stucco house, a wood-frame visitor center, and a substantial block of vines, dates back almost as far as wineries date in Gilroy.

Alfonso Bertero opened the doors in 1917. The second and third generations carry the name forward in somewhat enlarged premises. The founding Bertero built his winery of redwood, having dug a 4-foot-deep center-aisle cellar as an insulating device for the redwood tanks. (It is almost a sure thing that a winery with such a device was designed and built by an Italian.) His building has been augmented by a concrete block addition.

The pavilionlike tasting room, handsomely set in the vineyards, is the starting point for visitors. From it, the Berteros launch tours of the vineyard and winery proper, throwing in asides on an enormous oak tree and the whereabouts of marker stakes from the original Spanish land grant, all of which are well to the rear of the property from the tasting room.

The wine list, all of it available for tasting, spreads more widely than most in the area: Barbera, Cabernet Sauvignon, Grignolino, Pinot Noir, and Zinfandel are the reds. A couple of whites and a rosé round out the table wine roster. There are also sparkling wines, Vermouth, Dry Sherry, Cream Sherry, and Tawny Port.

Conrotto announces its winery with a standard rural mailbox—no more, no less. The modesty is too much. This is a good-sized establishment of its kind.

The wines—red, white, and rosé—go mostly to the restaurant trade, but the proprietor will sell them on the premises in lots of a case or more, mainly in jugs.

There is no tasting. Neither is there a tour of the premises, which run for a surprising distance beyond the front wall.

Fortino Winery is yet another case in which a new proprietor shifted the production of a one-time jug winery over to vintage-dated varietals.

Ernest Fortino bought the old Cassa Brothers winery in 1970, and has been upgrading the property ever since, although without modernizing it very much. A Willmes press bought for the harvest of 1978 is one concession to contemporary winemaking. An automatic bottling line is another. Otherwise, Fortino is the sort of man who believes that the old ways are best.

His fermentors, in a building to the rear of the main cellar, are open-topped redwood. In the main cellar he ages his wines—nearly all of them reds—in redwood and good-sized oak tanks. Time is his favorite filter.

Fortino's list of wines includes Carignan, Charbono, Cabernet Sauvignon, Petit Syrah, Zinfandel, several varietal rosés, and Sylvaner, as well as regular generic bottlings. All are on hand in a spacious tasting room and gift shop at the front end of the winery. So are occasional limited bottlings of white wines from black grapes.

Emilio Guglielmo Winery, a mile east of U.S. 101 at Morgan Hill, recommends itself to visitors for several reasons.

Most directly to the point, the owning family has taken pains to make its tasting room and picnic area inviting. Inside, the tasting room is quiet and cool. The focal point is a serving bar fashioned entirely from tank staves, but there is ample space to step back between tastes. Outside, vines trellised along one side of the building allow the picnic area to be as sunny and warm as a winter day can get, or as cool as a summer day can be. Umbrellas over the four tables add shade in summer.

An appointment to tour the winery can be worth the effort because of the winery's unusual aspects. Foremost of these is a double file of stainless steel fermentors patterned after a type developed in Australia. The tank floors, instead of sloping in one direction, are conical so that grape solids empty automatically through doors at the very bottom of the cone. At the other end of tradition, the Guglielmos keep a sizable collection of oak oval casks that predate Prohibition. Some are in a cellar beneath a residence—the original winery. The rest are in the main aging cellars along with steel and redwood tanks and a growing collection of oak barrels.

The Emilio Guglielmo label is new in the 1970s, though the winery dates back to 1933. The new label reflects a shift from jug generics to vintage-dated varietals. (The jugs still are available under the original Emile's label.) The list includes Semillon, Sylvaner, and Johannisberg Riesling in whites; a Grignolino Rosé;

Wine Barrels

and Barbera, Cabernet Sauvignon, Ruby Cabernet, and Zinfandel among reds.

One final reason to visit the property is the availability of small lots of selected older wines at the winery.

Hecker Pass Winery belongs to Mario and Frances Fortino, who launched their small cellar in 1972, but did not open it for tours until their first wines were ready for tasting in 1974.

Mario Fortino came to the United States from Italy in 1959 and worked for other cellars in the Santa Clara region—full-time until he founded his own winery, part-time until the business was well established. Some outgrowths of his earlier employment show up in the working winery. The basket presses and redwood fermenting tanks at the rear of the small stucco building are typical of old-line Gilroy, but inside, the proprietor has a temperature-controlled stainless steel fermentor for his whites, sophisticated pumps, and other equipment to suggest he learned a good deal while he was getting ready to launch his own venture. The aging cellar has redwood tanks and oak barrels.

The table wines, most of them vintage-dated and labeled as "Estate Bottled include Chablis, Carignane, Petite Sirah and Zinfandel. There are also dessert wines on the list.

Kirigin Cellars occupies one of the oldest properties in the Hecker Pass district but is one of the newest wineries.

Nikola Kirigin Chargin bought the one-time Bonesio vineyards and winery in 1976, and forthwith gutted the time-weary main cellar. The building now houses three rows of temperature-controlled stainless steel fermentors and racks of oak barrels in place of the old redwood tanks. The cellar also holds modern filters and bottling equipment, all visible on the leisurely tour.

Even the exterior of the cellar got a face-lift: buff stucco walls replace the old board-and-batten ones.

The proprietor, fifth generation of a Croatian winemaking family, had both university training and experience in other California wineries to lead him toward modern equipment and techniques.

The results are on hand for tasting in a pleasant

building next to the cellar, and at another tasting room on Business U.S. Highway 101 in Morgan Hill. The roster includes Chablis, French Colombard, Cabernet Sauvignon, Pinot Noir, and a flavored dessert specialty called Vino de Mocca.

In front of Kirigin Chargin's residence—originally the home of a local cattle baron named Henry Miller—a pine-shaded picnic ground can accommodate as many as 30 people.

Thomas Kruse Winery,

Thomas Kruse Winery, across the Hecker Pass Highway (State Highway 152) from the end of County Road G8, more or less started the revolution that is changing this region from a country jug producer to a source of vintage-dated varietals.

A Chicagoan until wine caught his interest, Kruse acquired the property in 1971 and forthwith set about doing things differently from his neighbors of that time. He has not changed since: he ferments all his wines in oak barrels, sticks to varietals, and insists on bone-dry wine as his style.

The list is uncommon, too. It includes a white sparkling wine from Zinfandel, a Carignane, a dry rosé from Cabernet Sauvignon, Pinot Noir, Grignolino, and a bottling of Thompson Seedless.

The winery is a classic wooden barn. Kruse spent several years rehabilitating a weather-weakened structure, but never violated its appearance inside or out. The tasting room, in a back corner, is all old wood: a serene nook in keeping with the rest of an unfailingly cheerful and informal atmosphere.

Live Oaks Winery advertises itself best of the several wineries along U.S. 101. A platoon of signs on the north side of the road invites visitors to turn and drive along beside an eclectic lot of frame buildings until the drive dips downhill and ends alongside a white-painted, board-and-batten winery.

In all its casual and good-humored aspects, this winery typifies what the Hecker Pass district used to be in its entirety: a source of modestly priced, unpretentious, everyday wine made in and offered from an appropriate kind of winery.

Live Oaks' tasting room has a paneled wall on one side, stainless steel bottling tanks on the other, stuffed birds and animal heads wherever space permits, and case goods stacked as owner Peter Scagliotti's need requires. The tasting room is at the lower level, at the rear of the building. Tours of the upper-level fermenting area go on only during the vintage season.

The Live Oaks label, which has been around since 1912, appears on red, white, and rosé—two wines of each type. Scagliotti offers a line in bottles and, for even less cost, a line in jugs.

Pedrizzetti Winery is most accessible at its roadside tasting room and gift shop on Business U.S. 101 at the north side of Morgan Hill. However, visitors who make appointments can tour the producing winery and taste its wines there.

The building's history goes back to 1946 with the Pedrizzetti family, and originates in 1923, when Camillo Colombano made wine on the property. Inside the rectangular cellar, two rooms full of well-seasoned redwood tanks are much as they have been from the be-

ginning. However, the rest of the property has gone modern. Outside, two rows of stainless steel fermentors flank a processing deck with a new continuous press. Another row of steel tanks snugs against an outside wall, and still more steel tanks fill the white wine aging cellar inside.

The office and tasting room are in a small building at the rear of a courtyard on the opposite side of the winery from the fermenting area. The roster of wines is mostly varietal and vintage-dated. Included are Zinfandels of every hue—white, rosé, and red—Petite Sirah, Barbera, and—rare bird—a white wine from Barbera.

Rapazzini's Los Altos Winery, a bit more than 2 miles south of Gilroy on U.S. Highway 101, has grown slowly but steadily in the years since its founding by Jon and Vic Rapazzini.

For many years the square stucco building housed only a tasting room and stored cases. Recently, however, Rapazzini moved its aging and bottling cellars onto the property.

The range of wines under the Rapazzini label is a wide one, including nearly all of the familiar table and dessert types, and sparkling wines. All are available for tasting here and at two other locations.

Richert & Sons Winery houses itself in an impressive hulk of a building, one with concrete walls imposing enough to summon up thoughts of a fortress.

However, there is nothing formidable about the welcome. All comers on weekends get a leisurely tour of the cellars, full of Sherries and Ports slumbering in oak. Weekday visitors need appointments.

The winery dates back to 1953 as the property of founder Walt Richert, and now, his son Scott. From the beginning, they have stuck to the task of making dessert wines.

San Martin Winery makes life easy for people who would like to taste its wines near the source. The company maintains three sizable tasting rooms within a close radius of its producing winery.

The main tasting room adjoins the winery, on Business U.S. 101 near its intersection with San Martin Avenue. There is another tasting room on the freeway, U.S. 101, near Dunne Avenue in Morgan Hill, and yet a third, also on the freeway, a shade more than 2 miles south of Gilroy.

At all three, wines are offered in sequences governed by the traditional rules of professional tasters. A host comments on each wine as it is poured. These exercises—frequent, brief, and never formidable—show wine in its wide diversity of flavors.

The roster of San Martin wines is dominated by vintage-dated varietals, and includes Sauvignon Blanc, Johannisberg Riesling, Muscat di Canelli, Chenin Blanc, and Chardonnay among whites; Zinfandel, Pinot Noir, Petite Sirah, and Cabernet Sauvignon among reds. A specialty of the house is a separate line of wines called "Soft" because they are fermented with an alcohol content lower than the normal percentage. In this list are Chenin Blanc, Johannisberg Riesling, and Gamay Beaujolais.

The winery is open to group tours only, and only by

(Continued on page 73)

Wine & the performing arts

Several wineries offer musical accompaniment to the clinking of wine glasses during the summer. A roundup of events includes winery telephone numbers to call for further information. If you prefer to plan well in advance for these popular attractions, you can write to the wineries at the address provided in the appropriate districts.

Geyser Peak Winery sponsors annual performances of the Brown Bag Opera from the San Francisco Opera Company on Sunday afternoons in June. The free concerts in the winery's picnic grove last approximately one hour. Complimentary wine tasting takes place prior to performances. The audience is encouraged to bring picnic lunches and pillows or blankets to sit on. For details on performances, call (707) 433-6585.

Guild Wineries offers the Winemasters Concert Series each summer at their Lodi facility. Past programs ranged from jazz to pops. Complimentary wines are served during intermission at the outdoor evening concerts, held on the lawn of the Winemasters' House. For information on programs and ticket prices, call (209) 368-5151.

Johnson's Alexander Valley Winery has pipe organ concerts one weekend each month for wine-sippers. For information on dates, call (707) 433-2319.

Charles Krug hosts the popular August Moon Concerts at their winery in St. Helena. While the concerts are always held in August, the program varies each year, resulting in different admission fees. Information on this series can be obtained by calling (707) 963-2761.

Paul Masson Vineyards originated the tradition of performances of classical music among the vines in 1957 with their "Music at the Vineyards" series. More recently they started a companion series of jazz and folk music concerts called "Vintage Sounds." For ticket and program information on both series, call (408) 257-4735.

Robert Mondavi Winery presents a Jazz Festival on the last Sunday in June and every Sunday in July at 7 P.M. Picnics are allowed after 3:30 P.M. and wine and cheese tasting is offered during intermission. For additional information, call (707) 963-9611. For information on the Shakespeare Festival held at the winery in August, call the Napa Valley Association of the Performing Arts at (707) 944-2462.

Sonoma Vineyards have presented a concert series for a number of years. Only one concert is scheduled for 1979. For further information, call (707) 433-6511.

Souverain offers a schedule of theatre, opera, and concerts throughout the year. Some events are free, others require an admission fee. Information on upcoming programs is available by calling the winery at (707) 433-6918. You can request to be added to their mailing list for future events.

Paul Masson's *old mountain winery is the backdrop to a concert of chamber music.*

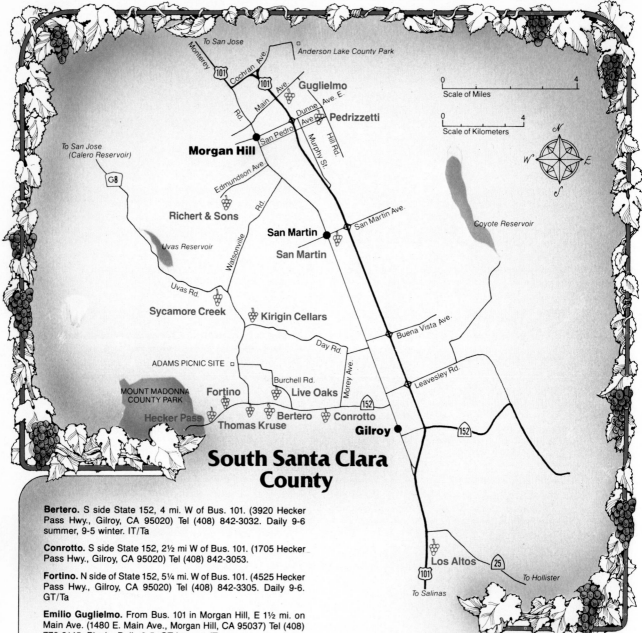

South Santa Clara County

Bertero. S side State 152, 4 mi. W of Bus. 101. (3920 Hecker Pass Hwy., Gilroy, CA 95020) Tel (408) 842-3032. Daily 9-6 summer, 9-5 winter. IT/Ta

Conrotto. S side State 152, 2½ mi W of Bus. 101. (1705 Hecker Pass Hwy., Gilroy, CA 95020) Tel (408) 842-3053.

Fortino. N side of State 152, 5¼ mi. W of Bus. 101. (4525 Hecker Pass Hwy., Gilroy, CA 95020) Tel (408) 842-3305. Daily 9-6. GT/Ta

Emilio Guglielmo. From Bus. 101 in Morgan Hill, E 1½ mi. on Main Ave. (1480 E. Main Ave., Morgan Hill, CA 95037) Tel (408) 779-2145. Picnic. Daily 9-5. GT by appt./Ta

Hecker Pass. N side of State 152, 5½ mi. W of Bus. 101. (4605 Hecker Pass Hwy., Gilroy, CA 95020) Tel (408) 842-8755. Daily 9-6.

Kirigin Cellars. From Bus. 101, W 5 mi. on State 152, N 2½ mi. on County G8. Winery on E side of rd. (11550 Watsonville Rd., Gilroy, CA 95020) Tel (408) 847-8827. Picnic; groups must reserve. Daily 10-6. GT/Ta

Thomas Kruse. S side State 152, 5 mi. W of Bus. 101. (4390 Hecker Pass Hwy., Gilroy, CA 95020) Tel (408) 842-7016. Picnic. Sa-Su 12-5, or by appt. IT/Ta

Live Oaks. N side State 152, 4 mi. W of Bus. 101. (3875 Hecker Pass Hwy., Gilroy, CA 95020) Tel (408) 842-2401. Daily 8-5./Ta

Pedrizzetti. Tasting room: N limit of Morgan Hill, E side of U.S. 101. Winery: from Bus. 101 in Morgan Hill, E on Dunne Ave. to Murphy, S to San Pedro Ave., then E. (1645 San Pedro Ave., Morgan Hill, CA 95037) Tel (408) 779-7774. M-Sa 9-5:30. Tours by appt.

Rappazzini's Los Altos Winery. E side U.S. 101, 3 mi. S of Gilroy. (PO Box 247, Gilroy, CA 95020) Tel (408) 842-5649. Daily summer 9-7, winter 9-6./Ta

Richert & Sons Winery. From Bus. 101 in Morgan Hill, SW 2 mi. on Edmundson Ave. just short of intersection with Oak Glen Ave. (1840 W. Edmundson Ave., Morgan Hill, CA 95037) Tel (408) 779-5100. M-F by appt, weekends 11-4. GT/Ta

San Martin. E side Bus. 101, 2 mi S of Morgan Hill; 5 mi. N of Gilroy. (PO Box 53, San Martin, CA 95046) Tel (408) 683-4000. Daily 9:30-5:30. Group tours by appt./Ta

Sycamore Creek Vineyards. From Bus. 101 in Morgan Hill, 3.9 mi. on Watsonville Rd. to Uvas Rd. (12775 Uvas Rd., Morgan Hill, CA 95037) Tel (408) 779-4738. Weekdays by appt., weekends 12-5. GT/Ta

Key: GT (guided tour); IT (informal tour); Ta (tasting).

. . . Continued from page 70

appointment. Under previous owners the property was archaically equipped. Now, after an end-to-end rehabilitation, its equipment is typical of contemporary California winemaking. The temperature-controlled stainless steel fermentors are outdoors, next to stainless steel dejuicing screens and continuous presses. White wine storage is in stainless steel in a cold cellar. Reds and selected whites age in oak barrels.

The tour leads to private tastings in a romantic room in the oldest and finest building on the property, a brick structure that was once full of redwood tanks, but now is primarily used for bottling.

Sycamore Creek joined the roster of South Santa Clara wineries in 1976. Its proprietors, Terry and Mary Kaye Parks, had acquired the old Marchetti winery and vineyards earlier, and could think of no better use of the property than to resume with the winemaking.

The producing winery is a classic wooden barn, cut into a gentle slope that looks out to rolling vineyards. Crushing and pressing take place on a concrete pad on the uphill side of the steep-roofed white building. Just inside the building, on a sort of mezzanine, is the bottling department. Below it, at the downhill grade level, is a fermenting and aging cellar full of neatly stacked barrels and a trio of small oak tanks.

Tasting goes on in a second barn a few feet away from the first one, by appointment and primarily on weekends. The list includes Cabernet Sauvignon, Carignane, and Zinfandel in its white, rosé, and red forms. A new planting of chardonnay in the home vineyard will add that wine to the list when it matures.

More wineries. Another three cellars are located in South Santa Clara, two of them new and one old. All three are too small to court many visitors. The new two are Ronald Lamb and Sarah's Vineyard. The old-timer is the Peter & Harry Giretti winery, which sells red wine in demijohns to a local clientele.

Other Than Wineries

Several pleasing and temptingly diverse parks line the hills on either side of the southern Santa Clara Valley.

Dry and parched as the east hills appear from U.S. Highway 101, they hide a string of reservoirs, each developed for recreation.

The most highly developed of the lot is Anderson Lake County Park, in the first range of hills east of Morgan Hill. Cochran Road (the temporary connector between Business U.S. Highway 101 and the new freeway U.S. 101) goes directly to the main area. Although primarily developed for boaters, the shore has a large picnic area. At the southern tip of the same lake is a second picnic area, this one reached via East Dunne Avenue.

Henry W. Coe State Park lies directly east of Anderson Lake on an extension of East Dunne Avenue. The distance from downtown Morgan Hill is 14 miles.

A one-time working ranch, the headquarters of Coe is in the old ranch buildings at an elevation of 2,600 feet. Both these and the park's rolling, grassy hills attract watercolorists by the score, especially in late April and May when the wildflowers bloom. There are some picnic sites and a few campsites. Expect a day-use fee.

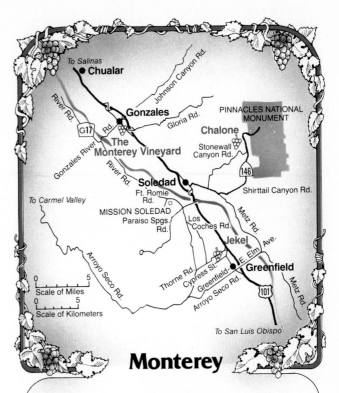

Monterey

Chalone Vineyard. From Soledad, State 146 10 mi E to Stonewall Canyon Rd., NW ¼ mi to winery road. (PO Box 855, Soledad, CA 93960) Appt. required from S.F. office: (415) 441-8975.

Jekel Vineyards. From Bus. U.S. 101 in Greenfield, W on Walnut to winery. (40155 Walnut, Greenfield, CA 93927) Tel (408) 674-5522. Th-M 10-5. GT/Ta

The Monterey Vineyard. From U.S. 101 at S side of Gonzales, Alta exit N ½ mi to winery. (800 S. Alta St., Gonzales, CA. 93926) Tel (408) 675-2326. Daily 10-5. Groups by appt. GT/Ta

Outside Map Area

Durney Vineyard. Directions to winery with appt. (PO Box 1146, Carmel Valley, CA 93924) Tel (408) 659-2690 or 625-1561. By appt. only.

Monterey Peninsula Winery. Jct. of Monterey-Salinas Hwy. and Canyon Del Rey. (2999 Monterey-Salinas Hwy., Monterey, CA 93940) Tel (408) 372-4949. Daily 10-dusk. /Ta

Key: GT (guided tour); IT (informal tour); Ta (tasting).

Farther south, Coyote Lake County Park offers a third choice. Again, a reservoir is the prime attraction, with shoreside picnicking as a most welcome supplement to the charms of the place. Access is from Gilroy via Leavesley Road.

Over in the west hills, Mt. Madonna County Park has its main entrance at the summit of the Hecker Pass. Like Henry W. Coe State Park, this area has been built out of a one-time working ranch. Cattleman Henry Miller owned it and left some formal gardens to posterity.

Also, the park has a herd of albino deer as a special attraction. Roads meander through the oak-forested hills at the upper elevations.

At the foot of the hills, next to a creek and pond, are picnic sites in the shade of oak and other trees. The

Divergent qualities *make the Central Coast a fascinating place to explore. At David Bruce's property (above) high in the Santa Cruz Mountains, autumn storms bump and scrape along at vine level. At The Monterey Vineyard in the Salinas Valley (left), autumn sun casts soft light through stained-glass windows.*

entrance is from State Highway 152. There is a day-use fee for this park, too.

There is also a small county picnic park next to County Road G8, opposite the end of Burchell Road. Several tables are in the shade of mature trees.

A water-oriented park in the west hills is at Chesbro Reservoir, some miles north and west of Morgan Hill via G8, as that wayward road pokes and dawdles its way northward to a junction with State Highway 17 near Los Gatos.

Plotting a Route

U.S. Highway 101 brings traffic into southern Santa Clara County from both north and south. State Highway 152, called the Hecker Pass Highway west of U.S. 101 and the Pacheco Pass Highway east of it, handles the cross traffic.

U.S. 101 is principally a divided freeway now, except for one stretch between Morgan Hill and the southern fringe of San Jose and another one just south of the Santa Clara County line. The road keeps to the flat but also runs close enough to the hills to remain more pleasant than many freeways.

The Pacheco Pass Highway, winding and scenic, carries a great amount of truck traffic in and out of the Central Valley and also serves as a link in the much-traveled road to Yosemite National Park. It is hardly ever lonely. The Hecker Pass segment of the road does not climb so high nor serve so many uses. Connecting Gilroy and Watsonville, it is popular enough, mainly for the views from the summit.

Not many local roads supplement the major highways. Business U.S. 101 runs through the business districts of Gilroy and Morgan Hill.

County Road G8 is a narrow and winding way between Gilroy and San Jose and also the means of getting to several reservoirs and picnic parks.

Where G8 forks left toward the hills, Watsonville Road eases right and back toward Morgan Hill. It stays alongside farms and houses, including one zinnia patch and one tiny commercial mushroom farm.

Monterey County

In the mid-1970s, Monterey County exploded into prominence as a vineyard district. Between 1963 and 1973, acreage devoted to vineyards had gone from a few hundred to more than 30,000.

Nearly all of that acreage is concentrated in the Salinas Valley between the towns of Greenfield and King City. Most of the vines are on steep, photogenic alluvial fans at each side of this long, broad furrow in the Coast Ranges. The richer, thicker soils at the bottom of the valley still hold the more traditional crops of this part of the world: strawberries and all sorts of leafy vegetables (above all—lettuce). U.S. 101 plows through farmland steadily all the way from Salinas to King City, but grapes cannot be viewed from the highway half so well as they can from local roads to either side.

In spite of all its vines, Monterey remains relatively modest as a district for vinous touring. Only five wineries had formal visitor policies in spring, 1979. Of

these, four were small, the fifth middle-sized.

This curious state of affairs owes itself to the fact that Monterey vineyards were originally a response to urban pressure against old vineyards just to the north, in Alameda and Santa Clara counties. Great volumes of Monterey grapes belong to or are bought by Almaden, Paul Masson, San Martin, Mirassou, Wente Bros., and other firms with long histories in those neighboring counties.

The roster of Monterey wineries is likely to grow longer soon. In the meantime, the short existing list offers a remarkable diversity to both eye and palate.

The Wineries

Except for The Monterey Vineyard, which looms up right next the freeway, a trip to Monterey County wineries requires taking local roads for anything from a quick detour to a genuine pilgrimage. Jekel is the quick detour. The Monterey Peninsula Winery is some miles west of U.S. 101 on an easy road. Chalone and Durney tuck away high in hill country to either side of the valley.

Chalone Vineyard occupies a special niche in Monterey in every sense of the term: it is in a separate place, and both vineyard and winery are the oldest in the county.

The vineyards roll across limestone slopes high above the east side of the Salinas Valley floor. The topmost rows almost reach the foot of a striking geologic curiosity, The Pinnacles. (An abstraction of the near-vertical basalt outcrop decorates Chalone's labels. Another representation of it is set in tile in the bottling room walls.) The next nearest vineyards are miles west and hundreds of feet lower.

The oldest Chalone vines go back to 1919, planted then by a man named Bill Silvear, who put his grapes on the site of a still-older vineyard. After Silvear died in 1957, the vines endured ups and downs until 1965, when the current owner bought the property. The owner is the Gavilan Corp., directed by Richard Graff and Phil Woodward.

First, the proprietors set the old vines right. Then, beginning in 1972, they began to expand their plantings. The original plot approached 30 acres. Current acreage is a bit more than 100.

Interim owners, between Silvear and the Gavilan Corp., had built a small winery. The white-walled, oak-shaded original served through 1974. Now dwarfed by a new cellar upslope, it serves to hold bottled wines.

Scaled to hold the expanded vineyard's full production, the handsome newer building cuts into its hillside so that crusher and press are at the high side. The upper floor holds cased goods, lab, and bottling room. Underneath are three cavelike galleries filled with fat, French barrels from Burgundy.

Getting up to see the place requires an appointment and considerable effort, especially when rain softens unpaved roads near the winery. But diligent admirers of California wine make the trip gladly.

The shy-yielding vineyards do not give enough to allow tasting of a short, predominantly Burgundian list of wines: Chardonnay, Chenin Blanc, Pinot Blanc, and Pinot Noir.

Cannery Row

Durney Vineyards stands in the same sort of lonely splendor as Chalone, but on the other side of the county, on the sea-facing side of the Santa Lucia Mountains, rather than looking down into the Salinas Valley.

William Durney's vineyards and winery occupy one of a mere handful of reasonable slopes in some seriously steep hill country, a few miles east of Carmel Valley Village.

Again, for dedicated students of California wine, a visit well repays the effort of assembling the required group, arranging for an appointment, and making the trek up Cachagua Road. The winery, founded in 1977 and not yet full-grown, occupies a handsomely renovated hay barn. Crusher and press stand just outside the back wall. Inside, stainless steel fermentors occupy one end, oak barrels the other. In time, there is to be a separate oak aging cellar.

Vineyards run across a series of gentle hills and dips on the downhill, north side of the winery. The roster of wines includes Chenin Blanc, Johannisberg Riesling, Cabernet Sauvignon, Gamay Beaujolais, and Zinfandel.

Jekel Vineyards hides away in an anonymous quarter of Greenfield, north and west of the main business district.

The winery is housed in a classically red, barn-shaped building. But this is mostly illusion. A steel building with eight inches of insulation sandwiched between its walls, the Jekel winery is modern to the minute. A fermenting room full of temperature-controlled stainless steel tanks is directly behind the front wall. Just outside stands a big crusher and a Willmes basket press. Alongside the fermenting room is a cellarful of oak barrels. In one corner of this room is a sterile bottling room. And so it goes.

A comfortable tasting room is but a few paces from any of these elements in the compact winery, so tours are effortless.

Vineyards surrounding the cellar are planted to chardonnay, chenin blanc, johannisberg riesling, gamay beaujolais, and cabernet sauvignon. These are the wines on the list.

The owning Jekel family planted its vineyards be-

ginning in 1972 and built its winery just in time for the harvest of 1978.

Monterey Peninsula Winery nestles into various corners of the mazelike bottom story of a fine stone building alongside State 68, more or less at the east end of Monterey airport's main runway.

A tasting room is at the front door, wherein a knowledgeable staff helps sort out the differences between wines from a wide range of districts. The grottolike room makes as romantic an impression as one might wish. Dim light and stone walls are supplemented by barrels that cannot be fitted anywhere else in the winery's crowded space.

Because the cellars are so crowded and built on such uneven floors, the tasting room is as far as visitors may go, except on one day of each year, when people on the mailing list are invited to an old-fashioned, barefoot grape stomp staged to help local charities.

Deryck Nuckton and Roy Thomas launched the winery in 1974 after some years as hobby winemakers. The focus is on reds—especially Cabernet Sauvignon and Zinfandel—but the list includes other varietals as well as some generics.

The building, incidentally, also houses offices, shops, and a restaurant. It gained earlier fame as the home of the original Cadematori's restaurant.

The Monterey Vineyard winery buildings—dramatic structures—loom up alongside U.S. 101 on the south side of Gonzales, in a region with very few large buildings.

Architecturally, the buildings' style is called "early California" by the proprietors, which is to say an amalgam of mission, adobe, and other Spanish colonial influences. Arches and towers are the main distinguishing marks, along with tile roofs.

Visitors work their way through the whole complex on a carefully engineered route that takes them past the crushers and presses, into a large fermenting hall, and through aging cellars full of large and small oak cooperage, before it finally arrives at the tasting room.

Close attention to the gear will show any number of unusual details. One example is a system of closed conveyors for moving pomace and lees (solid residues) out of the fermentors and into presses or filters. Another is a metal pallet for barrels in the small wood aging cellar. Most of these details were designed by winemaker-president Dr. Richard Peterson.

There is another family touch to the winery. Peterson's artist wife, Diane, designed the tall stained-glass windows that grace the towering side walls of the cellar.

In the second-story tasting room, the wines are varietal: Chardonnay, Chenin Blanc, Grüner Sylvaner, Gewürztraminer, a Botrytis Sauvignon Blanc (when nature smiles right), Cabernet Sauvignon, Pinot Noir, and Zinfandel.

The original scheme for The Monterey Vineyard was a grand one. The existing building was to produce only red wines from a huge acreage. A companion building was to be added for white winemaking. That enterprise sank before it could swim. However, an expansion of the original structure has been announced by the company's new-in-1978 owners, The Coca Cola Co.

A small proportion of the facility makes wines for The Monterey Vineyard label under Coke's ownership.

The rest is a producing cellar for another Coke winery, Taylor of New York.

More wineries. As Monterey gathers speed as a wine district, several relatively new cellars have opened for business without yet being ready for steady visitors at the time of publication. One of these is at Ventana Vineyards on Los Coches Road west of Greenfield. The property of Douglas Meador, the winery had a first small crush in 1978, in temporary quarters. Another winery with a slightly longer track record is Carmel Bay Wine Co., owned by stockbroker Fred Crummey. It is located in a one-time airplane hangar at the Monterey Peninsula airport.

Other Than Wineries

In addition to its vineyards and wineries, the Salinas Valley has an engaging admixture of the works of God and of the works of man on behalf of that God.

The pure article is Pinnacles National Monument, an imposing array of columnar basalt and lava caves left over from one of the more explosively formative moments of the local landscape. The monument is high in the hills that form the east side of the valley.

Much the greater development—including the visitor center and campgrounds—is on the east side of the monument, reached from Hollister along State 25. No road crosses the monument from west to east, but a fair sampler of the lava caves and some lunar-looking terrain crops up at the end of State 146, which departs from downtown Soledad and arrives some 40 minutes later in the monument.

Incidentally, the fogs and breezes that cool the valley floor do not penetrate to the Pinnacles, which, though temperate in spring and fall, are downright hot in summer.

Two of California's 21 Franciscan missions are in the vineyarded reaches of the Salinas Valley. They are Soledad and San Antonio. A third, San Miguel, is no great distance to the south along U.S. 101.

Soledad Mission—Mission Nuestra Señora de la Soledad, to give it its full name—has only one mostly melted adobe wall surviving from the original complex. (A chapel of newer style flanks it.) In its forlorn way, the old wall tells the history of the region. Soledad was essentially a desolate, lonely failure among the missions. The primary lack was available water. The Franciscans had no idea that the Salinas River was so full of water because none showed on top. One of the many crops they could not grow was grapes.

Nowadays, the new wave of vineyardists does a joyous victory dance right on the spot. Each September brings a mission festival and treading of the grapes on the grounds. Fair maidens compete to see which among them has the most efficient feet for crushing grapes. The results of their labors are fermented by Mirassou Vineyards and sold at auction during the following year's festival. Proceeds go to a restoration fund for the mission.

The mission stands west of U.S. 101. It is reached via Paraiso Springs and Fort Romie roads.

A far truer look at how life went in the mission days can be had at Mission San Antonio de Padua, located in a high valley west of the main Salinas River Valley,

approximately level with King City. Jolon Road leads to it from U.S. 101.

Most completely and most accurately restored of all the Franciscan missions along El Camino Real, San Antonio has the priceless further advantage of a location with even fewer inhabitants now than it had at the height of the mission era. In short, the broad, grassy plain in front of the mission and the oak-covered slopes behind it look much as they did between 1780 and 1830.

Within, the building has restorations or replicas of a great deal of working mission gear. Included is the old wine cellar, a structure guaranteed to gladden the hearts of all who drink wine from newer, more manageable fermentors and aging cellars.

Picnickers in search of a table in the Salinas Valley have only a handful of choices. A few flank the chapel grounds at Mission Soledad. The other choice is a sizable municipal park at King City, on the east side of U.S. 101 midway between the two freeway exits leading into town.

Plotting a Route

Monterey County is long on its north-south axis and slender on its east-west axis. More important, two lofty ranges of coast hills—the Gavilans on the east and the Santa Lucias on the west—trend northwest to southeast. As a result, the coast side of the county has two-lane State 1, and the Salinas River Valley has freeway U.S. 101 to transport people directly along that north-south axis.

The trouble for wine-fanciers is that the wineries string themselves out east to west, at about mid-county. Local roads tying them together get into and over the hills as best they can, but expressways they are not.

State 68, from Salinas to Monterey, links coast and valley toward the north. It is a fairly level two-laner for most of the distance.

Arroyo Seco Road-Carmel Valley Road is the other, more southerly tie-route. It is sometimes two lanes and sometimes a lane and a half, high, winding, and usually gloriously scenic.

State 46 (Stonewall Canyon Road), leading up to the Pinnacles, echoes on the east side what Carmel Valley Road does on the west.

For those who would rather see flowers than freeways, River Road and Fort Romie Road along the west hills are an expedient alternative from Salinas south to Greenfield.

San Benito County

San Benito County is something of a curiosity as far as vinous visitors are concerned. Almaden Vineyards owns or operates nearly all of the vineyards in the county, is the largest employer there, has two large wineries there, but is open to visitors only at a tasting room miles from either. Meanwhile, three small-to-tiny wineries with no more than 200 acres among them *are* open to visitors.

Except for Hollister and San Juan Bautista on its northern boundary, this is a sparsely settled region,

MISSION SAN JUAN BAUTISTA

San Juan Bautista

Scale of Miles 0 — 5

Scale of Kilometers 0 — 5

Enterprise Rd.

Union Rd.

Hospital Rd.

Southside Rd.

Tres Pinos

San Benito River Rd.

Cienega Rd.

Calera
Grass Valley Rd.

Cygnet

Paicines

Limekiln Rd.

Enz

San Benito

Almaden Vineyards. Pachecho Pass: at jct. of State 152 and 156. Daily 10-4:30. /Ta (Outside map)

Calera Wine Company. From Hollister, State 25 (San Benito St., Nash Rd.) to Cienega Rd. S on Cienega Rd. 11 mi., W on pvt. rd. 200 yds up hill to winery. (11300 Cienega Rd., Hollister, CA 95023) Tel (408) 637-9170. Picnic. Sa 11 a.m. by appt. GT

Cygnet Cellars. From Hollister, State 25 (San Benito St., Nash Rd.) to Cienega Rd. S on Cienega Rd. 11¼ mi., W on winery rd. (11736 Cienega Rd., Hollister, CA 95023) Tel (408) 637-7559. By appt. only.

Enz Vineyards. 16 mi. S of Hollister via Cienega Rd., then W on Limekiln Rd. (1781 Limekiln Rd., Hollister, CA 95023) Tel (408) 637-3956. Weekdays by appt.

Key: GT (guided tour); IT (informal tour); Ta (tasting).

especially in the Cienega District, where all of the visitable wineries and one of Almaden's pair are located. The only alternate point of interest is a park for off-road motorcycle riding.

The Wineries

All three of the small wineries in the district—Calera, Cygnet, and Enz—are on the uphill, or west side of Cienega Road, running southward from Almaden's Cienega winery.

Almaden Vineyards welcomes visitors to an agreeable tasting room at the junction of State Highway 152 and State Highway 156, in the Pacheco Pass country east and north of Hollister. Here, the wide range of Almaden wines is accessible for study and purchase.

Though not open for tours, the company's producing wineries are worth driving past to get an impression of the scope of Almaden's activities. The winery on Cienega Road devotes itself primarily to reds; the one just off State 156 at Paicines produces whites.

Calera Wine Company is yet another dramatic new start among California wineries. It is under construction on the still-born frame of a limekiln in the west hills of San Benito County. By spring, 1979, the

first two stages of a proposed eight-level building were snugged into a steep hillside above Cienega Road.

From every level, the view is spectacular: down an oak-clad slope to a small pond, then out across a low range of hills, then a higher one, and finally, on clear days, to the distance-hazed Sierras.

There is a functional reason for choosing the steep site. Proprietor Joshua Jensen's winery is being built so that gravity will do most of the work once grapes arrive on the premises. They will come in at the high side, level with crusher and press. Calera's stainless steel fermentors will be one step lower. Each succeeding move of wine toward bottle will go another level downhill.

Construction began toward the middle, with the oak barrel aging cellar. Early succeeding stages are to head back upslope, starting with the tasting room, then the fermenting area (the latter was in a temporary building for the first crush on the premises, in 1978). Once those are in place, progress will head downhill again, to include a second barrel cellar, a bottling room, and last—a warehouse for bottled wines.

Completion of the tasting room was planned for summer, 1979. If early arrivals do not find it ready, they can find consolation in a tree-shaded picnic ground for 25 that flanks the crusher area at the top of the site. Jensen allows visitors only by appointment, and only on Saturday.

The wines are Zinfandels, made from purchased grapes, and Pinot Noirs from the winery's own vineyards. Both varietals come in several separate bottlings.

Cygnet Winery occupies a modest metal building on an oak-studded grassy site just off Cienega Road. Within, the small cellar is conservatively equipped with a basket press, a small crusher, and American oak barrels. The unusual note is a series of 500-gallon fermentors made of fiberglass.

Cygnet is directed by two partners, James Johnson and C. Robert Lane. Their principal wine is a late-harvest Zinfandel. They also produce small lots of Cabernet Sauvignon and a dry white wine.

Enz Vineyards is tucked away toward the top of Limekiln Canyon, in a spot so peaceful and agreeable that it looks like the setting for a Disney movie, or maybe an episode from some nostalgia piece like *The Waltons*.

This is almost an anachronism: a small winery run along the lines of a family farm. In the midst of the vineyards—the oldest blocks date back to 1895—are the family home, a white barn converted to an aging cellar, fermentors and crusher set on an open pad, and a metal building, well upslope and last in line, which serves as both barrel and bottle aging cellar.

All hands in the Enz family turn out for various tasks in the producing and selling of wines made on the ranch from its own vines. Bob is the winemaker, Susan the business manager. Their children work without titles.

The roster of wines is relatively short, focused on Pinot St. George and Zinfandel, and on a proprietary aperitif, called Limekiln in tribute to the fact that a now-disused part of the property holds the remains of a once-active lime industry. The surviving bits include walls from some old kilns, and a stray stone building

(Continued on page 81)

Currier & Ives *could not have printed a better Central Coast vineyard scene than this one belonging to Almaden (above) near Paicines. At right, visitors start tour of Almaden aging cellar near Los Gatos.*

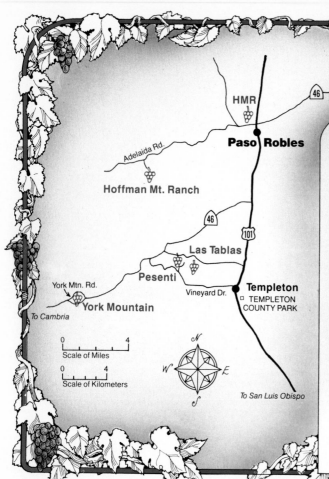

San Luis Obispo County

Estrella River Winery. From U.S. 101 at Paso Robles, exit E on State 46 6½ mi. Get directions to winery at farm house. (Shandon Star Rt., Paso Robles, CA 93446) Tel (805) 238-6300. Daily 10-4. IT/Ta

Hoffman Mountain Ranch. Tasting room in Paso Robles 1 block W of State 46-East exit from U.S. 101. (Adelaida Rd., Star Rt., Paso Robles, CA 93446) Tel (805) 238-4945. Tasting room open M-F 11-7; Sa, Su, holidays 9-7. Winery tours by appt. only.

Las Tablas Winery. From U.S. 101 Las Tablas exit, W 3 mi. on Las Tablas Rd., S on winery rd. (PO Box 697, Templeton, CA 93465) Tel (805) 434-1389. Daily 9-6./Ta

Pesenti. From U.S. 101, Vineyard Dr. exit, W 2½ mi. on Vineyard Dr. (Rt. 1, Box 169, Templeton, CA 93465) Tel (805) 434-1030. M-Sa 8-6, Su 10-6./Ta

York Mountain. From U.S. 101, W 9 mi. on State 46, then N on York Mtn. Rd. (Rt. 1, Box 191, Templeton, CA 93465) Tel (805) 238-3925. Daily 10-5. /Ta

Key: GT (guided tour); IT (informal tour); Ta (tasting).

Santa Barbara County

Firestone Vineyard. From U.S. 101 N of Buellton, 2 mi. E on Zaca Station Rd. (PO Box 244, Los Olivos, CA 93441) Tel (805) 688-3940. M-Sa 10-4. GT/Ta

Los Alamos Winery. From Los Alamos 5 mi. W on State 135. (PO Box 5, Los Alamos, CA 93440) Tel (805) Ask operator for Los Alamos 2390. Tu-Su 10-5. IT/Ta by appt.

Rancho Sisquoc. From Santa Maria S on U.S. 101 to Betteravia Rd. exit, then E 15 mi. on State 176 & Foxen Canyon Rd., 2 mi. on pvt. winery rd. (Rt. 1, Box 147, Santa Maria, CA 93454) Tel (805) 937-3616. M-Sa 10-4. GT/Ta by appt.

Sanford & Benedict. 9 mi. W of Buellton on Santa Rosa Rd., S side of rd. (Santa Rosa Rd., Lompoc, CA 93463) Tel (805) 688-8314. By appt. only.

Santa Barbara Winery. From U.S. 101, 1 block W on Anacapa St. (202 Anacapa St., Santa Barbara, CA 93101) Tel (805) 962-3812. Daily 10-5. /Ta (Outside map)

Santa Ynez Valley Winery. From Solvang, 2 mi E on State 246 to Refugio Rd., S 1 mi. to winery drive. (365 Refugio Rd., Santa Ynez, CA 93460) Tel (805) 688-8381. Daily. GT/Ta by appt. only.

Zaca Mesa Winery. From U.S. 101 N of Buellton, E 9 mi. on Zaca Station/Foxen Canyon rds. (PO Box 224, Los Olivos, CA 93441) Tel (805) 688-3310. Daily 10-4. GT/Ta

Key: GT (guided tour); IT (informal tour); Ta (tasting).

. . . *Continued from page 78*

or two left over from what was once a bustling community of some 200 souls.

Like most such small wineries, this one requires an appointment to visit.

Other Than Wineries

The sparsely settled Cienega district offers no particular diversions from winery touring. However, the agreeable old mission village and stagecoach stop of San Juan Bautista serves as a gateway to the county for those traveling along U.S. Highway 101.

In addition to the Mission San Juan Bautista and other historic buildings on the old plaza, San Juan's main street is lined by an inviting miscellany of specialty shops.

Picnickers are hard-pressed to find a spot in this region unless they arrange to stop at one of the wineries.

Plotting a Route

Since all three of San Benito's visitable wineries stretch out along Cienega Road on the west side of the valley, the only question is where to pick up that road.

From downtown Hollister, San Benito Street runs west to its end. A left turn is made there onto Nash Street, which leads in two blocks to the head end of Cienega Road.

Those coming from the west via State 156 can turn south short of Hollister at Union Road (marked by a round-backed hill planted to grape vines), joining Cienega Road a shade less than 5 miles farther.

San Luis Obispo County

San Luis Obispo County dawdled along for decades after the repeal of Prohibition as an even more one-dimensional wine district than Gilroy, farther to the north. A handful of small wineries around Templeton made Zinfandel and/or country jug wines for a local trade. Then, with the wine boom in the 1970s, vineyards and wineries sprang to a new and more diverse life.

Now, both vines and wines are concentrated in the area around Paso Robles, stretching east to Shandon and south to Templeton. Reflections of the old days linger, particularly near Templeton, but the new wineries are larger, occupied with making a wide range of varietal table wines and selling to distant markets.

The miles are not many from one winery to the next, but the philosophic distances can be much greater—the contrasts both agreeable and instructive. Other contrasts help make the district a pleasing one to visit: the break from steep and wooded hills west of U.S. Highway 101 to low, rolling terrain east of the highway, where a light dusting of oaks gives visual relief to broad expanses of grass.

The Wineries

In 1979, the roster of active wineries in San Luis Obispo County numbered five, all of them offering tasting within easy reach of U.S. 101. Only Estrella River has regular guided tours, but appointments at Hoffman Mountain Ranch and Pesenti will lead to looks into cellars different from Estrella and from each other.

Estrella River Winery became a landmark on the road between Paso Robles and Shandon as soon as the building went up in 1977.

It could not be otherwise, given the size of the stucco-walled main cellar, its lofty observation tower, and its location at the high point of some 600 acres of rolling vineyard.

Estrella River is the propriety of a private corporation headed by Cliff Giacobine and W. Gary Eberle, the business manager and winemaker, respectively.

There is a particular effort here to court visitors, beginning with the observation tower, and continuing with a well-mapped tour route on elevated walkways inside the cellar. Planned for 1979 construction were a separate tasting hall and a picnic ground.

The observation tower looks north to the Gavilan Mountains and west to the Santa Lucia Mountains. Both views are striking. The foreground scene of rolling vineyards falls easily on the eye, too.

Below the open-air tower, a closed-in gallery gives close views of the crusher-stemmer and adjoining continuous press.

Inside the main walls, an open platform looks first across a spacious fermenting room full of stainless steel tanks, then into an aging cellar full of oak upright tanks and barrels, the latter piled high on metal pallets. At the foot of stairs leading down from the platform, a large window looks into a modern sterile bottling room.

Estrella River offers only varietal table wines from selected lots of its own grapes. The roster includes Chardonnay, Johannisberg Riesling, and Muscat Canelli among whites; Cabernet Sauvignon, Zinfandel, and small lots of Syrah are among the reds.

Hoffman Mountain Ranch wines can be tasted with little trouble, but having a look around the winery requires a bit of a journey into dramatic hill country west of Paso Robles.

The firm maintains its most accessible face a block or two west of the State Highway 46 exit from the freeway, U.S. 101, at Paso Robles. Tasting and sales are housed there in a red building that looks as if it were designed by a man who was too late to invent the caboose.

The winery itself is some miles west. For the serious student of wine, getting an appointment and trekking up Adelaida Road to the ranch repays the effort.

Hoffman Mountain Ranch lives up to every part of its name. It is the property of Dr. Stanley Hoffman and his sons, winemaker Michael and vineyardist David. Its vineyards range in elevation from 1,100 up to 1,800 feet, sometimes on breathtaking slopes.

Finally, the property yields other crops, and looks entirely the part of a traditional ranch, white rail fences included.

The winery building fits its dramatic setting. A broad roof swoops up to a peak above the open-walled fermenting room. Stainless steel fermentors and a see-

Spanking new *wineries now dominate San Luis Obispo County. Hoffman Mountain Ranch (left) has an ultramodern bottling line with a superior scene outside its picture window. At Estrella River Vineyards (below), visitors are guided through the winery's big fermenting room full of stainless steel tanks.*

through bottling room with a fine view of grassy hills share the upper level. Parallel and downhill, the oak aging cellars hold upright tanks on the lofty side, and barrels on the downhill side, where the roof sweeps low toward the ground. The whole building is built of unpainted wood. It was completed in 1975.

The original 1962 vineyards of cabernet sauvignon, pinot noir, sylvaner, and chardonnay do not come as part of the tour. They are up and over the ridge-top, in four-wheel-drive terrain. In 1979, additional plantings were to begin on slopes facing toward the winery.

The HMR label is used only for varietal table wines, especially from the grapes noted above.

Las Tablas Winery is a new start on the oldest active winery property in the Templeton district.

The new start began late in 1976, when John and Della Mertens bought the property that had been the Rotta Winery since 1907, and before that the Adolph Siot winery going all the way back to 1856.

In 1979, the Mertens continue the patient process of upgrading outworn cooperage and equipment. While they renovate the winery proper, they are making essentially the same list of wines as their predecessor: dry, off-dry, and sweet Zinfandel, and a Muscat. The lone addition is a white table wine.

The tasting room is housed in an old redwood tank attached to the front of the main aging cellar. There is no tour of the working cellar, located upslope to the rear, in an ingeniously elevated and insulated Quonset-type building.

Pesenti Winery is the youngster in the Templeton district. Founder Frank Pesenti planted his first vines in 1923, built the first part of his winery in 1934, and added what is now the major building in 1947.

The winery continues in Pesenti family hands, now represented by the second and third generations. The white-walled cellars and their rows of redwood and oak tanks do not lend themselves to casual wandering; tours are by appointment only. However, the spacious tasting room is open to all comers.

The list of wines ranges from varietal table wines through several dessert types.

York Mountain Winery is the westernmost cellar of the three in Templeton, and several scores of feet higher in the hills than its neighbors.

Andrew York established his first winery in 1884 to use surplus grapes from his own vineyard. The property went two more generations in York family hands, until 1970, when a veteran winemaker named Max Goldman bought what had become a time-wearied place.

Goldman's original intention was to turn the one-time Zinfandel winery into a *methode champenoise* sparkling wine house. Sparkling wines remained a thought for the future in 1979, but Goldman and his family have replanted the first 10 acres of York's old vineyard, and are making small lots of varietal table wines from their own grapes and those of neighbors. The roster includes Chardonnay, Cabernet Sauvignon, and Merlot, as well as the traditional Zinfandel.

The brick-walled tasting room, with its big fireplace and miscellaneous memorabilia of earlier days (the most surprising of which is an ancient motorcycle), makes a comfortable stop in any season.

York Mountain Road loops north of State 46, up on the hill slope at its west end and down in verdant bottomland toward the east.

Other Than Wineries

This is not an easy part of the world for picnickers, or for families who need to offer small children a respite from tasting rooms and winery tours.

There is a county picnic park on the east side of U.S. 101 at Templeton. The big recreational park in the region is at Nacimiento Reservoir, several miles into the west hills from Paso Robles.

Accommodations and restaurants are both plentiful at Paso Robles. A listing may be obtained from the Paso Robles Chamber of Commerce, P.O. Box 457, Paso Robles, CA 93446.

Plotting a Route

Complications in getting around the region do not exist. The State Highway 46-East exit from U.S. Highway 101 at Paso Robles leads directly to two of the five cellars. Either the State 46-West or Vineyard Avenue exits at Templeton lead straight to the other three. Indeed, no other roads lend themselves to local exploration.

Santa Barbara County

Santa Barbara County's vineyards and wineries are close to well-established vacation spots, especially the polyglot town of Solvang, where traces of the early Franciscan mission and the cowboys have become overlaid with a thick layer of Danish.

Vineyards and wineries alike hide in the rolling hill country on either side of U.S. Highway 101 from Buellton north to Santa Maria. All are far enough off the freeway to be invisible from it, but not so far as to make visits difficult. In fact, quite the opposite is true: a well-articulated web of secondary roads allows easy access to the wineries, rewarding pike-shunners with superior scenery between tours and tastes. The price in extra miles is small indeed.

The Wineries

The county's cellars are new additions to this landscape, all but one of them founded since 1970, most of them since 1975. At publication time, the roster stood at 7, but the promise was for more in the near future.

Two of the six wineries between Solvang and Santa Maria are readily visitable, as is the lone cellar in the city of Santa Barbara. The rest require appointments.

Firestone Vineyard's winery building soars dramatically above the southernmost ridgeline of the mesa called Zaca. Rooflines set at varying angles to each other give the place a bold, sculptured quality. Beneath those roofs the architectural drama continues, with the highest peak giving the fermenting room an almost cathedral-like atmosphere. A swooping roof over the oak aging cellar finally comes so close to earth that barrels can be stacked only two high along the downhill wall, and then only because the floor drops a level to make a separate gallery.

Well-trained tour guides explain winemaking from one end to the other, beginning with the vineyards that surround the cellars, and ending with tastes in a wood-walled room in which an upper set of windows looks out to nearby hills, while a lower set gives views into the cool darkness of the lower wood aging cellar.

Founded in 1974, Firestone is the largest winery in the Santa Ynez Valley, and likely to remain so for some time to come. A partnership of the Leonard Firestone family and Suntory, the Japanese distillers and wine-makers, the firm offers estate-grown varietal wines, including Chardonnay, Gewürztraminer, Johannisberg Riesling, Cabernet Sauvignon, and Pinot Noir, plus Rosés of Cabernet Sauvignon, and Pinot Noir.

Los Alamos Winery is one of the smallest in the district, with one of the biggest vineyards to supply its needs.

The small concrete block structure sits, along with several other buldings, in a clearing amid a rolling sea of vines.

The winemaker is the owner's mother-in-law. Mary Vigoroso (the name is apt) sticks to Zinfandel for the most part, fermenting it in stainless steel tanks that remind one of the building's original purpose—they are dairy tanks, and it was a dairy—then aging the wine in French oak barrels.

Other Los Alamos wines may be made elsewhere, although only from grapes on the property.

Because the winemaker is also the tour guide and chief salesman, she requests the courtesy of an appointment. A sign on the winery door explains how to find her when she is not in the cellar.

Rancho Sisquoc hides away about as well as a winery can: deep in the Sisquoc River Canyon, two miles beyond public roads—about halfway between the small town of Los Olivos and the village of Sisquoc.

Most California vineyard properties are known as ranches. This one puts the rest in the shade, not because of its 200 acres of vines, but because of the other 38,000 acres, most of it grazing land for cattle.

The winery building is quietly unobtrusive, hidden among older work buildings and dwellings at ranch headquarters, as the vines are in the rangeland. Still, even as a miniature cog in a giant wheel, the cellars are pleasing to visit.

The first crusher is nailed to one wall of the cozy tasting room. It is a baseball bat, too short and light to do the work now, but not by much.

Behind the tasting room, with its front wall of local river rock, lies the small barrel aging cellar. Fermentors, presses, and other working gear are in the other wing of an L-shaped board-and-batten building.

Behind the winery is a pleasant picnic lawn. All around it, the ranchhouse grounds come close to being an unofficial arboretum, with oaks, peppers, palms, peaches, avocados, pecans, and pines growing in harmonious confusion.

Although the ranch goes back beyond the turn of the century, the first major block of vines dates only from 1970. Owner James Flood of San Francisco bonded the winery just in time for the harvest of 1977.

The list of wines is almost as short as the vinous history: Franken Riesling, Johannisberg Riesling, Rosé of Cabernet Sauvignon, and Cabernet Sauvignon are made each year from small, selected lots of grapes. Most of the crop is sold to other wineries.

Although there is almost always someone around to sell wine to droppers-in, tours require an advance appointment.

Sanford & Benedict's vineyards suddenly loom out of the grassy landscape alongside Santa Rosa Road between Buellton and Lompoc.

Aside from getting rid of the barley and garbanzo beans that used to grow on their property—and still do on much of the surrounding landscape—the proprietors have kept the original flavor of their ranch intact.

A weathered barn, complete with classic corrugated iron roof, dominates a trio of ranch buildings. The outside is a complete charade: inside is a tidy winery—and a handsomely finished one. The floor is flagstone, taken from local bedrock. The walls are smooth-sawn redwood.

Sanford & Benedict's red wine fermentors are rare these days; they are open-topped oak tanks. They nestle between rows of oak barrels, and in one case, next to a Willmes press painted baby blue.

The open fermentors are but one clue that things are done in the old-fashioned way here. Mostly it is a matter of choice, but also imposed by the complete lack of electricity on the ranch. (Gas lamps illuminate night work at harvest time. A portable generator powers the machinery.)

Like most wineries in the county, Sanford & Benedict is quite new. The vines went in in 1972; the first crush was in 1976.

The roster includes Chardonnay and Pinot Noir as particular specialties, and also lists Johannisberg Riesling and Cabernet Sauvignon.

Santa Barbara Winery occupies a one-time warehouse near the waterfront of the city for which it is named.

It is the old-timer in the county. Proprietor Pierre LaFond bonded a cellar in 1962, which grew enough to require a move to the present premises by 1965. The winery has continued to grow enough to need several expansions since then.

Although the cellars are well apart from the others in the county, the vineyards are not. LaFond grows grapes for his varietal table wines along the lower reaches of the Santa Ynez River west of Buellton. The varieties include Chardonnay, Chenin Blanc, and White Riesling among whites; and Cabernet Sauvignon and Zinfandel in reds. All of these, along with some jug generics, may be tasted at the winery.

Santa Ynez Valley Winery is one of a considerable number of new California cellars housed in old dairy buildings. This bespeaks a trend toward more small wineries and fewer small dairies, and saves the pouring of a great many new concrete floors, but—in this case—causes a good deal of extra walking for winemakers and visitors.

Inside the plain walls at Santa Ynez, bottled wines are stored at three different levels in one room, wines in oak barrels or steel tanks are stored at two levels in two rooms, and the stainless steel fermentors are outdoors. If the floor plan is a bit unorthodox, the equipment is not. An appointment is required to take a tour, but this winery is as instructive as most small wineries are in the sequence of winemaking steps.

Santa Ynez Valley Winery was founded in 1976 by a trio of partners, all residents of the region. Their vineyards—most of them at the winery, some a few miles away at Los Olivos—supply the winery with grapes for Chardonnay, White Riesling, Sauvignon Blanc, Semillon, a white from Cabernet Sauvignon, and Merlot.

The property, not incidentally, once held the forerunner of St. Mary's College, hence the signpost reading "Old College Ranch" at the head of the entry drive.

Zaca Mesa offers a complete look at a thoughtfully designed, flawlessly equipped, small California winery of the sort that draws bits and pieces from everywhere and still manages to look as native as the oak trees growing on grassy hills all around it.

The propriety of Marshall Ream, a retired oil executive, Zaca Mesa houses itself in a prim, cedar-sided refinement of a classic wooden barn, set into a small hollow along the Foxen Canyon Road side of the mesa from which it takes its name.

Out back, the crusher is a new French design that looks like a collection of cockle shells whirling around in a metal sleeve. The stainless steel fermentors are from Santa Rosa. Inside the windowless building, a lofty, wood-walled aging cellar holds oak barrels from coopers in several different corners of France. Next to the cellar is a sterile bottling room based on a German model. The building dates from 1978.

The small scale of Zaca Mesa makes for easy understanding of the whole process of winemaking.

Tours of the cellars depart from a tasting room housed in a separate building.

Behind the tasting room and alongside the cellar, picnic tables string out in the shade of native oaks.

Wind Towers

(Save for a ceremonial patch of grapes, all landscaping is of native plants.)

Most of the vineyards are on top of the mesa, but one block runs alongside Foxen Canyon Road, starting a shade more than a mile south of the winery.

The varieties planted include chardonnay, johannisberg riesling, sauvignon blanc, cabernet sauvignon, pinot noir, and zinfandel. All are available as varietal wines.

Other Than Wineries

This region, though new as a wine district, has been a major destination of tourists for years. Solvang, with its Danish flavor, draws as many as 5 million visitors per year. Pea Soup Andersen's at Buellton seems to get almost that many.

The *Sunset Travel Guide to Southern California* provides detailed information on these two towns, the missions of Santa Ynez and LaPurisima, and the ocean shore resorts at Santa Barbara, Gaviota, and more northerly points.

For picnickers, the parks closest to the wineries are Santa Rosa County Park, a tree-shaded slope high above the Santa Ynez River west of Buellton via Santa Rosa Road, and Los Alamos County Park, just west of Los Alamos town.

Santa Rosa has many picnic tables and a couple of games courts, and fewer users than most parks in this part of the world. Los Alamos County Park adjoins a school athletic field. Flatter than Santa Rosa, it has agreeable picnic sites under mature oaks.

The biggest, most versatile park in the region is some miles east of Santa Ynez via State Highway 154. It is Lake Cachuma County Park, where there is swimming and boating as well as a picnic ground.

Accommodations and restaurants are abundant in the region. In addition to Solvang and Buellton, Santa Maria offers well-developed visitor facilities. For lists, write to Solvang Chamber of Commerce, P. O. Box 465, Solvang, CA 93463, or Santa Maria Chamber of Commerce, P. O. Box 277, Santa Maria, CA 93546.

Plotting a Route

U.S. Highway 101 neatly divides the vineyarded reaches of northern Santa Barbara County into western and eastern sectors. It is a freeway for the whole duration of its run through the winemaking district, though the rolling hill country keeps it from being monotonously straight and out of touch with the countryside.

When speed is required, the freeway can be used in getting from one winery to another. However, local roads east of the freeway are bucolic, but straight enough and uncrowded enough to add very little time to a tour while improving the scenery and the feeling of being in wine country.

From Santa Ynez, Refugio Road connects with State Highway 154 at Los Olivos; from Los Olivos, Foxen Canyon Road rambles north to a junction with State Highway 176. The latter rejoins U.S. 101 at Santa Maria. Four wineries are on or very near these routes.

West of U.S. 101, Santa Rosa Road, State Highway 1 and State Highway 85 make a loop, anchored either at Buellton or Los Alamos.

The East Bay

Mostly urban, but famous for white wines

Although Alameda and Contra Costa counties have long traditions as sources of wine, both had long sinking spells lasting into the early 1970s. The Livermore Valley was the last remaining district with not only a reputation, but a sizable acreage in vines. Mission San Jose and other early districts had long since replaced vines with houses and factories.

With the wine boom has come a considerable new technology for handling grapes, and a curious resurgence of winemaking on the east side of San Francisco Bay. There are not many new vineyards growing in this populous part of the world, but numerous new wineries have sprung up to use grapes grown elsewhere.

The Livermore Valley, with its open spaces, continues to look the part of a wine district, as it has since the 1880s. However, the greater number of East Bay wineries are located on the populous bay shore from Fremont north to Berkeley.

To the north, Contra Costa County and neighboring Solano County make a tidy loop drive.

The Livermore Valley

Say "Livermore" to a student of California wine, and he will make the automatic associations of "white wine" and "gravelly soil." It is an early wine-producing community.

Pioneer vineyardists Charles Wetmore and Louis Mel brought cuttings of vines from Chateau d'Yquem very early in Livermore's wine history and made Sauterne-like wines from the resulting grapes. The original Carl H. Wente and the original James Concannon concentrated on white wines, too. Winemakers have branched out from white wines, but never left them.

The whole county of Alameda produces much less than 1 percent of the state's wine each year. However, the families making wine in Livermore still include families that made wine there in the beginning—in the 1880s.

The Wineries

Livermore's two wineries are side-by-side pioneer firms still in the hands of their founding families, the Concannons and the Wentes. In Pleasanton, five miles west, Stony Ridge and Villa Armando are a pair of relatively new firms housed in wineries that go back to earlier times.

Concannon Vineyard, in the hands of the third generation with the fourth coming up, proves conclusively that Irishmen can make wine if given a reasonable climate to do it in.

As with any Irish enterprise, there is a fine story about how it got started. In the 1880s the then Archbishop of San Francisco, Joseph S. Alemany, was a bit short of sacramental wine. His solution was to suggest to James Concannon, printer and stamp maker, that he should buy a vineyard and make wines. Concannon had a flexible enough mind to make the professional jump.

While the printing talent has lapsed in all subsequent Concannons, the winemaker has stayed in them. And they have stayed in one place, on Tesla Road 2 miles southeast of the Livermore city flagpole.

For the most part their cellar appears unhurried and informal. The oldest part of the building dates from the early years of the winery. Subsequent additions have been made out of need for space rather than any desire to add frills. Some sections of wall are brick; others are clapboard. A fair proportion is made of corrugated iron, to match the roof. Inside, old oak upright tanks and oval casks from the founder's day run in orderly but crowded rows.

In case anyone is deceived by these appearances, it should be noted that the family has its feet firmly in the present. It is not only abreast of research at the University of California at Davis, and at other centers; it actively participates in the research itself. The Concannons have contributed a few acres from their small vineyards to serve as test plots for grape varieties not commonly grown in Livermore, and for experimental combinations of rootstocks and fruiting varieties. (Vines, like humans, marry for better or for worse. California needs rootstocks resistant to both phylloxera and nematodes to carry its classic grape varieties. Some combinations work. Some do not. Some work in certain conditions but not in others. Researchers are very busy at the mating game.)

A more instantly visible reflection of modern thought is the collection of stainless steel fermentors along the winery's west wall.

White wines under the Concannon label include Chenin Blanc, Sauvignon Blanc, White Riesling, and Muscat Blanc. Among the reds are Cabernet Sauvignon, Petite Sirah (which the winery was the first to offer as a California varietal), and Zinfandel. From time to time the family offers Sauvignon Blanc, Cabernet Sauvignon, and Petite Sirah in limited bottlings. The rarest Concannon wine of all, though, is Rkatsiteli, a white wine from a Russian grape variety brought to this country by a member of the U.C. Davis faculty.

The Concannon tasting room is as easy-going as the rest of the property. On all but special occasions it consists of a trestle table amid cases of wine aging in bottles next door to the bottling line. (On special occasions there are more tables, but no more formality.) Just outside, 10 picnic tables under shading trees look out across the family vineyards.

Tree-shaded picnic *between vines and winery is a relaxing interlude for Livermore visitors.*

Richard Carey Winery. From Nimitz Fwy./17 exit E on Davis, S ¼ mi. on Martinez. (1695 Martinez, San Leandro, CA 94577) Tel (415) 352-5425. F 11-6, Sa 11-4. GT/Ta

Concannon. From Livermore flag plaza, S 2 mi. on Livermore Ave.-Tesla Rd. (4590 Tesla Rd., Livermore, CA 94550) Tel (415) 447-3760. Picnic. M-Sa 9-4, Su 12-4:30. GT (on the hour)/Ta

J.W. Morris Port Works. From Eastshore Fwy./80 take Powell St. Exit E ¼ mi. to Hollis St., ½ mi. S then E on Park Ave. (1215 Park Ave., Emeryville, CA 94608) Tel (415) 655-3009. M-F 9-5. Tours by appt.

Oak Barrel. University Ave. 1 block E of San Pablo Ave., in Berkeley. (1201 University Ave., Berkeley, CA 94702) Tel (415) 849-0400. M-Sa 10-6:30. /Ta

Stony Ridge. From Main St. in Pleasanton, E on Ray St.-Vineyard Ave. 3½ mi. Winery at end of pvt. drive, S off rd. (1188 Vineyard Ave., Pleasanton, CA 94566) Tel (415) 846-2133. Ltd. picnic. Weekdays 9-4:30, weekends 11-5./Ta

Veedercrest. From Eastshore Fwy./80 Powell St. exit E., 1¼ blocks on Hollis St., W 50 yds. in driveway. (1401 Stanford Ave., Emeryville, CA 94608) Tel (415) 652-3103. GT/Ta by appt.

Villa Armando. From Main St. in Pleasanton, N ½ block on St. John St. (553 St. John St., Pleasanton, CA 94566) Tel (415) 846-5488. Daily 9-5. Tours by appt./Ta

Weibel. From Mission San Jose, S 1 mi. on State 238, E on Stanford Ave. ½ mi. (1250 Stanford Ave., Mission San Jose, CA 94538) Tel (415) 656-9914. Picnic. GT M-F 10-3/Ta Daily 10-4.

Wente Bros. From Livermore flag plaza, S 2½ mi. on Livermore Ave.-Tesla Rd. (5565 Tesla Rd., Livermore, CA 94550) Tel (415) 447-3603. M-Sa 9-5, Su 11-5. GT (M-F)/Ta

Wine And The People. University Ave. 1 block W of San Pablo Ave. in Berkeley. (907 University Ave., Berkeley, CA 94702) Tel (415) 549-1266. M-Sa 10-6, Su 11-5./Ta

Key: GT (guided tour); IT (informal tour); Ta (tasting).

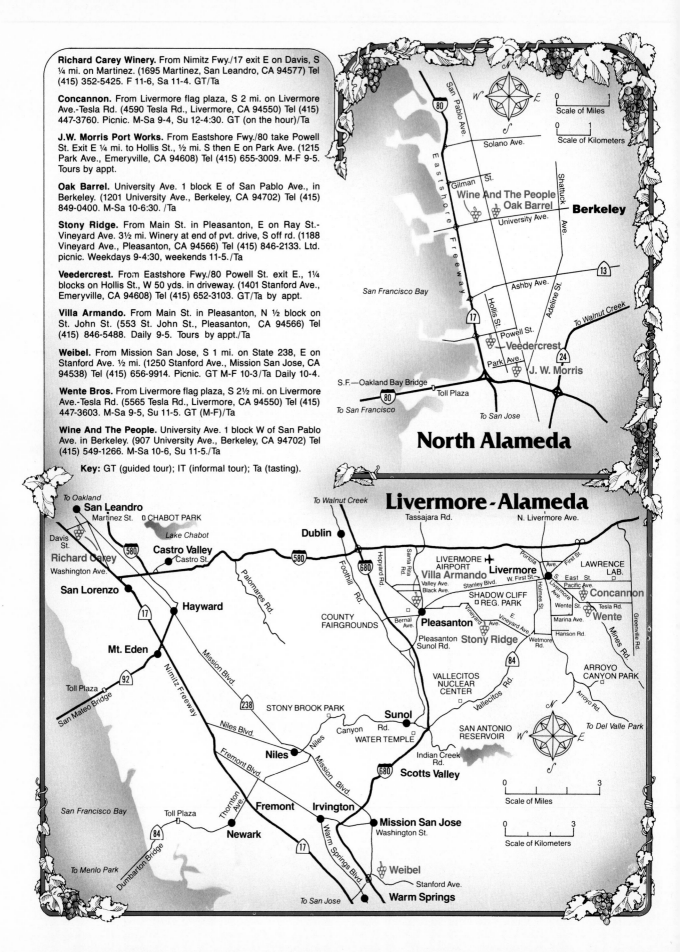

Stony Ridge Winery dates only from 1975, but houses itself in a cellar that goes back to 1887, and looks it.

Partners Harry and Len Rosingana and Marc Berardinelli are making small lots of Chardonnay, Johannisberg Riesling, Semillon, Zinfandel, and Gamay while they rehabilitate a building that had become a veritable museum of winemaking.

A man named John Crellen founded the winery, then named Ruby Hill, and it remained in his family until 1921, when Ernest Ferrario bought it. Ferrario kept the property going through a little bit of thick and a lot of thin until, in 1973, he sold it to Southern Pacific Land Company without having done much modernizing during his long tenure.

On the outside, this is all for the best. Crellen had an eye for architecture. He set his 60 by 185-foot brick and stone building into a gentle hillside, and capped it with some graceful cupolas. Inside, however, the lower floor was gravel, the wiring sparse, and the plumbing even sparser. The current operators have begun their attack on these shortcomings and have also rooted out many of the ancient redwood tanks in favor of stainless steel tanks and oak barrels. Still, in 1979 there remains enough from the old days to give a real flavor of pre-Prohibition winemaking.

The tasting room is in the winery during the warm months and in a big house between the winery and Vineyard Road during winter.

(In early 1979, there were two wineries for the price of one. Lanny Replogle has a sublease on one part of the building for his Ventana winery, but also plans to acquire a separate structure before the 1980 harvest.)

Villa Armando Winery in Pleasanton is less well known among Californians than among Atlantic Seaboarders, because most of the wine made at this middle-sized cellar goes east for sale.

Anthony D. Scotto acquired the winery from the founding Garatti family in 1962, coining the current name then. In 1971, Scotto opened a tasting room designed in a Spanish style. It was only then that the wines became available to the home audience. The tasting room is still the prime local source. The wines are also available in a restaurant the Scottos operate in conjunction with the winery and tasting room.

Tours of the old, workaday winery buildings directly behind the Pleasanton Hotel are by appointment only. Most of the gear is conventional, but students of winemaking techniques will find some unusual fermentors to think about. The Scottos extract the color from red wine grapes before—rather than during—fermentation, the latter being the conventional way. (Frank Garatti, who founded the winery in 1902, doubtless would be amazed.)

Most of the production is of proprietary types, labeled as Vino Rustico, Rubinello, and Orobianco.

Wente Bros. is the oldest wine business and the newest working winery in the Livermore Valley, in one of those odd turnabouts that is not at all uncommon in vinous California.

The first Wente in Livermore was Carl H. Wente, who arrived in 1883, a year or so ahead of James Concannon. The two men were close in age. Subsequent generations of the two families have grown up within

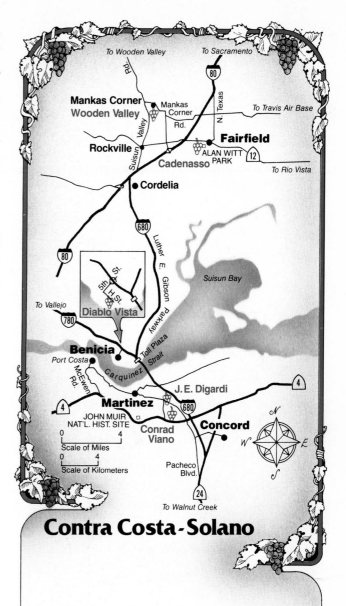

Contra Costa-Solano

Cadenasso. From I-80, Fairfield-Rio Vista exit, S ¼ mi. (PO Box 22, Fairfield, CA 94534) Tel (707) 425-5845. Daily 8-6. Tour by appt./Ta

Diablo Vista. From I-780 at Benicia take 5th St. exit S to H St., then E 3 blocks to mfg. complex. (mailing address: 1610 Ridgewood Rd., Alamo, CA 94507) Tel (415) 837-1801. Tours and tasting by appt.

Digardi. From Martinez, SE 2¼ mi. on Pacheco Blvd. (3785 Pacheco Blvd., Martinez, CA 94553) Tel (415) 228-2638. M-F 9-3. Tour by appt.

Conrad Viano. From State 21, W 1 mi. on Hwy. 4, N 1 mi. on Morello Ave. (150 Morello Ave., Martinez, CA 94553) Tel (415) 228-6465. Picnic. Daily 9-12, 1-5. IT/Ta

Wooden Valley. From I-80 at Fairfield, NW 4½ mi. on Suisun Valley Rd. (Rt. 1, Box 124, Suisun, CA 94585) Tel (707) 864-0730. Tu-Su 9-5./Ta

Key: GT (guided tour); IT (informal tour); Ta (tasting).

Livermore invites *visitors to tour on bicycles. A group leaves the main gate at Concannon (right). One of the accessible vineyards is El Mocho (below), a Wente Bros. property originally planted in the 1880s with vines from Chateau d'Yquem in France.*

a stone's throw of each other. But there is no stone-throwing; they get along so well that it is traditional for the oldest child to take charge of both broods when the parents go somewhere together.

The Wentes, on the opposite side of Tesla Road from Concannon and a few hundred yards east, retained their original cellar until 1966. By then the old frame building had become a small part of the winery and had to yield to a more efficient structure. With the original building's dismantling, all of Wente took on a modern appearance. There have been subsequent additions to the concrete cellars, the age of the ivy on various walls helping to peg the different construction dates.

Few wineries offer visitors a clearer picture of how wine is made from start to finish than Wente. Behind the main aging cellars, four horizontal basket presses adjoin several rows of temperature-controlled stainless steel fermenting tanks. Next to the presses are some specialized devices used to handle field-crushed grapes hauled up from the family's distant vineyards in Monterey County. The whole works is out-of-doors and accessible for close inspection (except during harvest time). Guides on the weekday-only tours gladly explain the fine points.

The aging cellars, for their part, contain a remarkable diversity of cooperages: stainless steel, glass-lined steel, redwood uprights, oak ovals, and oak barrels. Again, the purpose of each type is well-explained.

Finally, the visitor can get within arm's reach of an automatic bottling line. Automatic bottling lines have a hypnotic effect on mechanically minded people. They have dozens of moving parts, all going at a synchronized rate. Bottles get washed, filled, corked or capped, topped with a capsule, and labeled fore and aft, all with little or no human assistance.

In front of the winery, the tasting room is an adobe building designed expressly for the comfort of the guests. The basic notion is an Arthurian round table at which all comers are welcome to taste the full range of Wente wines, now being made by the young fourth generation. The Sauvignon Blanc, Semillon, and Grey Riesling are traditional in Livermore, going back to the earliest days. More recent additions include Chardonnay and Pinot Blanc. The most recent members of the roster come from the family's vineyards in Monterey County's Salinas Valley, notably including Gewürztraminer, Johannisberg Riesling, and a special blend of Cabernet Sauvignon, Malbec, and Merlot.

Other Than Wineries

Reliably warm and sunny, the Livermore Valley has spawned several picnic parks within easy reach of the wineries and vineyards.

The handiest of the lot is Shadow Cliffs Regional Park, nestled into the old arroyo bed alongside Stanley Drive between Livermore and Pleasanton. It has tree-shaded picnic sites, some playground gear, and a bit of water to splash in. Stanley Drive, not incidentally, has a bike path connecting the two towns.

Del Valle Regional Park, another part of the fine East Bay Regional Parks system, hides away in beautiful rolling hills southeast of Concannon and Wente. The park encompasses much of a reservoir lake's shoreline. It has abundant picnic sites in the shade of oaks,

as well as swimming beaches and a boat launch. The park entrance is a bit more than 7 miles south of Tesla Road by way of Mines and Del Valle roads. The junction with Tesla Road is midway between the Wente and Concannon wineries, and is well marked with signs.

A lower-key park is Arroyo Canyon, on the road that passes the old Cresta Blanca winery and the veterans' hospital. The park is a chain of tree-shaded picnic tables along Arroyo Creek. Arroyo Canyon Road starts in downtown Livermore as South L Street.

At Sunol, the San Francisco Water District maintains picnic tables and other comforts around its water temple. The entrance to the grounds is at the intersection of State Highway 21 with State Highway 84, just at the head of Niles Canyon.

Pleasanton's main street has an early American flavor about it still, in spite of the town's being ringed with contemporary housing tracts. The focal point is just west of St. John Street, where the landmark Pleasanton Hotel and the Pleasanton Cheese Factory face one another across the roadway. The cheese factory is a useful source of picnic fare to go with whichever of the local wines one might choose.

The Alameda County Fair, July 1–15 at Pleasanton, demonstrates that a good many cows remain in the area—and encompasses much more, including local winemaking.

For information on restaurants and overnight accommodations, write to the Livermore Chamber of Commerce, P.O. Box 671, Livermore, CA 94550.

Plotting a Route

The Livermore Valley is crisscrossed by a pair of freeways. Interstate Highway 580 goes east-west; Interstate Highway 680 runs north-south. One or the other will get a visitor into the region from almost anywhere at maximum speed.

I-580 turns toward Livermore from the San Francisco Bay basin at Hayward and connects with Interstate Highway 5 in the San Joaquin Valley. Heading east, the first real vista is the Livermore Valley, which springs into full view at the crest of a long upgrade. A second and much larger panorama is the San Joaquin Valley from the top of Altamont Pass on the east side of Livermore.

I-680 courses for most of its length in the shelter of the East Bay hills. The route begins at its junction with Interstate Highway 80 and ends at its intersection with U.S. Highway 101 at San Jose, so it is useful to visitors from the Sacramento Valley or the South Bay.

For the traveler heading up to Livermore from the south end of San Francisco Bay, State Highway 84 from Newark or Mission San Jose offers a low-speed alternative to the freeway.

South Alameda

Alameda County's southwest corner was a flourishing vineyard district before Prohibition and remained a fairly sizable one through the years before World War II. But by 1965, the roster of surviving wineries and vineyards had dwindled to one, and there it remains.

(Continued on next page)

. . . Continued from page 91

Weibel Champagne Vineyards leans east into a steep and photogenic line of hills and looks west out over baylands at Warm Springs. Look from Weibel toward the hills and time has changed nothing: except for vine rows, the hand of man shows but little. Look the other way and the story is different: westward, beyond a tract of houses, lies an automobile assembly plant which advertises itself as the world's largest building under one roof. It is the south end of an industrial-residential chain that runs unbroken to Oakland and beyond.

Being caught on the boundary between the worlds causes certain difficulties for the Weibels, but they go on in good humor at a winery that once belonged to Governor Leland Stanford.

Some of the buildings still would be recognizable to Stanford if he could stop by today, but the originals of 1869 have been supplemented since the Swiss family Weibel acquired the site in 1940. The winery is several hundred yards off State Highway 238. The access road, bordered on one side by eucalyptus trees and on the other by olive trees, runs alongside the vineyard until it comes to the small adobe-style building which houses Weibel's tasting room. Just north of it, a long, low, red brick building houses all of the Champagne-making and most of the stored still wines aging in bottle. Uphill from these are two rows of stainless steel aging tanks, the outdoor Sherry soleras, and the original winery building. A good deal of the redwood and oak cooperage in it holds Weibel table wines, most of them made at a new-in-1972 Weibel winery near Ukiah, in Mendocino County (see page 32), and transported to Mission San Jose for aging and bottling. Some wine is still made at Mission San Jose, the crusher being at the topmost level of the winery complex.

The brick Champagne building gives a clear view of the equipment for making both bottle-fermented and Charmat sparkling wines; this is one of the few cellars in which visitors can make a direct comparison between the two methods of winemaking and then go taste the results. The tasting room host pours sparkling wines of several sorts ranging from a Champagne Brut to a Charmat Sparkling Burgundy. The range of table wines encompasses nearly all of the generic and varietal types, and finally, there are several appetizer and dessert wines. Weibel, unlike other wineries, chooses to make its Green Hungarian a fairly sweet table wine. Among its dessert types is a relatively unusual Black Muscat. A house specialty liqueur is called Tangor.

The Weibels have an arbor-shaded picnic table alongside the tasting room.

North Alameda

Take Bay Area Rapid Transit to the wine country, one cellar waggishly advises its customers. The definition of wine country may be argued, but BART does go right by the Richard Carey winery door. City buses come about as close to four other wineries in this region.

There is no growing of grapes in Berkeley, Emeryville, or San Leandro, but the industrialized east shore of San Francisco Bay is right in the center of other places where grapes do grow well: Napa and Sonoma are not far north; Livermore is across the hills to the

John Muir Home

east; Santa Clara, Monterey, and San Luis Obispo stretch away to the south. Once freeways, field crushing, and other technical solutions had come into being, no great difficulties stood in the way of making wine downtown. And, lo, there is an urban wine country growing up in the East Bay, in one-time bakeries, refrigerated warehouses, and other structures.

The Wineries

All five of the wineries in North Alameda welcome visitors, although three do so with limitations imposed by small size. The only difficulty the small places pose for visitors is scheduling. Weekends, especially, can be difficult to organize.

Richard Carey Winery occupies better than half of a massive concrete building, a block from the San Leandro BART station and next door to the Greyhound depot.

Once a refrigerated warehouse, the structure lacks external charms but is ideally suited to making and storing wine. The winery occupies two separate bays. The larger one holds a 1927-model crusher-stemmer called Blue Max, a remarkably small continuous press, a remarkably modern bottling line, and the usual range of cooperage—all in neat array. The smaller segment holds the office, tasting room, and new bottles waiting for wine.

This is the winery's second home. Founded in 1972 in another building nearby, it was for a time known as Chateau Vintners. Proprietor Richard Carey brings grapes—transported in half-ton fruit bins on a stakeside truck—from as far north as Lake County, and as far south as San Luis Obispo to make his wines. In harvest season, visitors can observe the whole winemaking process on Fridays and Saturdays.

The list of wines includes Blanc Fumé and Chenin Blanc in whites, Cabernet Sauvignon and Zinfandel among the reds.

J. W. Morris Port Works houses itself on a side street in Emeryville, in what was once a bakery. The winery shares space with Oakland Paper & Supply. Their brick building is one of the handsomer examples in a whole street full of attractive buildings, though it pales somewhat in comparison with the gaudy Emeryville Town Hall, a block west.

The name, J. W. Morris Port Works, has become something of an anachronism during the company's short history. At the founding in 1975, vintage Port made from coast county grapes was to be the sole wine produced. Since then the partners have added red table wines to their roster. However, port-making is still the prime reason for having a look around these cellars.

Grapes—mostly from Sonoma vineyards—arrive at a side window and are dumped through it into open-topped redwood fermentors just inside. The rest of the process unfolds in the immediate vicinity.

The table wines age in a separate cellar beneath the port works.

Because this is a family partnership, visitors are likely to be shown about by J. W. himself, or his son-in-law and winemaker, Jim Olsen.

Oak Barrel is the older of two enterprises on University Avenue in Berkeley that are both wineries and suppliers to home winemakers.

There is no tour of a working winery here, but visitors can buy everything they need to start one of their own, along with wine by the barrel or bottle to tide them over while they get started. The propriety of partners John Bankuti and Ivo Gardella, Oak Barrel has a tasting room which more or less doubles as a clubhouse for some of the area's home winemakers.

Veedercrest is set somewhat apart from its neighbors in the East Bay flatlands by the fact that it also is a Napa Valley winery.

That is, although the winery is housed in a severely modern concrete building in Emeryville, proprietor A. W. Baxter owns one sizable vineyard in the Mayacamas Mountains and buys grapes from another in the Carneros district for most of his production.

The property is unmistakable. Stainless steel fermentors almost surround a buff-and-rust cube of a building alongside a railroad track, a larger and handier location than the original Baxter basement cellar.

Tours and tastings are by appointment only. The roster of possibilities includes Chardonnay, Gewürztraminer, and White Riesling among whites. Cabernet Sauvignon is the principal red. The labels are Veedercrest and Ringsbridge Cellars.

Wine and the People is the newer of the two companies on Berkeley's University Avenue that function both as wineries and suppliers to home winemakers.

At this one, the range of supplies stretches to include not only all of the equipment, but—in season—grapes from a wide range of California districts.

As for available wine, proprietor Peter Brehm makes small lots of Zinfandel, Cabernet Sauvignon, and other varietals—most of them from the grapes of the same vineyards that send fresh fruit to the firm for sale to home winemakers, so tastings here are doubly informative to all who contemplate making their own.

Other Than Wineries

Set in the midst of the populous East Bay, these cellars are handy to every sort of diversion from the Oakland Raiders to an afternoon at the movies, a tour of the Oakland Museum, or picnics in any of dozens of parks. The *Sunset Travel Guide to Northern California* provides detailed looks at the possibilities.

Plotting a Route

State Highway 17—the Nimitz freeway—connects with Interstate Highway 80—the Eastshore freeway—at Emeryville. All five of the North Alameda wineries are less than a mile from the freeways. For those who would test the possibilities of public transportation, the San Leandro station of BART is the wine country stop. Alameda-Contra Costa Transit coaches serve the whole district. For information, telephone (415) 653-3535.

Contra Costa County

Contra Costa County contained only one active producing winery and one aging cellar in spring, 1979. The county seldom has had more than those two active cellars in recent years and is urbanizing at a rate which suggests that this state of affairs will continue.

J.E. Digardi Winery goes back a good way as a building in Martinez. It was built as the Joost winery in 1886.

The city has come to engulf the old property, which at this point has a small retail store alongside Pacheco Boulevard, a fine frame house behind that, and the substantial wooden winery still farther to the rear. These days, the cellars serve mainly to age wines.

The Digardi label appears on a fair range of table and sparkling wines in the retail store. Any further examination of the property requires an appointment.

Conrad Viano Winery, on one edge of Martinez, has much of the air of a country winery. The family home has a rear corner of the basement set aside for tasting and retail sales. Three other smallish buildings of painted concrete block are behind that and slightly downhill. They are the winery and storage buildings.

Beyond, on the upslope, several acres of vineyard look back at the clustered structures (and several neighboring residences).

There is not enough gear on hand to call for a guided tour. A few minutes' poking about will reveal the crusher and press at the back of the hindmost building and an array of small redwood upright tanks inside it. Otherwise the scene is mostly farm tools and stored cases.

The tasting room takes longer. The Vianos have under their well-designed label Barbera, Burgundy, Cabernet Sauvignon, Gamay, Zinfandel (which they prize), Zinfandel Rosé, Chablis, Grey Riesling, and among appetizer and dessert types, Muscatel, Port, and Sherry.

The family bought the vineyard in 1920, founded the winery in 1946, and had to build a bigger cellar in 1967 and an addition in 1971. The third generation of Vianos is at work today.

There is a picnic lawn under a small grove of almonds next to the winery for those who would tarry over a bird and a bottle.

Solano County

Habitually, Solano County is appended to Napa to form a single wine district. The statistical reasons might be sound, but traveling from one county to the other does not go half so quickly as a trip between Solano and Contra Costa County. For this reason Solano here is attached to the region east of San Francisco Bay.

Specifically, it is only 21 miles—25 minutes—from Fairfield to Martinez by State Highway 21, a four-lane freeway, but it is 45 miles—an hour or more—from Fairfield to St. Helena over an admixture of state and county two-lane roads.

The Wineries

Three wineries were active in Solano County in spring, 1979. Cadenasso, in Fairfield, is the old-timer of the group. Diablo Vista in Benicia is the newcomer. Wooden Valley falls between the other two in age and physical location.

Cadenasso Winery is a traditional stop for wine-bibbers who travel regularly between the San Francisco Bay Area and the Sacramento Valley. The ivy-darkened concrete block walls of the main building are visible to motorists on I-80 just as they approach the Fairfield—Rio Vista—State Highway 12 exit ramp on the west side of Fairfield. Inside, an eclectic collection of oak ovals and small redwood uprights marches in four close ranks from one end to the other.

The tasting room, in the cellar beneath owner Frank Cadenasso's home, has as its entry an arched concrete tunnel. Downstairs the walls are mostly painted a vivid pink to match the company stationery.

Cadenasso began in 1906 when father Giovanni Cadenasso planted vines north of Cordelia. It continued when he moved to Fairfield to plant vines across the street from the present winery. That vineyard became county hospital grounds after the senior Cadenasso sold the land and dismantled the winery as a sensible response to Prohibition. The present site dates from 1926 (the main building came later, in 1942).

Cadenasso wines, served for tasting with great pride but no pretense, include Chenin Blanc, Grey Riesling, Chablis, and Sauterne among whites; Burgundy, Cabernet Sauvignon, Grignolino, Pinot Noir, and Zinfandel among reds. The Zinfandel and all of the generics can be had in jugs as well as bottles, and a considerable part of each day's sale goes out the door in the generous container.

Ordinarily there are no tours. A look through the winery requires an appointment, very nearly the only formality Cadenasso allows, let alone asks. The staff is too small, though, to lay down its work without planning ahead for visitors.

Diablo Vista Winery houses itself in, of all places, a one-time cafeteria in an old manufacturing plant in Benicia.

The proprietors say their location is ideal. First, it is handy to their homes and their source vineyards. Second, the cellar is substantially below grade, and thus easy to keep cool.

The property of the Leon Borowski and Kermit Blodgett families, Diablo Vista is open to visit only by appointment. Tours take in every step of winemaking from crusher-stemmer to bottling. There is tasting of varietal table wines from a wide range of places—Chardonnay from Placerville, Malvasia from Livermore, Zinfandel from Dry Creek in Sonoma and from Lodi, and, finally, Cabernet Sauvignon from Napa.

Wooden Valley Winery has an appealing informality about it. There is no tour. The tasting and sales room is one of four frame buildings grouped around a sizable courtyard, but is unmistakable. On weekends, especially, the court is full of parked automobiles and the tasting room full of local patrons exchanging empty jugs for full ones. The proprietor is Mario Lanza, but unrelated to the singer.

The wines on hand include several generic table wines (in bottles and jugs) and a broad spectrum of varietals in bottles only. A complete list of appetizer and dessert wines is also there to be tasted. Sparkling wines are not offered for tasting.

Other Than Wineries

Solano County offers no great abundance of picnic parks or other recreational diversions close to its wineries.

One exception, directly next to the Cadenasso Winery on West Texas Street, is Alan Witt Park, a spacious collection of playgrounds and picnic lawns.

Back on the Contra Costa side of the river, the tiny, waterside town of Port Costa offers another kind of diversion altogether.

Port Costa was once a teeming Sacramento River port, but bridges and other aspects of progress caused it to become technologically unemployed during the 1930s. Beginning in the 1960s it revived itself as an antique collection of shops and restaurants, and it has played host to crowds of visitors ever since.

The village is just off State Highway 4, a few minutes downstream from Martinez.

Plotting a Route

Interstates 80 and 680 form a T that gets to the heart of the region from any direction.

I-680 has some agreeable moments as it slips along the flat from Cordelia down to the Sacramento River at Suisun, where the U.S. Navy's mothball fleet provides a wistful vista. But the freeways are mainly the means to get from Point A to Point B in a hurry.

The joys of driving in this part of the world belong with Suisun Valley Road, Wooden Valley Road, State Highway 121 from Cordelia to Lake Berryessa (and on across into the Napa Valley if time does not weigh heavily), and whatever connecting roads seem promising on the spot.

The Suisun and Wooden valleys, both small, look fine in all seasons. They even smell good early in March when their abundant orchards bloom a fragrant cloud of white and pink above carpets of indelibly yellow mustard and beneath canopies of blue sky.

The hills west, in this season, are bright green with new grass and dull green with old oaks.

These are old roads, narrow and curving. Summer drivers bustle along in hopes of finding some cooler place; but in late winter or early spring when the weather is balmy, some of them tend to grow forgetful of their goals. On such days the wheels of progress grind as slowly as those of justice, but the views are exceedingly fine.

The tasting game

The names of wines do little to explain how they will taste. Colombard and Pinot Blanc do not sound much alike. Pinot Blanc and Pinot Noir sound more alike. But when you get down to cases, the wines of the first pair taste more like each other than the wines of the latter pair.

Most wineries run tasting rooms to help overcome the semantics of the business. The hosts will help organize a sequence of wines so each sample will show off to its best advantage. (Dry whites are served first, followed by rosés, reds, sweet wines, appetizers, then desserts. Sparkling wines come last.)

Newcomers usually find it useful to explore at least one candidate from each of the five classes (see the chart on page 37). Experienced tasters sometimes organize a day in the wine country just to taste one class or even one variety.

All "tasting" amounts to is making a considered judgment about whether or not a wine pleases the drinker. This is a purely personal exercise, but is most rewarding if it includes some basic tests by which professionals make their decisions.

Sight. The appearance of a wine reveals something of its character. The liquid should be clear to brilliantly clear. Table wines should not have brownish tints (whites range from pale gold to straw yellow, reds from crimson to ruby or slightly purplish, rosés from pink orange to pink). Most dessert wines will have a brownish tint and some may even be deep amber, depending on type.

Smell. Table wines should have a fresh, fruity quality of aroma. The many types add a wide range of subtle variations. The fruitiness may be overlaid with bouquet. (Aroma is the smell of grapes, bouquet the smell of fermentation and aging.) But one seldom encounters bouquet when drinking new wines at the winery. Appetizer and dessert wines have little aroma but substantial bouquet.

Taste. In fact, taste is simply sweet, sour, bitter, and salty. Most "taste" is an extension of smell. Some qualities can be perceived only after the wine is on the taster's palate: acidity (liveliness versus flatness), astringency (young red wines will have a tannic puckeriness in most types except mellow ones), and weight or body (light versus rich).

One further note. "Dry" describes the absence of sugar, nothing else. Dry wines are sometimes thought to be sour because acidity and tannin are more evident.

Tasters take different poses at different places. At Sterling, one tastes while seated (left). At Mirassou (below), the job is done standing at a bar. Sometimes people just gather around an upturned barrel in a cellar. In any case, the nose is a taster's most important asset.

Lodi & the Mother Lode

Two adjoining districts are worlds apart

Lodi Brick Barns

When a wine industry official says "Lodi," the word encompasses most of northern San Joaquin County, Sacramento and its surroundings, and several bits and pieces of Sierra Nevada foothills.

Using one town's name to cover all that territory is excusable shorthand. From the end of Prohibition until the early 1970s, the dozen or so wineries right around Lodi outnumbered all the others in the district two to one. Several of them individually made more wine than all of their distant district relatives combined.

However, this district is divided into two regions now, as different from one another as red is from white. Lodi still dominates in gallons, but a much-revitalized Gold Country has a greater number of wineries to visit. Sacramento offers a few tasting rooms.

Lodi, town & country

Lodi is a genuine Central Valley agricultural center. Most of its 30,000 people live in tidily kept, tree-shaded residential districts around the main shopping area. Vineyards and other farmlands come right up to the edge of town.

Local farmland is, by force of geography, compact.

Lodi nestles within the angle formed by the meeting of the Sacramento and San Joaquin rivers. To the east, the Sierra Nevada foothills form the third leg of a triangular boundary. Though there are other crops grown, grapes predominate. The town has long been a table grape center, a brandy capital, and a natural source of sherry types. In more recent times, new grape varieties produced by the University of California at Davis have helped refocus local production toward table wines.

The Wineries

For one reason or another, Lodi has been—and still is—a traditional home for wineries owned by cooperatives of grape growers. Two of its six visitable cellars are co-ops. Probably because so many of its growers have a piece of the co-op action, Lodi has lacked for small, family-owned cellars in recent years. But that appears to be changing: another two of its visitable cellars are indeed family-owned and small.

Barengo Vineyards, known a bit less formally by local visitors as just Barengo's, looms up alongside Acampo Road in an expansive and rather pleasing brick building which dates back to 1868.

It became the Barengo winery in 1944 when Dino Barengo bought it to establish his own business. The property now belongs to Ira and Kent Kirkorian, who also own several hundred acres of vineyard here and elsewhere in the San Joaquin Valley. They bought the winery from an interim owner in 1976, the founder having sold his interest in 1973.

The principal changes since Barengo's proprietorship are two. First, a shed full of concrete fermenting tanks has given way to a battery of stainless steel fermentors. Second, the main cellar has been extended to house stainless steel storage tanks along with the existing complement of redwood tanks and oak barrels, and also to house a modern bottling line. (The cellar crew is particularly grateful for the new bottling line. The old one might have served as the original inspiration for the Toonerville Trolley.)

No tours go into the cellars. But the tasting room— brick-walled, oak-beamed, softly lighted—has windows cut into its inside walls so visitors can keep an eye on the main cellar while exploring the wine list.

One of the winery's specialties has been Ruby Cabernet, which Dino Barengo helped pioneer as a varietal wine in 1949. (It is a UC-bred offspring of Cabernet Sauvignon and Carignane.) Other specialties include a varietal dessert sherry type called Pedro Ximinez, a flavored after-dinner drink called Cremocha, and Dudenhofer, a woodruff-flavored white patterned after German May wines, but distinct from them. The winery also has estate Chenin Blancs from the owners' vineyards, and other varietals from as far away as Santa Barbara County.

The name Barengo is also closely associated with wine vinegar made in the traditional Orleans method. Veteran visitors may recall that a small, boomerang-shaped building next to the main cellar served as the vinegary. It is now an office, and the vinegar is housed in a sizable new building across an open field. The tasting room hosts will explain vinegar as patiently as they explain wine.

Across from the tasting room door under a row of trees are four picnic tables, available on a first-come, first-served basis.

The firm has several tasting rooms elsewhere in the state. It will forward a list on request.

Borra's Cellar is one of two recently established small family wineries in Lodi. It is the only one in the district entered through a good, old-fashioned storm cellar door, the kind that angles up against a wall to cover the cellar stairs beneath.

An appointment is required to get through that door, which is at the rear of the Stephen Borra family residence. In the cellar, full of tidily stacked American oak barrels, proprietor Borra pours tastes of whichever wines are available. The list includes Barbera, Carignane, and late-harvest bottlings of Mission and Zinfandel. Borra can be talked into strolling out beyond an equipment shed to give a visitor a look at his crusher, press, and fermentors. The latter include both open-topped redwood and stainless steel tanks. The family vineyard stretches away beyond them.

Coloma Cellars operates from an adobe-faced building on the State Highway 99 frontage road just north of Lodi.

Visitors to the small aging cellar find a variety of table, dessert, and specialty wines available for tasting. There are no tours of the cellar or the adjacent building

where grape concentrate is produced for home winemakers.

The label, incidentally, originated in a long-defunct cellar in the Gold Rush town of Coloma.

East-Side Winery, known by its label as Royal Host, has its tasting room inside a retired 50,000-gallon redwood wine tank.

The vessel, tailored to its new purpose with a man-sized door and interior varnishing, still gives a clear impression of how it feels to be inside a wine tank. It gives the optical illusion of being even bigger inside than outside.

The main winery buildings stretch southward from the roadside tasting room. As is often the case with cellars built in the 1930s, the architecture does not conform to romantic notions of a winery. Still, at East-Side the scenic deficiencies are only external. The interiors are full of handsome cooperage, all of it in admirably clean and orderly surroundings.

East-Side, as much as any winery in the district, reflects the increasing interest in making table wine. Members of the grower cooperative that owns it have responded strongly to the grape varieties developed at U.C. Davis; the Royal Host label appears on varietal bottlings of Emerald Riesling, Ruby Cabernet, and the rarer Gold. (Gold, a muscat-derived grape, was originally intended to be eaten fresh, but it would not ship successfully. The wine resulting from it falls within the general classification of light, sweet Muscat.)

East-Side demonstrates equally well the lingering and probably unquenchable Lodi enthusiasm for making Sherry. In one building on the comprehensive tour is a large and informally organized Sherry solera.

After the tour, which is long, and the tasting, which can encompass a substantial list, visitors can retire to picnic tables just outside the tasting tank. On the lawn, tables are shaded by a mixture of tall trees. Family groups need give no advance notice, but larger groups are required to reserve in advance. The grounds will accommodate no more than 100.

Guild Wineries & Distilleries, largest producer of wine among the state's cooperatives and one of the farthest flung associations of vineyardists, has its ancestral home and much of its presence in or near Lodi.

For visitors, the action is all at the central winery just off Victor Road (State Highway 12) on the east side of town.

No wine is crushed on these premises. They are the aging and bottling facility. Like other firms engaged in enticing great numbers of Americans to drink modestly priced wine as a daily dinner beverage, Guild is required to have wines of many types. To meet this need, it crushes grapes of many varieties from sharply differing climate regions.

Two wineries in Lodi, two more near Fresno, and one at Delano ferment the wines, then feed them into the central cellars for aging and bottling. In addition, Guild owns the Cresta Blanca winery at Ukiah (see page 31) and the B. Cribari winery at Fresno (see page 113); the wines from both of these are brought to Lodi for bottling, too.

A modern, spacious, and cool tasting room is out in front of the main aging cellar. Some of Guild's visitors limit their explorations to this oasis, especially when

The end of winter *sees pruners at work in Lodi tokays as a storm gives way to clearing skies.*

the summer sun heats Lodi into the 100°F/38°C range, or when winter rain pelts the countryside. However, the hosts willingly conduct tours in the worst of weathers as well as the best.

Visible in the big cellars during the tours are concrete storage tanks of great capacity and steel tanks of still greater volume, a complete Charmat Champagne cellar, a huge bottling room (that clanks and rattles at a furious enough pace to satisfy *The Sorcerer's Apprentice*), and, not least, the cased goods warehouse. There is an immense amount of wine at Guild, and the people there have worked out ingenious arrangements for dealing with it. For example, a sunken lane goes straight through the middle of the warehouse. It is just wide enough to accommodate flatbed truck and trailer rigs and just deep enough for forklifts to drive right on and off the flatbeds to load them.

On an entirely separate plane, Guild maintains a display vineyard adjacent to the Winemaster's House. In this vineyard the proprietors have planted three or four of each of the wine grape varieties recommended for California. Nowhere else can visitors see with so few steps how varied the vine is.

Back in the tasting room, Guild offers its full line of table, appetizer, dessert, and sparkling wines. Most are under the Winemaster's label, but included prominently is the company's long-time trademark, the red and white checkered label of the Vino da Tavola wines. Also on hand for sale are Guild brandies and Guild's rarity, Silverado, the first vodka produced from grapes in California.

D. Lucas Winery is Lodi's newest and smallest cellar, and the only one that shares its equipment with home winemakers.

The crusher and press are housed in an old-fashioned red barn during the off-season and are pulled out in the open air during harvest. A small, tidily kept frame building between the barn and the proprietor's residence holds several small racks of barrels full of aging Zinfandel, some white, some light, some full-bodied, and a bit of it sweet.

David Lucas makes wine mostly for local customers, having started in 1978. Much of it he sells to a mailing list. The rest sells, first-come, first-served, at the cellar door between Thanksgiving and Christmas. Home winemakers are welcome in harvest time, when Lucas sells grapes from his 30-plus-acre vineyard of old zinfandel vines, with crusher privileges available to buyers. Visitors with appointments are welcome all year around.

More wineries. In the course of poking around Lodi, one is bound to encounter other wineries. Most are marked by the tall towers that house their column stills. (Lodi is a center for beverage brandy, as well as for the production of dessert wines.)

One of the most striking wineries architecturally in the Lodi district is on Woodbridge Road at Bruella. Once the Cherokee Co-op, later Montcalm, still later Filice, it now belongs to Robert Mondavi. The other Lodi wineries are purely in the bulk trade and not open to visit. They include Woodbridge Vineyard Association, Lodi Vintners, Community Winery in the northwest quarter of town, and Liberty Winery in the northeast.

Other Than Wineries

The year-round attractions of the wineries are supplemented by an annual festival with an uncommonly long name—the Lodi Grape Festival and National Wine Show. It takes place all over town on a weekend in mid-September, usually the one following Labor Day.

Most of the festivities are in the Grape Bowl, a fairground near State Highway 99 northeast of Lodi. Wineries mount exhibits, and the local wine growers' association sponsors daily wine tasting in the midst of general farm displays and the most widely advertised feature of the festival, the grape mosaics.

The mosaics are what their name suggests—pictures or designs wrought by placing grapes one at a time on wire mesh. Panel sizes range up to 5 by 10 feet. Club women spend hours plucking thousands of grapes and poking them into words and pictures that follow a preannounced theme. (A typical motif is "Early California.") Grapes come in a wider range of colors than many people would suspect. The mosaics are as much a lesson in grape physiology as they are an art study.

Elsewhere on the grounds concessionaires operate the usual quick food stands and carnival rides.

The main event is an hours-long parade with bands, floats, and drill teams. It assembles on the west side of town, winds through the business district, and finishes up 2 to 3 miles later under the summer sun at the Grape Bowl.

Everybody who is not in the parade watches it from a curbside vantage point and contributes to a formidable, postparade traffic tie-up. Agricultural communities lead more relaxed lives than manufacturing centers do, though, and all resolves itself in good-humored cooperation.

Several wineries hold open house during the festival just as they do all year. But they augment their staffs to run comprehensive tours for festival crowds that have numbered 50,000 to 60,000 in recent years.

Lodi also offers two recreational parks. Lake Lodi Park, on Turner Road a mile west of State 99, rings the municipal lake, a diverted part of the Mokelumne River. Trees shade the shore and the picnic tables. The park has rental boats and swimming beaches.

Micke Grove, south of town in a large stand of valley oaks, has a small zoo, gardens, and fine picnic sites. It is west of State 99 on Armstrong Road.

For a listing of restaurants and accommodations in the area, write to the Lodi District Chamber of Commerce, P.O. Box 386, Lodi, CA 95240.

Plotting a Route

The town of Lodi straddles State 99, the quick route from almost any of the other San Joaquin Valley towns north or south.

For visitors coming from the San Francisco Bay region, the all-freeway route is Interstate Highway 580 through Livermore to Tracy, then north along the connector Interstate 205 to Interstate 5. To change from I-5 to State 99 requires a brief descent onto some local road. Lathrop Road does the job as well as any. (It is about 4 miles north of the junction of I-205 with I-5.)

Another speedy route between the San Francisco Bay area—especially the northern half—and Lodi com-

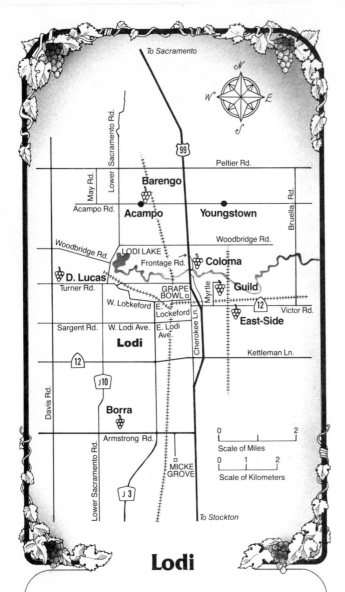

To Sacramento

Peltier Rd.

Barengo

Acampo Rd.

Acampo   **Youngstown**

Woodbridge Rd.

LODI LAKE

Frontage Rd.   **Coloma**

Woodbridge Rd.

D. Lucas

Turner Rd.   GRAPE BOWL   **Guild**

W. Lockeford   E. Lockeford   Myrtle

Victor Rd.   12

Sargent Rd.   W. Lodi Ave.   E. Lodi Ave.   **East-Side**

Kettleman Ln.

Lodi

12

J 10

Borra

Armstrong Rd.

0   2
Scale of Miles

0   1   2
Scale of Kilometers

MICKE GROVE

J 3

To Stockton

Lodi

Barengo Vineyards. From State 99, Acampo exit, W 1 mi. on Acampo Rd. (PO Box C, Acampo, CA 95220) Tel (209) 369-2746. Daily 9-6./Ta

Borra's Cellar. From State 99, Armstrong Rd. exit, W 2 mi. on Armstrong Rd. (1301 E. Armstrong Rd., Lodi, CA 95240) Tel (209) 368-5082. Appt. only.

Coloma Cellars. N side of Lodi, cross Mokelumne River Bridge, on frontage rd., E side of State 99. (PO Box 478, Lodi, CA 95240) Tel (209) 368-7822. Daily./Ta

East-Side (Royal Host). From State 99 State 12-East exit, E 1 mi. (6100 E. State 12, Lodi, CA 95240) Tel (209) 369-4768. Picnic. Daily 9-5. GT/Ta

Guild. From State 99, State 12-East exit, E ¾ mi. to Myrtle Ave.. N ¼ mi. to winery dr. (PO Box 519, Lodi, CA 95240) Tel (209) 368-5151. Picnic. Daily 10-5. GT/Ta

D. Lucas. From State 99, State 12/Kettleman Lane exit, W 3½ mi. to N. Davis Rd., N 2 mi. to winery. (18196 N. Davis Rd., Lodi, CA 95240) Tel (209) 368-2006. Appt. only.

Key: GT (guided tour); IT (informal tour); Ta (tasting).

bines Interstate Highway 80 as far east as Fairfield, then the two-lane State Highway 12 from Fairfield to Lodi.

State 12 traverses a great deal of wine country. For the eastbound motorist, the road begins at Sebastopol, loops north through Santa Rosa and runs south in leisurely fashion through Sonoma town. From there it cuts east through the city of Napa and skims along the southern marches of Solano County until it joins I-80 for a short run to Fairfield. From Fairfield it passes first through grassy hills, then along one slough and another in the Delta country until it straightens out and streaks for Lodi.

At one point the road offers an overview of the aircraft based at Travis Air Force Base. It also offers endless opportunities to study small boats while they pass the river bridge at Rio Vista.

A slower, somewhat more scenic variation of the I-80–State 12 route between the Bay region and Lodi stays closer to the Sacramento River delta for a longer time. This route requires getting to the Contra Costa County town of Concord by whichever route is most efficient, then working east to Antioch on State Highway 4, and from there to Rio Vista along the levee road, State Highway 160. At the Rio Vista Bridge, change to State 12 for the ride to Lodi.

Late fall or early winter, when great flights of ducks darken the skies, has no peer as a season for driving between Antioch or Rio Vista and Lodi. Sometimes a tule fog comes in, rendering the day unsuitable for touring. But when the December or January weather is crisp and clear and the river runs full and the lines of trees have no leaf, few places in California tell a clearer story of the season. Even the farms in the bottom lands show no plants, only rich black soil, tilled and waiting for spring.

Spring can hardly be described as plain in these parts. The grasses wave long and green on every side. Cottonwoods and lesser trees brighten the riverbanks with fresh foliage. And local people turn out in numbers to fish for catfish in the sloughs, which are full to the brim—no more than a foot lower than the wheels of a car on the road—while farm crops on the dry side of the road wax healthy in ground a good 10 feet lower than the dike tops.

State Highway 88 is one of the most scenic ways to get between State Highway 49 in the Gold Country and State 99 down on the flat at Lodi. State 88 joins State 12 just west of the Camanche Reservoir, and the two proceed together through Lockeford into Lodi.

Going through Lodi to get to the Gold Country offers not only a scenic route but also a pleasant way to stop at one of the Lodi wineries for those who do not wish to make a specific visit for winery tours.

Within the neighborhood of Lodi, getting around requires little effort. West of State 99, Turner, Woodbridge, and Acampo roads serve well for east-west travel. The main north-south roads other than the freeway are De Vries and Lower Sacramento.

East of the highway, things spread out a bit more, but the same east-west roads (with the important addition of Victor Road) continue. The north-south roads are Kenneffck and Bruella.

Within these grids the terrain is flat, given over mainly to vineyards but with occasional surprises, such as a line of olive or palm trees, an old dry river course with its bottom full of vineyard, or maybe a home garden.

A few vineyards are being trained up for trellising, a harbinger of mechanical harvesting; these are all young vines. A few are trellised in the ancient Italian style, almost like arbors, with trunks bare to head height. Still others—mostly very old tokay vineyards—have six-foot-high vines, heavy and craggy and planted so close together that in winter, from even a slight distance, they appear to be a solid black mass.

The Mother Lode

The Mother Lode is a region where local grapegrowers say of themselves, "We don't have to be crazy . . . but it helps."

Theirs is an altogether different weather from that of the San Joaquin Valley floor below. Spring frosts are but one major aspect of a climate that makes grapes a dubious crop for investment. Indeed, one scientist at the University of California at Davis says that a Sierra Nevada foothill winegrower will, over the long haul, harvest approximately 25 percent of what he might expect in easier climes.

People learned this soon after 1849, when local winemaking sprang up to help satisfy the thirsts of Gold Rush miners. The rigorous climate has been a damper on would-be vineyardists since; acreage in the Mother Lode never has been large.

Still, despite the chancy economics, Zinfandel from this region has enjoyed fame in every era of California winemaking. Vines have never disappeared from the region altogether, and now they are perhaps at the zenith. Not only are vineyard acreages and the roster of regional wineries at their peaks, but cellars in many other counties are making Amador Zinfandels in competition with the stay-at-home bottlings.

Even if the wines from this region were less well received by connoisseurs, the Mother Lode would be worth a vinous visit. The whole region is full of memorabilia from 1849, and full of people who keep some of that gaudy spirit. The winemakers are among the latter.

Some fairly long distances separate three main clusters of wineries— El Dorado, Amador, and Calaveras-Tuolumne counties — so the terrain is divided into those three segments.

El Dorado Wineries

As of publication time, El Dorado County has three active wineries. Two of them are close to U.S. Highway 50 and just east of Placerville; the third is some miles south of U.S. 50. Boeger Winery and Eldorado Vineyards, near the freeway, are readily visitable, while their away-from-the-highway mate, Sierra Vista, requires an appointment.

Boeger Winery is, like a great many other California wineries, both old and new. Here, however, the contrast is easier to see than almost anywhere else.

The current winery went up in 1977, a tidily designed concrete block structure with stainless steel fermentors, a Willmes press, and other processing gear out back, and racks of oak barrels and puncheons within.

Just a few yards downstream, along the creek that bisects the property, is an old stone building that originally was the Fossati-Lombardo winery in the 1850s, but now houses the tasting room. The upper floor held the hand-cranked crusher that currently sits in the tasting room. Two chutes above the tasting bar used to drop the newly crushed fruit into open fermentors.

In good weather, visitors can picnic just above the creek in a spot between the two buildings, and consider how today's winemaking differs from that of the old days.

The list of Boeger varietal wines includes Chardonnay, Chenin Blanc, Johannisberg Riesling, and Sauvignon Blanc in whites; Cabernet Sauvignon and Zinfandel in reds. The generics are called Hangtown Gold and Hangtown Red after Placerville's original name. They come from four patches of grapes, one in the pocket valley that holds the winery, the other three nearby.

Incidentally, the owning Greg Boeger family also grows pears and apples on the home ranch.

Eldorado Vineyards is the property of Earl and JoAnne McGuire, who will introduce themselves as Mick and Jody.

Their winery, which dates from 1975, is a workaday building, seen from the outside, as it is covered with shiny sheet metal. Inside, its frame turns out to be made from hand-adzed timbers. The McGuires give tours of their small cellar, from crusher to bottling.

Like the neighboring Boegers, the McGuires grow tree fruit as well as grapes. In season, they sell some of this produce, along with the wines, from a stand in front of the winery.

They also offer first-come, first-served picnicking at five tables which are not far from fine views of the distant Crystal Range of the Sierra Nevada.

Sierra Vista Winery is beyond the end of conventional roads, on one of several forest tracks. Visitors head in the right direction with help from wooden signs tacked to tree trunks wherever the track forks.

In spite of this, the winery is not remote from civilization, nor is it primitive. The rough-hewn roads owe themselves to the fact that a high ridge is just being developed into an extension of Pleasant Valley. The winery is not primitive because its owner is a scientist.

Proprietor John MacCready ferments his wines in one-time dairy tanks of stainless steel, directly in front of a trim, 20 by 30-foot, wood-sided cellar, and ages them inside the building, the whites mainly in other stainless steel tanks and the reds in American or French oak barrels. Sierra Vista is aptly named. MacCready can see the Crystal Range whenever he looks up from his old basket press.

The long-range plan is to make Sauvignon Blanc, Syrah, and Zinfandel—the latter in conventional and late-harvest styles—as the major wines on the list. Others, including Chardonnay, will make at least occasional appearances.

Founded in 1977 at its present tiny size, Sierra Vista is planning to increase its capacity in several phases over the first decade of its existence. For now, visits are by appointment only.

Amador Wineries

At the turn into the 1980s, Amador is the heart of the Mother Lode wine district. The county has 1,000 acres of grapes, compared to 200 for El Dorado and fewer than 100 for Calaveras-Tuolumne. Amador also listed seven active wineries, more than double the total of either neighbor, with several more on the horizon.

Of the tourable cellars, only D'Agostini had regular visiting hours at publication time. Amador Winery offered regular tasting hours. The other wineries required appointments.

The town of Plymouth is the focal point of the Amador wine district, with four wineries nearby. The other three cellars are at Ione, Jackson, and Sutter Creek.

Amador Winery, founded in 1966 by John Merrill, is middle-aged by local standards. The cellar and tasting room are housed together on the lower level of an aging stone and wood-frame building right next to State Highway 49 in Jackson. To taste here is to tour. The list of wines is basically generic.

Argonaut Winery is in the village of Ione, a shade down the Sierra Nevada foothill slopes from all the other Mother Lode cellars.

Perhaps the smallest of the regional lot, it belongs to several partners who otherwise work in the aerospace industry. One of the partners lives at the winery site, but weekends are the only time visitors are allowed to have a look at the small cellar and its collection of oak casks. An appointment is required.

In accordance with local tradition, the list of wines is led by Zinfandel.

D'Agostini Winery is the genuinely durable one in this lofty region. The first vines on the site east of Plymouth belonged to a Swiss named Adam Uhlinger, who planted them in 1856. For a good many years, Uhlinger made wine under his own label. The present owners, the D'Agostini family, bought vines and winery in 1911 and have been on the property ever since.

Uhlinger built for the long haul. He laid stone walls and strung heavy beams. The D'Agostinis have kept his handiwork intact, though the winery has prospered substantially and required a series of additions. They have also kept several of the oak casks that were coopered on the site by a neighbor of Uhlinger.

The buildings, old and new, are set at the foot of a gentle, vine-clad slope. Beyond the 125 acres of vineyard are hills wooded more thickly than is common in California wine districts.

Tours start with the fermentors and end with the tasting room. Burgundy and Zinfandel head the list of table wines. Malvasia Bianca is the signature white.

Monteviña contends for the title of largest winery in Amador County, and is clearly the most widely distributed label among the current roster. This does not mean it is large by state-wide standards, however. Indeed, it would rank among the smaller cellars in Napa or Sonoma counties.

Owned by W.H. Fields and winemaker Cary Gott, Monteviña was founded in 1973. At publication time, the winery was housed in a prefabricated steel build-ing. The proprietors looked forward to an early addition to their space, barrels being stacked more than head high in close rows, everywhere they could be stacked. The new construction would include a separate barrel aging cellar and tasting room, leaving the present building to hold only larger tanks.

Monteviña is an estate winery by the classical definition. All its wines come from 160 acres of vines owned by its proprietors. The emphasis is on Zinfandel, much of it from an 80-year-old vineyard. Also in the roster of varietal wines are Sauvignon Blanc, a white wine from Cabernet Sauvignon, and among reds, Barbera and Cabernet Sauvignon. Specialties include carbonic maceration reds from Cabernet Sauvignon and Zinfandel, and—for the first time in 1978—a port type. (To explain carbonic maceration in detail is beyond the scope of this book, but essentially it means fermenting whole clusters of fruit rather than crushed single grapes. The intention is to achieve a fresh, zesty wine for early consumption.)

Until the new cellar is built, visits are by appointment; tours include looks at the big Vaslin press, and stainless steel fermentors, as well as the aging cellar full of oak.

Shenandoah Vineyards occupies a lofty knoll overlooking the Shenandoah Valley. The property of Leon and Shirley Sobon since 1977, the ranch belonged for many years to a prominent local family named Steiner, which directly explains the outward appearance of the place. "Stein," in German, means "stone," and Mr. Steiner took his name very seriously indeed. All of the house walls and one wall of what is now the winery have stone walls, made of river rock, carted up from the nearby Cosumnes River and mortared in place by the former owner. The stonework has a sort of landmark status locally; old-timers come now and again to see that the new proprietors have not damaged the Steiner legacy.

The Sobons have not, although they more than tripled the size of the winery building in 1978 by adding two levels, with concrete block walls, to the stone-and-wood original. The addition is on the reverse slope of the knoll, invisible from Steiner Road.

The expanded winery is tidy and well equipped. At the upper level, crushers, basket presses, redwood red wine fermentors and a wizard Italian juice separator (for making white wine out of black grapes) stand under a shed roof, while two rooms inside are full of barrels for fermenting and aging Chenin Blanc, white Zinfandel, and a white Mission del Sol. The lower levels house several oak tanks and about a hundred American and French oak barrels for aging Cabernet Sauvignon and Zinfandel. Visits are by appointment only.

StoneRidge Winery is a thinking man's small cellar, designed into its site—or sites—to ease the burdens of moving both grapes and wine.

The crushing, fermenting, and pressing go on in a small shed at the high side of the property. There, grapes feed into a crusher set on a platform so it can pivot to fill any of three open-topped redwood fermentors. On a lower level is a stainless steel tank used for the first racking. It ties into an underground line that allows new wine to flow by gravity to an aging cellar

Automatic bottling lines *are endlessly fascinating. At blurring speed (above), they sanitize bottles, fill them with wine, cap or cork them, cover the neck with a capsule, and slap on labels fore and aft. The bottling room at Guild in Lodi, shown at left, is one of the largest visitable ones in the state.*

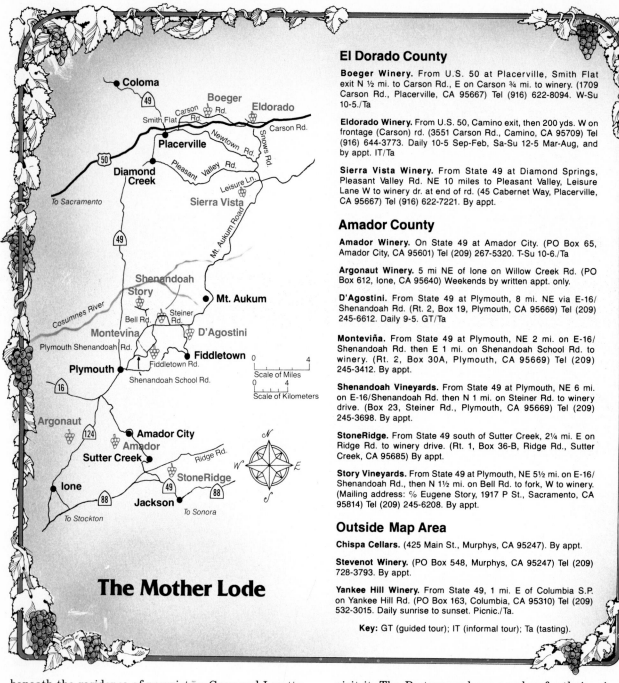

El Dorado County

Boeger Winery. From U.S. 50 at Placerville, Smith Flat exit N ½ mi. to Carson Rd., E on Carson ¾ mi. to winery. (1709 Carson Rd., Placerville, CA 95667) Tel (916) 622-8094. W-Su 10-5./Ta

Eldorado Winery. From U.S. 50, Camino exit, then 200 yds. W on frontage (Carson) rd. (3551 Carson Rd., Camino, CA 95709) Tel (916) 644-3773. Daily 10-5 Sep-Feb, Sa-Su 12-5 Mar-Aug, and by appt. IT/Ta

Sierra Vista Winery. From State 49 at Diamond Springs, Pleasant Valley Rd. NE 10 miles to Pleasant Valley, Leisure Lane W to winery dr. at end of rd. (45 Cabernet Way, Placerville, CA 95667) Tel (916) 622-7221. By appt.

Amador County

Amador Winery. On State 49 at Amador City. (PO Box 65, Amador City, CA 95601) Tel (209) 267-5320. T-Su 10-6./Ta

Argonaut Winery. 5 mi NE of Ione on Willow Creek Rd. (PO Box 612, Ione, CA 95640) Weekends by written appt. only.

D'Agostini. From State 49 at Plymouth, 8 mi. NE via E-16/Shenandoah Rd. (Rt. 2, Box 19, Plymouth, CA 95669) Tel (209) 245-6612. Daily 9-5. GT/Ta

Monteviña. From State 49 at Plymouth, NE 2 mi. on E-16/Shenandoah Rd. then E 1 mi. on Shenandoah School Rd. to winery. (Rt. 2, Box 30A, Plymouth, CA 95669) Tel (209) 245-3412. By appt.

Shenandoah Vineyards. From State 49 at Plymouth, NE 6 mi. on E-16/Shenandoah Rd. then N 1 mi. on Steiner Rd. to winery drive. (Box 23, Steiner Rd., Plymouth, CA 95669) Tel (209) 245-3698. By appt.

StoneRidge. From State 49 south of Sutter Creek, 2¼ mi. E on Ridge Rd. to winery drive. (Rt. 1, Box 36-B, Ridge Rd., Sutter Creek, CA 95685) By appt.

Story Vineyards. From State 49 at Plymouth, NE 5½ mi. on E-16/Shenandoah Rd., then N 1½ mi. on Bell Rd. to fork, W to winery. (Mailing address: ℅ Eugene Story, 1917 P St., Sacramento, CA 95814) Tel (209) 245-6208. By appt.

Outside Map Area

Chispa Cellars. (425 Main St., Murphys, CA 95247). By appt.

Stevenot Winery. (PO Box 548, Murphys, CA 95247) Tel (209) 728-3793. By appt.

Yankee Hill Winery. From State 49, 1 mi. E of Columbia S.P. on Yankee Hill Rd. (PO Box 163, Columbia, CA 95310) Tel (209) 532-3015. Daily sunrise to sunset. Picnic./Ta

Key: GT (guided tour); IT (informal tour); Ta (tasting).

The Mother Lode

beneath the residence of proprietors Gary and Loretta Porteous.

The aging cellar has a romantic antique touch (or rather, several of them). The Porteouses salvaged several ancient oak casks and puncheons from a one-time miner's boarding house which had made wine for its clientele in the gaudy days of the Gold Rush. These are the majority of the oak cooperage, though they are supplemented by newer French and American barrels.

The production focuses on Zinfandel from an old vineyard nearby, and Ruby Cabernet from the home property.

The winery is small enough that the tasting room consists of a barrel, set on end in the aging cellar. It is also small enough that an appointment is required to visit it. The Porteouses have no plan for their winery to grow much in the next few years.

Story Vineyard concentrates on Zinfandel, in the best tradition of this region, but also makes a white wine from mission grapes, as a limited-production specialty.

This is an instructive small winery. Owned by veterinarian Eugene Story, the yellow brick building on Bell Road is flanked by his 40-year-old vineyard. Between the first row of vines and the main door, crusher and press occupy a concrete pad. Inside, a row of temperature-controlled stainless steel fermentors runs along one wall while racks of American oak barrels take up most of the rest of the space. A small bottling line is at the rear. Thus the cellar allows the whole process of winemaking to be seen from beginning to end without moving a step, though for clear looks at some of the details it is advisable to stroll a few feet.

Story founded the business in 1973 as Cosumnes River Vineyard, and built his cellar the following year. He changed the name to Story in 1979, after finding that almost nobody but locals could pronounce Cosumnes.

Appointments are required to visit the cellars. By specific arrangement, the proprietor permits picnicking at one or another of several wooded sites around his rolling vineyard.

Calaveras – Tuolumne Wineries

Three small wineries are close to the Calaveras-Tuolumne county line, one on the Tuolumne side near Columbia, the other two at Murphys in Calaveras County. The two at Murphys are so small (or new, or both) that they do not have formal visitor policies.

Yankee Hill Winery, a mile east of Columbia State Historic Park, is the property of the Ron Erickson family. It is the largest (and since it includes a direct predecessor) the oldest cellar of the three.

One small wood-sided building holds both aging cellar and tasting room. The building dates to 1972, when it was built as Columbia Cellars by a former owner.

The Ericksons offer vintage-dated Zinfandel and Grenache, as well as several generics and sparkling wines under the Columbia Cellars label. They also offer picnicking under an arbor alongside the winery.

More wineries. In Murphys are two wineries, Chispa Cellars and Stevenot Winery. Chispa is the property of Jim Riggs and Bob Bliss, and houses itself in the cellar of an 1856 building. Stevenot is the property of Barden Stevenot, who founded his winery in 1978. An appointment is best in each case.

Other Than Wineries

The Mother Lode, like several other California wine districts, gains considerable appeal from having a romantic nineteenth century history. Unlike the others, the early appeal was only slightly vinous. The real story in these parts was gold.

Although large-scale mining is in the distant past, the countryside still shows a good many signs of the time: headframes of old mines, washes from sluicing operations, and not least, towns with some uncommon architecture dating back to an era of easy spending.

The landmarks are too many, in too many different places, to be covered here. An engaging guide is the *Sunset* book *Gold Rush Country*.

Plotting a Route

A plethora of state highways ascends from the San Joaquin Valley floor to intersect with State Highway 49, the Mother Lode's north-south artery.

The fastest way up is not one of those, but rather the freeway, U.S. Highway 50 from Sacramento to Placerville.

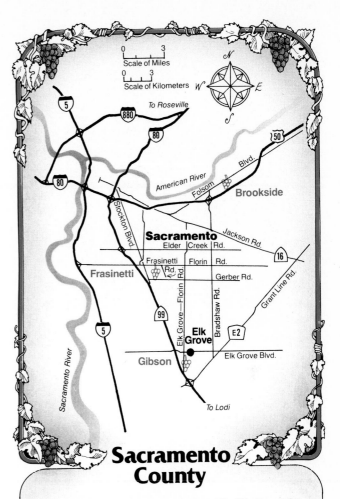

Sacramento County

Brookside. S side of Folsom Blvd. 4½ mi. NE of Perkins. (9910 Folsom Blvd., Sacramento, CA 95827) Tel (916) 366-9959. Daily 9-6. IT/Ta

Frasinetti. On Frasinetti Rd. ½ mi. S of Florin Rd. and W of SP RR tracks. (PO Box 28213, Sacramento, CA 95828) Tel (916) 383-2444. M-Sa 8:30-7, Su 11-6./Ta

Gibson. Tasting room: jct. of State 99 and Grant Line Rd. (Elk Grove, CA 95624) Tel (916) 685-9211. Daily 10-7./Ta

Harbor Winery. (7576 Pocket Rd., Sacramento, CA 95831) By written appt. (Not on map.)

Sequoia Cellars. (738 Anderson Rd., Davis, CA 95616) Tel (916) 756-3081. By appt. (Outside map.)

Key: GT (guided tour); IT (informal tour); Ta (tasting).

Of the slower state routes, State Highway 88 from Lodi to Jackson is ranked by more than a few connoisseurs at the head of the list for scenic beauty. Almost as attractive is State Highway 16 from Sacramento to Plymouth. The latter road has the further advantage of arriving in the heart of the most vinous part of the Mother Lode.

Within the region, winery visitors can make a tidy and efficient loop by using U.S. 50, State 49 and Amador County Road E16 (which becomes Pleasant Valley Road in El Dorado County). Nearly all of the wineries in Amador and El Dorado counties are on these routes, or very close to them. The Calaveras wineries are near State 49, some miles south of the loop.

Not all the color *went out of the Sierra foothills with the gold. Vineyards and wineries there are among the state's most picturesque. The barrel aging cellar (above) is at Monteviña. The tiny cellar (right) belongs to StoneRidge. Below, sheep mow the winter cover crop for an independent vineyardist near Plymouth.*

Sacramento

Sacramento is mainly the state capital, but it also has some enduring associations with the grape. Three old-line wineries continue to operate within or close by the city limits. In recent years, two tiny newcomers have joined the ranks. One of the greatest ties, just a few minutes west on Interstate Highway 80, is the Davis Campus of the University of California. Davis is the home of the university's Department of Viticulture and Enology, one of the world's leading centers of research and training for grape growers and winemakers.

Wine touring in Sacramento, though, is not the day or weekend activity it can be elsewhere in the district. Here, it is more of a respite from the road, or an interval in some larger scheme.

The Wineries

Of the five wineries in or near Sacramento, only Brookside has a tour, and it is informal. Two others have tasting rooms. Both of the small newcomers are visitable only by appointment.

Brookside's Sacramento facility was founded as Mills Winery in 1910, had new owners in 1946, then became a part of the Southern California-based Brookside Company in 1968.

A parchment document displayed in the tasting room attests to the winery's role in California history. The first railroad on the Pacific Coast was laid at the entrance to the winery property, and the Pony Express route used the adjoining property.

The winery is open daily for self-guided tours and tasting. A limited number of wines (mostly dessert) are still available by the barrel (an original distinction of Mills). All of the Brookside wines are available in bottles and jugs.

Frasinetti and Sons dates back to 1897, a long career by local standards. Its founder, James Frasinetti, died in 1965 at the age of 91. His sons and grandsons continue the family tradition.

After the original building burned to the ground in 1924, it was replaced by a utilitarian collection of corrugated iron structures. During the early 1970s, the family added warm-hued stucco faces to the main cellar and the bottling building, made a handsome tasting room, and otherwise turned the property into a peaceable, even serene, island at the end of a busy industrial street running alongside the railroad right of way.

There is no tour, only tasting of a longish list of table and dessert wines. Two specialties are N B Tween (a dessert wine in between sweet and dry) and Cerasolo, a pale, soft red developed by the founder for those customers who found his regular reds too thick and dark.

Gibson Wine Company is best known as a pioneer in the making and marketing of fruit and berry wines, but the firm also makes a range of table, dessert, and sparkling wines.

The winery was started in 1934 by Robert Gibson, who died in 1960. The company was then bought by a grower cooperative and continues to operate under that ownership.

There is no tour of the substantial winery, but the wines may be sampled at the Gibson tasting room, located a mile south of the winery on the East Frontage Road of State Highway 99, at the Grant Line Road exit.

More wineries. The two small newcomers to winemaking in the Sacramento district are Harbor Winery and Sequoia Cellars. Harbor Winery is the property of a college teacher of literature named Charles Myers, who makes small lots of varietal table wines from Napa and Amador grapes, and a rare dessert wine from mission grapes grown in Amador. The cellar is in a riverfront building at the edge of the city, and has been active since 1972.

Sequoia Cellars dates only from 1977 and is located in a leased corner of the old Woodland Ice Company building. It is the propriety of Carol Gehrmann and Patricia Riley, who make Cabernet Sauvignon, Zinfandel, and one of the state's pioneer Carnelians. (Carnelian is a grape variety cultivated at the University of California at Davis to yield claretlike wines in warmer climes than Cabernet Sauvignon will tolerate.)

Other Than Wineries

Though the Department of Viticulture and Enology at U.C. Davis is not open to the public, it deserves a bow from any appreciator of California wine who whistles past on I-80 or cruises by on State Highway 128 on the other side of the campus. The campus, 14 miles west of the capitol at Sacramento, is a pretty place to while away an hour or two in the midst of a great many trees and even more bicycles.

It would stretch matters to say that all of California's technical progress in winemaking owes itself to the academicians at Davis, but the school had a lot to do with creating the spirit of enlightened inquiry that marks professional vintaging in the state. Its staff members are in demand among Australian, French, South African, and Yugoslav wine people, and others. They cooperate with their colleagues in other countries on technical counsel and guest instruction, and they serve as judges in international competitions.

The Davis faculty is also in demand at home, where it cooperates with the staffs of commercial firms on investigations of everything from disease-resistant rootstock to the abilities of different wines to age.

Some of the most visible results of the work at Davis are noted here and there throughout this book. But some of the most important results of the school's research will not be covered here because they have to do with such esoteric (but vital) matters as the roles of tannins in red wines or the tensile strengths of main stems in grape clusters.

Plotting a Route

Sacramento, being at the hub of Interstate Highway 5, I-80, U.S. Highway 50, and State 99, is not hard to find. Since the local wineries are fairly closely tied to the freeway system, getting to them is an easy task as well.

The state capital is not vacation country, nor is it scenic vineyard country. There is little reason for wine buffs to explore local side roads. Main attractions in the city include the capitol building, Old Sacramento, and Sutter's Fort.

San Joaquin Valley

California's biggest vineyard of them all

Old Harvest Wagon

The San Joaquin Valley is not wine country in the compact sense of the north coast counties, where visitors can choose from among half a dozen to a score of cellars within a few miles. But this huge and implausibly diverse agricultural empire is wine country on a scale the coastal regions cannot match: its 35 wineries produce something like 70 percent of the state's annual volume of wine. Fresno County alone sends 500,000 tons of grapes to wineries in a good year, compared to 200,000 for all 14 coast counties combined.

This vineyard of the giants requires its visitors to wear seven-league boots. Some 200 miles of State Highway 99 separate Modesto on the north from Bakersfield on the south. In all that space, only 15 cellars had visitor facilities in the spring of 1979. What is more, the area's distance from other major population centers is an important consideration for all but valley residents. Modesto is 95 miles southeast of San Francisco; Bakersfield is 111 miles north of Los Angeles. For these reasons most winery visits come as diversions, either during travels between coast and mountains, or on north-south vacation trips.

The handful of survivors from the family farm era of winemaking lend spice to visits, but in the main the tourable wineries fit the size of this great valley.

In business terms, the San Joaquin is one huge district because the large wineries draw grapes from the length and breadth of the valley. For visitors, though, the region divides into at least three parts. The focal points are Modesto, Fresno, and Bakersfield.

Modesto & surroundings

Modesto and the wine business did not get together until the 1930s, but the two have prospered mutually ever since. The city's population doubled between 1950 and 1960, and has doubled again since. The total now approaches 100,000. The production of wine has grown even faster than that.

Modesto is well equipped to handle visitors in numbers. A gateway to Yosemite National Park, it has substantial numbers of motels and restaurants, most of them ranged along McHenry Boulevard and Yosemite Avenue.

The Wineries

No great distance separates Lodi from Modesto, but in those few miles the pattern of winery ownership changes markedly. Lodi is a capital of grower cooperatives. Modesto does not have a single one.

E & J Gallo is far and away the dominant winery

among the eight that ring Modesto. Some that seem small next to Gallo have impressive size when measured against the average cellar of other districts. A pair of genuinely small premises still give the region a diverse character.

Five wineries welcome visitors in one way or another. Bella Napoli, Delicato Vineyards, and Pirrone Cellars are on or near the freeway, State 99. Cadlolo and Franzia are east of the freeway on State Highway 120.

Bella Napoli evokes an era that seems to be passing in the San Joaquin Valley. The winery, a separate structure at the rear of the family home, is in every respect a small, old-fashioned country enterprise.

Because of this, proprietor Lucas Hat cannot encourage a tourist trade in the usual sense. There are no tours or tastings, only the agreeably uncomplicated opportunity to stand in the courtyard amid whitewashed farm buildings and buy a supply of country red or white in bottle or jug.

Lucas is the second generation of Hats—the family name is Neapolitan—to make Vine Flow table wines for sale to a mainly local trade.

The wines come from a sizable vineyard surrounding the house and winery. Hat takes only a small part of his crop for his own use. The rest he sells to a larger winery.

Cadlolo Winery, in the town of Escalon, presents a fresh face to the world. The main building of concrete and red brick looks almost new beneath its coat of pale cream paint. But it dates from 1913 when L. Sciaroni launched a winery on the site. Charles Cadlolo held the reins from 1937 until 1970. His sons, Raymond and Theodore, now own and operate the still-small family cellars. The only signs that hint at the age of the building are an old-style evaporative cooling tower on the roof and a mature tree that shades the front wall.

The brothers' pride in the premises is evident in more than the freshly painted appearance of the main building. The crusher alongside one wall has a well-scrubbed air. The interior of the winery is just as tidy.

Not-quite-formal tours (sometimes interrupted for a bit of work on the part of the guide) start at the crusher and go all the way through to the bottling department. Tasting is in a casual room just to one side of the main cellar, within sniffing range of its aromatic redwood tanks full of wine. On hand for sampling are several generic table wines, and appetizer and dessert wines.

Delicato Vineyards occupies a very considerable plot of ground just alongside the southbound lanes of State 99, on a frontage road near Manteca.

Signs give ample warning before the freeway exit leads onto what is very nearly a private lane. The winery has on each flank a residence of one or another branch of the owning family, the Indelicatos. (Given the family name, the proprietors must have taken great delight in naming the place. He who doubts the authenticity of the reverse twist has only to read the names on the mailboxes on either side of the winery.)

Delicato has grown greatly during the past decade. A few years ago an informal tour could cover all the ground within a small, iron-sheathed winery building

in a very few minutes. Now guided tours launch out from a new-in-1975 textured-block tasting room to take in impressive arrays of outdoor steel fermentors and storage tanks—almost 13 million gallons worth—and such esoteric contrivances as rotary vacuum filters. The immaculately clean original cellar, full of redwood tanks, is on the route. So is a much enlarged bottling line. An appointment is required to take this tour—the most complete and informative one of any sizable producing winery in the district. No appointment is required to taste the wide range of Delicato wines, including varietal and generic table wines, appetizer, dessert, and sparkling wines.

Franzia Winery is on State 120 east of Ripon. An attractively designed and furnished tasting room sits in the midst of a decorative block of vines next to the highway. The several large buildings of the winery proper stand farther back, amid larger blocks of vines.

Since 1971 the property of the Coca Cola Bottling Company of New York, Franzia started out as a family business. Giuseppe Franzia, having emigrated from Genoa, established the family in the California wine business in 1906. The untimely intervention of Prohibition necessitated a second start in 1933. Giuseppe and five sons had built the enterprise up to an annual production of 15 million gallons by the time the family sold.

The company offers tours of its vast, mechanically efficient plant only by appointment. Appointments are generally limited to groups.

Franzia wines include all of the familiar appetizer and dessert types, several sparkling wines, and a range of table wines. Most of the latter are generics. Some varietals have been on the list since 1974.

A tree-shaded picnic ground on lawns adjacent to the tasting room is open to casual drop-in visitors when it has not been reserved for groups.

Pirrone Wine Cellars, on the east side of State 99 just north of Salida's business district, is a family-owned winery dating back to 1936.

Its founder was Frank Pirrone, who had been an architect practicing in Garfield, New Jersey, until he started the winery on land he had purchased in 1923. (One of his uncles had managed the vineyard in the interim, selling the grapes to home winemakers.)

After the founder's retirement, two sons carried on for a time, selling wines in bulk. In 1964, Al Pirrone bought his brother's share of the business.

The main winery, built in 1946, can produce a million gallons a year. The production is dessert wine, sold in bulk to other wineries.

In the tasting room the proprietor offers a range of wines, including table and sparkling as well as dessert wines.

More wineries. Visitors to Modesto are likely to notice other wineries on the landscape.

By far the largest winery in Modesto (and probably the largest in the world) is E & J Gallo. At the present it is not open to visitors. Alas for that, because the Gallos have come from small and perfectly ordinary beginnings to a dazzlingly complex center for making wine under the most rational of conditions with the most efficient of equipment. Nothing is left to wayward chance. The Gallos even have their own bottle manufactory on the premises, yielding glass made to their own patented formula.

Gallo's made-on-the-spot bottles receive a complete range of varietal and generic table wines, sparkling wines, and appetizer, dessert and flavored types made from grapes grown the length and breadth of the state. The firm owns huge vineyard acreages in Modesto, Livingston, and the Sierra foothills, buys still more grapes on contract, and also buys the entire wine production of grower cooperatives in the Central Valley, Sonoma, and Napa.

Even though there is no admittance, serious students of California wine owe themselves a drive past the headquarters and winery on Fairbanks Avenue in the southeast quarter of Modesto. There is no crushing at this facility: that goes on at other Gallo wineries west of Livingston and in Fresno.

United Vintners has an old, little-used winery on State 120, about equidistant between Franzia to the west and Cadlolo to the east. This, the original Petri winery, is not open to visitors; instead, UV welcomes visitors at Asti in Sonoma County (see page 23) and at Inglenook in the Napa Valley (see page 41).

The other winery in the district is Bronco. At Ceres, it too is closed to visitors.

Other Than Wineries

Unlikely as it may seem, Modesto is in the midst of a great deal of water. The Tuolumne and Stanislaus Rivers join the San Joaquin just west of town. Just to the east, folds in the hills harbor three major reservoirs with recreational developments.

These reservoirs, along with Yosemite National Park, draw a great many vacationers through the Modesto district. But for casual visitors, they are too far away to combine with winery visits. Caswell State Park solves that problem. It extends along 4 miles of the Stanislaus River west of Salida. The river, shallow here, has a number of swimming holes. Picnic sites under spreading oaks are 10 to 15 degrees cooler than nearby farm fields. To get to the park, exit west from State 99 on Austin Road 2 miles south of Manteca. The park is about 5 miles west of the freeway.

Each of the major towns in the district has a tree-shaded municipal park for quick picnics.

For a list of overnight accommodations, write to the Modesto Chamber of Commerce, P.O. Box 844, Modesto, CA 95353.

Plotting a Route

All of the wineries open to visit in the Modesto area are either on the freeway, State 99, or the two-lane road, State 120. These two roads form an awkward, toppling T. State Highway 108, another two-laner, runs from State 120 at Escalon into Modesto, the third leg of a triangle that can turn a tour of all five wineries in the region into a tidy loop for anyone starting and finishing in Modesto.

On the San Joaquin Valley floor, these and all other roads are flat, with few or no curves.

The visual interests are subtleties on a vast canvas. A shift from row crop to orchard is gross change, especially when February and March light the orchards with blossom. Random occurrences of single oaks or small clusters in the fields produce eerie perspectives on a misty day. There is a prodigious number of unpainted, decaying small barns to consider in this era of large-scale agriculture. Residential architecture ranges from a rare brick colonial to a profusion of board-and-batten cottages.

To get into the region from the San Francisco Bay area, use Interstate Highway 580 to Tracy, Interstate Highway 5 to its junction with State 120, then the state route to get to or across State 99.

From Los Angeles, I-5 intersects both State Highway 132 into Modesto, and State 120.

Fresno

The highest point in Fresno is the 20th floor of its Rodeway Inn. Look out from that floor on a typical heat-hazy day in summer, and no hill of stature will appear in view. Fresno is flat.

The city has grown big enough to have traffic jams and other urban qualities. (In the last census, its 183,000 population was enough to rank it ninth largest among California cities, 73rd largest in the nation.)

Yet it manages to have charms. The main street of Fresno's original business district, fading a few years ago, has been turned into a spacious shopping mall with fountains, many trees (and shaded sitting places), and 20 specially commissioned sculptures. Nearby, a big convention center of unusual architecture is the stage for attractions both home-grown and imported.

To the north of the original city center, West Shaw Avenue has become a long, often architecturally distinctive, sequence of shopping centers and office buildings.

The central city may have begun to acquire a certain urbanity in this era of large-scale and mechanized farming (everybody in the Central Valley calls it "agribusiness" these days), but Fresno is, nonetheless, a farm center. The talk in the coffee shops has to do with one crop or another.

Among those crops, grapes figure most prominently. Fresno and neighboring counties north and south produce enough raisins for the Western hemisphere and enough table grapes for much of the United States. In recent years the district's share of wine production has slipped below its old level of 50 percent of all California wine, but only because other districts have added vineyards more rapidly than has Fresno.

Traditionally the production has leaned toward Sherries, Ports, Muscats, and other sweet dessert wines. The long, sunny summers favor sugar-laden grapes with their ancestral roots in Portuguese or Spanish soils. Here, as in Lodi and Modesto, specially developed warm-climate grapes for table wines are replacing other varieties or supplementing them.

Reading the founding dates of wineries, an innocent might assume that winemaking did not get going in Fresno until 1936 or so, as in the case of Modesto. Blame Prohibition for creating yet another false

In the vast *San Joaquin, mechanical harvesters pick the clock around to keep up with huge harvests.*

impression. A man named Lee Eisen planted the first vineyard in the district in 1873. (Three rail-sitters of the day volunteered to eat the entire crop, which they might have done the first year but never thereafter.) Grapes have flourished in Fresno from Eisen's time on, and a good many have gone into wine since 1876.

The Wineries

The Fresno district covers an awesome number of square miles from Madera on the northwest to Cutler on the southeast. Within that vast expanse, fewer than a dozen wineries welcome visitors. But sparse as the numbers might be, the wineries are of such diverse character as to make a complete sampler of everything from giant to miniature, from generalist to specialist, from ultramodern to entirely traditional.

California Growers Winery dates from 1936, but has been wearing a new face since 1973. Originally a grower cooperative, the firm was incorporated in the latter year under the leadership of one of its former members, Robert Setrakian. The winery capacity has been enlarged substantially since the change in ownership.

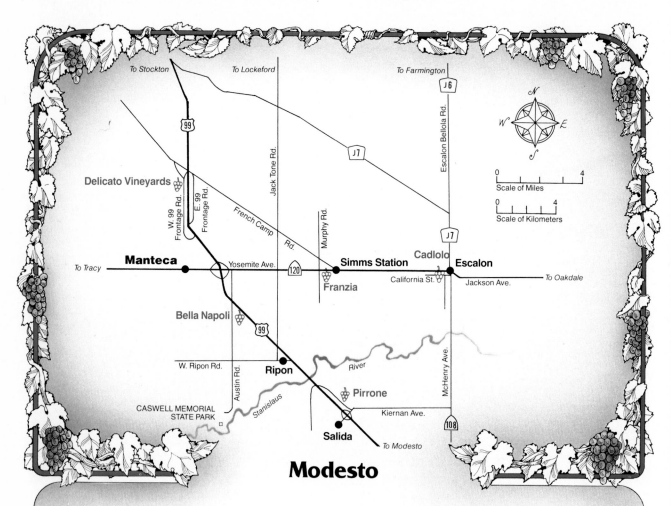

Bella Napoli. From State 99, Austin Rd. exit, S on Austin ½ mi. (21128 S. Austin Rd., Manteca, CA 95336) Tel (209) 599-3885. Daily 8-5. Tours by appt.

Cadlolo. From State 120 at W side of Escalon, S on Escalon Ave. across RR tracks, W on California St. 100 yards to winery. (1124 California St., Escalon, CA 95320) Tel (209) 838-2457. M-Sa 8-5. IT/Ta

Delicato Vineyards. From State 99, French Camp Rd. exit, S on westside frontage rd. ½ mi. (12001 S. Hwy. 99, Manteca, CA 95336) Tel (209) 982-0679. Daily 9-5. GT by appt./Ta

Franzia. From State 99, E 4½ mi. on State 120. (PO Box 697, Ripon, CA 95366) Tel (209) 599-4111. Picnic. Daily 9-5. Tours by appt./Ta

Pirrone. On frontage road E side State 99 between Hawthorne Rd. and Kiernan Ave. exits, ½ mi. N of Salida. (PO Box 15, Salida, CA 95368) Tel (209) 545-0704. Daily 9-5. IT/Ta

Key: GT (guided tour); IT (informal tour); Ta (tasting).

Calgro, as it is known for short, was then and is now a kind of eastern outpost of big valley wine. The winery nestles against the Sierra Nevada foothills near the town of Cutler, about 25 miles due east of Kingsburg.

For the time being there are neither tours nor tasting, but only retail sales of a full range of wines and brandies under the Growers, Setrakian, LeBlanc, and Bounty labels.

B. Cribari and Sons has been around since the 1920s, but it moved into a new home in 1978. Old hands who go looking for the Roma winery on Fresno's south side will find Cribari instead. There is an easy expla-

nation for this: Guild Wineries and Distilleries has owned the Cribari label for many years, and bought Roma in 1971, so the swap is all in the family.

When a man named John Cella was developing Roma in the post-Prohibition era, he meant to have a giant of a winery. The fact that the property is laid out on a grid of streets attests to his ambition. The winery is not the giant it once was because standards have changed, but it is big, covering more ground than many newer places. It is also a good deal more colorful than many contemporary wineries.

The proprietors took a huge, brick-walled aging cellar, removed the tanks from it, and turned it into a re-

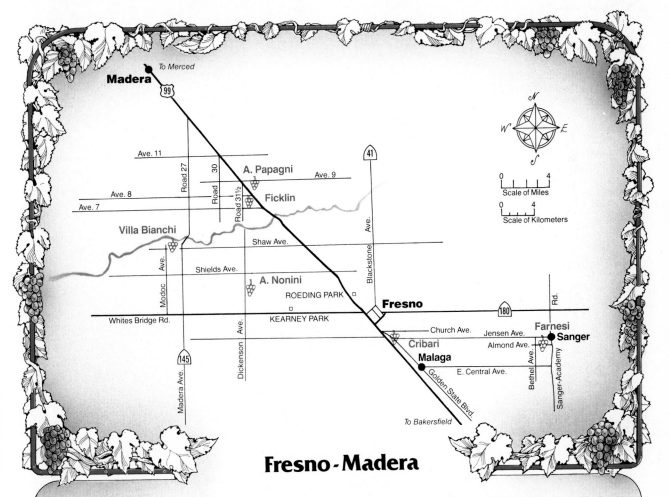

Fresno-Madera

Cribari & Sons. From State 99, Jensen Ave. exit northbound or Ventura Ave. exit southbound, change for Golden State Blvd. to Church Ave., then E ¼ mi. to winery. (3223 E. Church Ave., Fresno, CA 93714) Tel (209) 485-3080. Daily 10-5. GT/Ta

Farnesi. From Jensen Ave. in Sanger, S on Bethel Ave. ½ mi. to Almond Ave., E on Almond to winery. (2426 Almond Ave., Sanger, CA 93657) Tel (209) 875-3004. M-F 8-5, Sa 8-12./Ta

Ficklin. (30246 Ave. 7½, Madera, CA 93637) Tel (209) 674-4598. By appt.

Nonini. From State 99, McKinley Ave. exit W 7½ mi. to Dickenson Ave., then N ½ mi. to winery. (2640 N. Dickenson Ave., Fresno, CA 93705) Tel (209) 264-7857. M-Sa 9-6. GT/Ta

Papagni. In SE corner of Ave. 9 exit from State 99. (31754 Ave. 9, Madera, CA 93637) Tel (209) 674-5652. By appt.

Villa Bianchi. From State 99, W on Shaw Ave. to Modoc Ave., N on Modoc to winery. (5806 Modoc Ave., Kerman, CA 93630) Tel (209) 846-7356. M-F 8-4. IT (except during crush)/TA

Outside Map Area

California Growers. From Cutler S to intersection of Rd. 128, Ave. 384. (PO Box 21, Yettem, CA 93670) Tel (209) 528-3033. M-F 8-5.

Key: GT (guided tour); IT (informal tour); Ta (tasting).

Getting into it

On most winery tours, the guide will say that a full-grown man can crawl through the tiny gate in the front of an aging tank to clean it, but will not have anybody on hand to prove the claim.

A cellarman can and does crawl through the gate after each use of the cask or tank, to scrub it thoroughly and then burn sulphur in it.

The essence of getting in is entirely a matter of shoulders. First, the cellarman climbs a step just outside the manhole, then leans, and does something very much like the first half of a butterfly stroke in swimming. Once his shoulders clear the portal, he must wriggle his lower half inward until one knee clears the gate so that he can get a leg inside to stand on. Going out, the process reverses itself: he sticks one leg out, then the other; then wriggles backwards until his waist can bend outside the tank.

To wash a tank,
a man must crawl in through a gate just wide enough for a pair of middling shoulders.

ception and tasting hall for visitors. Fanciful flags and pennants hang from the lofty ceiling and on some of the tall walls. Hourly tours leave from the hall.

The route is along B Street to 4th, across to C, then back. Along the way it passes Cribari's huge crushers, goes through an aging cellar full of big redwood tanks and another one lined with 120 oak oval casks ranging up to the improbable size of 6,500 gallons each. Finally, in the brandy cellars, the tour provides the only close-up look at column stills to be had in all California.

Available in the tasting room is the full line of Cribari table, sparkling, and dessert wines.

Farnesi Winery

Farnesi Winery in Sanger is a small family enterprise founded in 1935 by a transplanted Tuscan named Corado Farnesi, and carried on since 1951 by his nephew, Danny Farnesi. The younger Farnesi, having had the benefits of practical instruction from the founder and academic work at Fresno State University, runs the winery alone in all seasons except harvest-time. Then the whole family joins in making two red table wines to satisfy a local clientele.

The winery, in an adobe building across the street from a row of tidy residences, requires no tour. The proprietor will talk shop over a cordial glass.

Ficklin Vineyards

Ficklin Vineyards, out of Madera, is one of the smallest wineries in the Central Valley, and certainly the most single-minded.

The specialty is a Tinta Port made entirely from four selected Portuguese grape varieties. Not only is it the specialty: it is nearly the sum of winery production. (The owners started making Emerald Riesling and Ruby Cabernet in the 1960s mainly for their own table, but this remains a very casual part of the enterprise.)

The Ficklin family ranch dates back to 1911, when Walter Ficklin, Sr. arrived in the Fresno area and immediately launched into grapes and other fruit growing. Wine entered the picture in the early 1940s when Ficklin responded to a request by scientists at the University of California at Davis to plant trial blocks of several Portuguese grape varieties that had shown promise in university tests.

David Ficklin, after studying at Davis, began as the winemaker and winery manager. He continues in those roles, assisted now by his son Peter, also a Davis graduate. The vineyardist is Steven Ficklin, son of the now-retired Walter Ficklin, Jr.

The winery was founded in 1946, and in 1948 the first wine was made from tinta cao, tinta madeira, alvarelhao, and touriga grapes. The alvarelhao grapes since have been abandoned in favor of souzao.

The main cellar, small and low in a flat sea of vineyards west of State 99, is of adobe block fashioned on the site by the family. It is a substantial tribute to the traditional bent of the Ficklins. So is a handsome cellar full of fat oak barrels and puncheons. However, the family is only bent toward tradition, not bound by it. For example, they have done away with their original concrete fermentors in favor of more practical stainless steel tanks. And they have abandoned binning their bottled wines in favor of storing them in their case boxes to minimize handling.

The Ficklins sell their Tinta Port (along with small lots of Emerald Riesling and Ruby Cabernet) in a retail room next door to the cellar. Because the winery and ranch are owned and worked by the family, the Ficklins can offer tours by appointment only, when their days are not too full of jobs that need doing immediately. They explain how to find the well-hidden premises when they make arrangements for visits.

A. Nonini Winery

A. Nonini Winery, on the west edge of Fresno, was founded in 1936 by A. (equally appropriate for Antonio and wife Angiolina) Nonini, and since has passed to the hands of three sons, Geno, Gildo, and Reno. The third generation now is entering the family winemaking arena.

Since the Noninis own all their own grapes, they lay claim to having the only estate-bottled wines in Fresno County. Production is limited to table wines, including Barbera and Zinfandel as well as generics.

A tour of a tidy wood-frame cellar takes in every step from crushing to bottling, ending up in a fittingly informal tasting room housed in a cottage just in front of the cellar's front wall.

Along with Bella Napoli, Cadlolo, and Farnesi, this is one of the last four survivors of a once-abundant roster of family wineries catering to a local trade. This one has not lost a bit of flavor from the days when Basque shepherds would fill botas, or buy barrels on the way from winter to summer pastures, and back. It is still possible to buy Nonini wine in small barrels, or to have your own filled.

Angelo Papagni Winery

Angelo Papagni Winery tucks into one quarter of a freeway cloverleaf just south of Madera.

The buildings went up in 1974–1976. Though the exterior walls are unornamented workaday warehouse metal, this is an impressive place nonetheless. The Papagni crushing facility rivals the nearby freeway cloverleaf for size. Inside, steel fermentors and aging tanks share space with an imposing collection of oak barrels.

The property was designed to make vintage-dated table wines, including the rare Alicante Bouschet, Barbera, and Charbono among reds Chenin Blanc and the delicately sparkling Moscato d'Angelo among whites.

Full-fledged tour and tasting facilities lie in the future. Meanwhile, the proprietors will give tours by appointment. Anybody lucky enough to wander through when the winemaking staff is tasting in the lab may be invited to share a glass.

Villa Bianchi Winery

Villa Bianchi Winery is the newest label in the Fresno district, launched in 1974 in a 1930s winery refitted for the purpose.

Just for the romance, owner Joseph Bianchi saved an old still tower fitted out to please the taste of a Henry the Eighth. Otherwise the property has been made into a modern San Joaquin-style cellar, but not quite a typical one: Villa Bianchi operates with a patented process for both red and white wines that keeps grapeskins and seeds out of contact with the juice as it ferments. Tour guides explain the details as part of a complete exploration of the premises.

The tasting room lets visitors judge the results for themselves. The roster includes French Colombard, a white wine from Grenache, and Zinfandel, as well as generics.

Wine Press

99 on Shaw Avenue. Forestiere was a Sicilian possessing Herculean powers with a pick and shovel. After digging for 38 years, he ended up with a maze of tunnels that runs beneath 7 acres of surface ground. The deepest rooms are 25 feet below ground and 20 degrees cooler than summery afternoons up top.

For information on accommodations and restaurants in the area, write to the Fresno Chamber of Commerce, 2331 Fresno Street, Fresno, CA 93721.

Plotting a Route

For people already in the San Joaquin Valley, State 99 is the obvious means of approaching Fresno-area wineries from either north or south. Anyone starting from the San Francisco Bay area can get across the coast ranges most efficiently on I-580, though State Highway 152, the Pacheco Pass Highway, is more scenic and only slightly slower.

In addition to being the basic approach route, State 99 is also a useful thread in getting from one winery to another since it makes a long, diagonal slice through the region that somewhat parallels the sequence of cellars.

Generally speaking, none of the roads leading to the wineries provides stunning scenery. The possible exceptions would be those roads in the Reedley-Sanger district that get close to the course of the Kings River. These lead past changing terrain and brightened colors.

Bakersfield

Bakersfield is the urban anchor for the southern end of the San Joaquin Valley. Unlike Fresno and other valley cities, Bakersfield is as involved in drilling for oil as it is in growing crops. In fact, it is not at all uncommon to see the bobbing heads of pumps at wells between vine rows. The other instantly noticeable fact of local life is a general passion for country and western music.

Grapes have been a part of Kern County agriculture for a good many years, but most of them went for table use or raisins until late in the 1960s. Then, new grape varieties and new grapegrowing techniques began to open new avenues in this hottest of California wine regions, and wine became a prime interest rather than an afterthought.

The Wineries

It is easy for visitors to get a taste of wines in this region. Three of its six wineries maintain tasting rooms. Seeing how the work gets done is harder, since only two offer tours, and then only by appointment.

The three sources of samples are Giumarra Vineyards, LaMont Winery, and A. Perelli-Minetti & Sons Winery. All are fairly sizable operations in a district which has no other kind.

Giumarra Vineyards first opened to visitors in 1974, at the same time the family-owned winery released its first vintage-dated varietal wines from local vineyards.

The winery occupies the western end of a long line

More wineries. A good many more large wineries operate within this sprawling district. Included in the roster are these: California Products, E & J Gallo, Guild, Sierra, Vie-Del, and Viking in Fresno; Almaden in Kingsburg; Bisceglia (Canandaigua), Paul Masson, and Mission Bell (United Vintners) in Madera; Cella (United Vintners) and Mt. Tivy (The Christian Brothers) in Reedley; and Selma in Rio Vista. These wineries have no visitor accommodations of any sort. They do not even sell wines at retail.

Other Than Wineries

Fresno has two excellent parks and a mysterious underground grotto as alternate diversions to winery tours.

Roeding Park, 157 acres tucked between the freeway, State 99, and State 99-Business and between Olive and Belmont Avenues, is a tree-shaded, quiet respite from the valley sun. There are several areas for children, including a storyland, a zoo, an amusement arcade, a sizable pond with rental boats, and spacious picnic areas beneath tall rows of eucalyptus.

Kearney Park is 7 miles west of Fresno on Kearney Boulevard. It is a huge, county-operated picnic park on the grounds of the old M. Theo Kearney estate. Several large areas are set aside for group reservations. Interspersed between these are a great many small areas for first-come, first-served family use.

The mysterious underground grotto of Baldasare Forestiere is north of Fresno, two blocks west of State

of buildings near Edison. The other structures house other aspects of a diverse farming business, and there are enough of them that it takes a couple of minutes to drive from the property entrance to the sculpted concrete building that houses the bottling lines and tasting room.

On the second floor, the tasting room allows visitors to watch work on the bottling line while they sample from a list that includes Chenin Blanc, Riesling, French Colombard, Cabernet Sauvignon, and Pinot Noir.

Groups can arrange for walking tours of the crushing area and aging cellars.

LaMont Winery has been a pioneer in Kern County winemaking in several ways. It started as a family-owned bulk winery in 1945, then was bought by a grower cooperative in 1966. During years as a cooperative, the winery was named Bear Mountain after a conical peak that looms up just behind a rambling array of cellar buildings and open-air steel fermenting and storage tanks. Also during that time, the winery began producing varietal table wines under the LaMont label, the latter name borrowed from a nearby town. These wines marked the first concentrated effort to produce and sell table wines from the Bakersfield district. LaMont became the name of the property in 1978 when it was bought from the grower cooperative by John Labatt, Ltd., a Canadian firm which owns a major brewery and three wineries in its home country.

Under the new owners, LaMont continues to produce varietal table wines, including Chenin Blanc, French Colombard, Gewürztraminer, a Rosé of Barbera, and Ruby Cabernet.

Visitors can arrange to tour the winery. The tasting room is open to all comers, even people who arrive by airplane, for this is the only tasting room in the state with an adjacent airstrip. Because the strip is private, fly-in visitors must write ahead to the winery for a "hold harmless" agreement.

A. Perelli-Minetti & Sons, near Delano, is the real pioneer winery still active in the region. The late Antonio Perelli-Minetti launched his cellars on the present site in 1937. His family still owns the winery and a marketing company called California Wine Association.

There is more history behind the name of CWA than a short book will hold. It was once the most pervasive name in California winemaking, and very nearly a monopoly marketer of the state's wines. Perelli-Minetti resisted joining the organization until it had lost much of its power, then succeeded in taking it over.

This link to a state-wide past explains why the tasting room holds bottles labeled as Guasti and Ambassador, names originally associated with the Cucamonga district east of Los Angeles, and why one of the appellations on those labels is Napa Valley.

The tasting room itself is an architectural tribute to a wine tank and to the idea of recycling. A round, redwood building, it uses an old wine tank as an outside wall, interwoven grapestakes as a ceiling, and other winery equipment for other parts of the construction. (The Perelli-Minettis are pleased to observe that the only material not scavenged from the winery and vineyards is the redwood for the interior walls.) There is no tour of the sprawling winery.

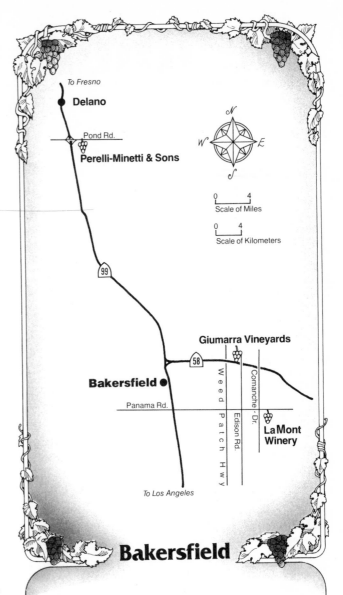

Bakersfield

Giumarra Vineyards. State 58 SE from Bakersfield 6.5 mi. to Edison Rd. exit, N ¼ mi. to Edison Hwy., W 100 yds. to winery entrance on right. (PO Bin 1969, Bakersfield, CA 93303) Tel (805) 366-5511. W-Su, 9-5. GT by appt./Ta

LaMont Winery. From State 99, Taft-Greenfield exit, W 10 mi. to Comanche Dr., S ½ mi. to winery. (PO Box 566, LaMont, CA 93241) Tel (805) 845-2231. Daily 10-5. GT by appt./Ta

A. Perelli-Minetti & Sons. In SE corner of Pond Rd. intersection with State 99. (PO Box 818, Delano, CA 93216) Tel (805) 792-3162. Daily 10-5./Ta

Key: GT (guided tour); IT (informal tour); Ta (tasting).

More wineries. Three other wineries make and sell wine only in bulk in the region. The most visible of them is California Mission Wines, alongside the freeway, State 99, at MacFarland. The others are Delano Cooperative and a dessert wine cellar belonging to Guild Wineries & Distilleries.

Southern California

New frontiers back where it all began

Time and the restless tide of population in Southern California have caused a whole series of shifts in vineyards of this oldest of California's wine growing regions.

Father Junipero Serra planted the first vines at the mission in San Diego circa 1769. As early as 1831 Jean Louis Vignes planted the first commercial vineyard in what is now downtown Los Angeles. All traces of these and some other early districts are long gone. The one reminder of early times is a small room at Mission San Gabriel, kept more or less the way it was when the Franciscans were making wine in it.

At present the greatest concentration of vineyards is in the Cucamonga district east of Los Angeles, between the San Bernardino County towns of Ontario and Fontana. However, as population pressures grow more severe with each passing year, this region too suffers a steadily tightening squeeze.

In searching for new land to plant, several vineyardists have turned south to Temecula in Riverside County. At least one has looked still farther south, to Escondido, only a few miles from the old mission in San Diego.

Despite the shifting focus in vineyard sites, winery touring south of the Tehachapi Mountains still concentrates itself in Cucamonga, where local cellars are among the state's busiest in welcoming visitors.

Cucamonga

A wide, relatively unpopulated strip separates Ontario from Fontana. Within it lies nearly all of the present-day Cucamonga wine district.

Cucamonga hardly exists as a specific place; it is an intersection of Archibald Avenue and Foothill Boulevard, or a post office. The more general description of the area these days would be Pomona Valley. But wine goes back to the 1830s in Cucamonga, and that will be the name of the wine district for as long as its vines endure.

Whatever its name, this is a curious countryside. The San Gabriel Mountains rise sharply on the north, effectively forming a wall on that side of the valley. At the foot of these mountains, a gently sloping and remarkably even alluvial fan runs more than a mile before it flattens out and becomes true valley floor. To the south, a less imposing range of hills called the Jurupas marks the limit for grapevines.

When the winds are westerly, visitors who fly into Ontario International Airport make their final approach over block after block of vines. Once on the ground and driving back through the vineyards, though, the visitors discover that a great many of them display "For Sale" signs on their corners. Some have not been harvested of late.

Industry and population press in from both east and west. A few years ago, San Bernardino County had 23,000 acres in bearing vines. By 1977 the figure had dwindled to 9,400. The owners of many of those acres are allowing vines to die by inches while they await a day of higher land prices.

Still, 9,400 acres is a great acreage, and the history of the vine in this district is long and strong. Furthermore, just because vines are in trouble does not mean wineries are. In these times of fast, efficient transport, grapes will be brought from elsewhere to keep wineries active hereabouts.

The Wineries

It has been a habit among Cucamonga proprietors to play the part of the traditional country winery, selling much—sometimes all—of their production at the cellar door. The custom continues, even though some of the larger cellars have had to build extra doors in favorable locations to make supply and demand come out right.

Get down to business, and there are four full-fledged, producing wineries to visit in the Cucamonga district. Tasting rooms, with and without aging cellars attached, expand the roster by three.

Brookside Vineyard Company says it is in Guasti. In fact, it nearly is Guasti.

The winery buildings are numerous and spread out over an uncommonly large plot of ground. Interstate Highway 10 sets limits on the north. Ontario International's main runway borders Brookside on the south. Turner Road on the east and Archibald Avenue on the west are the other limits to the main property. And there is more of Brookside than bewilders the eye at headquarters: two fermenting wineries and an aging cellar are elsewhere in the district.

The proprietors have made things easy for visitors. Only three of the home winery buildings are open—one is the stone-walled tasting room and retail shop; another is a luncheon restaurant; the third is the handsome main aging and bottling cellar.

Tours of the aging cellar depart from the tasting room. On weekdays, signs do the guiding; on weekends, a host or hostess leads the way.

The cellar is a startling structure. Looping curves atop the end walls suggest Roman inspiration. Built of dark gray river rock that must once have been abundant here, it measures 100 by 600 feet, suggesting Herculean ideas more than mere mortal ones. Inside those 3-foot-thick walls the two major points of interest are a huge undergound cellar full of barrels—in their turn full of sweet wines—and a museum of the winery's long, complex history.

The winery that is now called Brookside was built as the Italian Vineyard Company by Secundo Guasti in

Old line vineyards *in Cucamonga snug up against the steep-sided San Gabriels.*

the 1880s. As IVC, it was the biggest winery in the world just before Prohibition, with 5,000 acres of vines all in a block.

Meantime, Brookside had its origins in the same decade, but was built in Redlands by Emile Vache. Another Frenchman, Marius Biane, married the boss's daughter, then inherited the business. Biane's sons took the Brookside name with them when they revived the then-defunct Guasti property in the 1950s.

Bianes owned Brookside until 1972, when it was bought by Beatrice Foods, Inc. A third-generation Biane, Rene, still runs the place.

Wines on hand in the tasting room are labeled Assumption Abbey (produced under an agreement with the Benedictine order), Brookside, and Vache. Under one or more of these labels the company offers a wide range of table, appetizer, dessert, and sparkling wines.

In addition to providing tastes indoors, the winery will sell bottles for picnics at tables on a tree-shaded lawn facing the tasting room.

For those who cannot get this close, Brookside has another 30 tasting rooms, most of them in California, some outside the state. The company will forward a list.

Louis Cherpin Winery is housed in a main building that has undergone intermittent expansion ever since its foundation stone went down in 1934. The successive enlargements are marked by changes from brick to red block to concrete block. Large vines are trained up each section.

Inside, most of the cooperage is upright redwood. In early 1968, when the Adelanto Winery closed its doors forever, the Cherpin brothers bought several oak ovals that had been coopered in Germany on special order for the former owners. These now line one wall of the winery alongside the bottling equipment.

The winery, flanked by several frame outbuildings and equipped with an honor guard of various dogs (all friendly), is at the end of a short dirt drive off Valley Boulevard. The retail room in a small frame building faces the winery door. In it, the Cherpins offer jugs of table wines under the family name. They have another line of table wines in bottles, called *Pour le Gourmet* in tribute to the family's French origins. Several dessert wines round out the list.

Cucamonga Vineyard Company is a remarkable restoration, and therefore a remarkable winery to visit.

Built before the turn of the century by a pair of brothers named Vai, the winery carries California Bond No. 1. Until its current owner, Pierre Biane, acquired it in 1977, it *looked* like the first winery ever bonded in the state. But since Biane's arrival, he has built spanking new cellars in, on, and around the old-timer. As a result, they gave a look at the most modern of equipment side-by-side with some genuine museum pieces.

Brand new, refrigerated, stainless steel fermentors stand in tidy rows alongside ancient open sumps with old brine pipes, once used as chillers, running through them. Just across a walkway, a handful of open-topped redwood fermentors stand empty and disused, more mute testimony to how things used to be done here. It is a longer walk from the old crushers to the new ones with their companion dejuicers and continuous presses,

but the contrast is not lessened by the stroll.

Tasting goes on in an old aging cellar, emptied out and spruced up for the purpose. (No wines remain from the old days for contrast with the new production. A man can't hang on to everything.)

Cucamonga Vineyard Company plans to focus on table wines (both varietal and generic) and sparkling wine. There will be some specialty sherry types.

The winery's location on Eighth Avenue may seem a trifle remote until one pauses to consider that the Spanish-style main building fronts on a mainline railroad. Visitors park behind that main building, having entered the grounds through a gate at the west end.

J. Filippi Vintage Company, on the edge of Fontana and at the end of a row of industrial concerns, encourages visitors to limit their inspection of the premises to the tasting room, which is comfortably airy.

The working winery has grown right through the walls of its original building in a series of additions, with the result that there is no easy path to follow through it. The earliest walls date from 1934. The most recent additions—a row of foam-insulated steel fermenting tanks—stand outside of all the walls. The persistent visitor may have a look inside, where the working equipment is mostly modern.

On hand for tasting are a number of table, sparkling, and dessert wines. The varietal table wines are produced elsewhere. The generic types are made here, as are several dessert wines, including a specialty called Marsovo (Marsala with a trace of egg in it). The labels are Joseph Filippi and Chateau Filippi.

The winery and adjacent family home are surrounded by an expansive vineyard, all well trained, much of it planted since the mid-1960s. It makes a startling contrast to the dead and abandoned vines across Etiwanda Avenue and elsewhere in the immediate neighborhood.

The Filippi family maintains six tasting rooms elsewhere in Southern California. They will send a list of addresses on request.

Galleano Winery, after years of shy withdrawal from public attention, opened a tasting room in the early 1970s and now offers tours as well.

Founded by Domenic Galleano in 1933, the property is a perfect evocation of the sort of small, family enterprise that once dotted this whole countryside. The main cellar has tidy rows of ancient redwood tanks, plus some oak. Crusher and presses also go back to an earlier day.

The tasting room is housed in a modest frame building at the rear of a courtyard formed by the main cellar on one side and the family residence on the other. Within, visitors may taste the pride of the house, a local Zinfandel, usually with one of the owning Galleanos as host. The roster of wines includes other varietals, generics, and some dessert wines. Galleano wines are sold nowhere else.

Opici Winery has a tasting room open to the public. Tucked away at the end of a street next to a platoon of Alta Loma tract homes, the square, flat-roofed, cream-colored building offers a surprising range of wines made in facilities located elsewhere in the district and state.

This is headquarters for the company, which sells

(Continued on page 123)

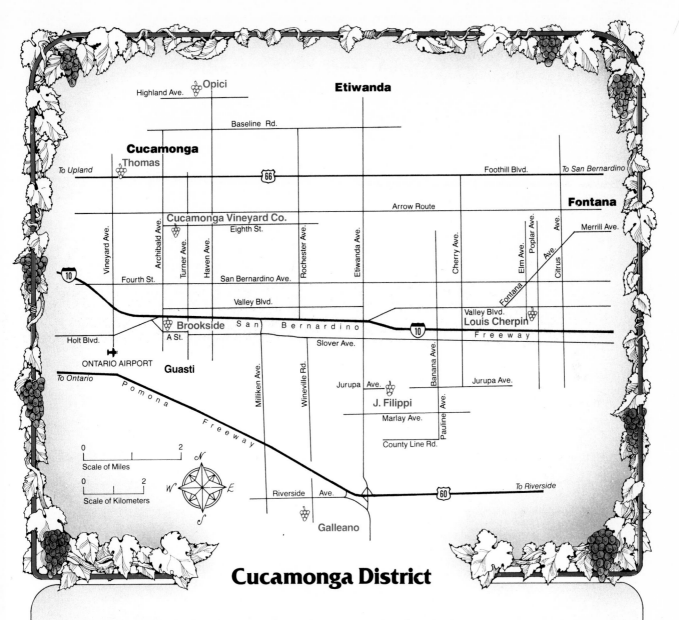

Cucamonga District

Brookside. From San Bernardino Fwy. (I-10), Archibald Ave. exit, S 2 blks to A St. (9900 A St., Guasti, CA 91743) Tel (714) 983-2787. Picnic. Daily 8-6. IT weekdays, GT weekends/Ta

L. Cherpin Winery. From San Bernardino Fwy., Citrus Ave. exit, N to Valley Blvd., then W ¾ mi. to winery drive S side of rd. (15567 Valley Blvd., Fontana, CA 92335) Tel (714) 822-4103. Daily 8-5./Ta

Cucamonga Vineyard. From San Bernardino Fwy., Archibald Ave. exit, N to Eighth, E to winery. (10013 E. Eighth St., Cucamonga, CA 91730) Tel (714) 987-1716. /Ta.

J. Filippi. From San Bernardino Fwy., Etiwanda Ave. exit, S 1 mi. to Jurupa Ave., the winery drive. (PO Box 2, Mira Loma, CA 91752) Tel (714) 984-4514. Picnic. Daily 9-6./Ta

Galleano Winery. From U.S. 60, Etiwanda Ave. exit, S to Riverside Ave., W to Wineville Rd., S to winery. (4231 Wineville Rd., Mira Loma, CA 91752) Tel (714) 685-5376. M-Sa 9-5./Ta

Opici. From San Bernardino Fwy., N 4 mi. on Haven Ave., W ½ mi. on Highland Ave. (10150 Highland Ave., Alta Loma, CA 91701) Tel (714) 987-2710. Th-M 10-6./Ta

Thomas. NE corner of Foothill Blvd. at Vineyard Ave. (8916 Foothill Blvd., Cucamonga, CA 91730) Tel (714) 987-1612. Picnic. Daily 8-6. IT/Ta

Outside Map Area

San Antonio (Los Angeles). From City Hall in downtown L.A., NE 1½ mi. on N. Main St. to Lamar St., S to winery. (737 Lamar St., Los Angeles, CA 90031) Tel (213) 223-1401. Picnic, by res. Daily 8-8. GT/Ta

Key: GT (guided tour); IT (informal tour); Ta (tasting).

It all begins with vines in the sun

A grape starts out in spring all acid and no sugar. As it ripens its acid level declines and its sugar level rises.

The winemaker's task is to harvest the grapes when the ratio of sugar to acid is right. The desired ratio differs from one class of wine to another. Port and other dessert types come from grapes with higher sugar and lower acid than grapes used for red table wines. Champagne, on the other hand, calls for unusually low sugar and very high acid.

In the end it comes down to the interactions of climate and grape variety. There is a "right" climate for each variety—or, more precisely, a right range of climate. California has richly diverse and complicated climate patterns. Furthermore, vineyardists in the state grow 130 varieties of *Vitis vinifera* in one amount and another.

After a long study, researchers at the University of California at Davis defined five climate zones based on heat summation. (Heat summation is the total number of degree-days above 50°F between (and including) April 1 and October 31. The measuring stick for degree-day calculations is mean temperature. For example, if the mean temperature was 70°F for 5 consecutive days, the summation would be: $70 - 50 = 20 \times 5 = 100$ degree-days.)

The five climate zones:

Region I (2,500 degree-days or fewer). Occurs in Anderson Valley, Carneros, Felton, and Gonzales, as examples. The university recommends table wine grapes as best suited to the region, especially such varieties as chardonnay, pinot noir, and white riesling.

Region II (2,501-3,000 degree-days). Occurs in Glen Ellen, Hollister, Oakville, and Greenfield, as examples. The university recommends table wine grapes for this region also, especially cabernet and sauvignon blanc. In both this region and Region I, in fact, it recommends nearly all of the grapes used in familiar varietal table wines.

Region III (3,000-3,500 degree-days). Occurs in Cloverdale, Livermore, Calistoga, Paso Robles, and Ukiah, as examples. This begins to be the margin between purely table wine country and dessert wine country. The recommended table wine varieties include barbera, ruby cabernet, sauvignon blanc, and semillon. The university gives qualified recommendations for many others, depending on specific local conditions. It also recommends a good many of the familiar muscats and some sherry and port grapes, again depending on precisely measured local climate factors.

Region IV (3,501-4,000 degree-days). Occurs in Guasti, Livingston, Lodi, and Modesto, as examples. The balance goes over to dessert wine grapes. Nearly every muscat, sherry, and port grape earns a university recommendation in this region. Among table wine grapes, emerald riesling, French colombard, barbera, and ruby cabernet get clear recommendations. As the presence of emerald riesling and ruby cabernet indicates, this is a region for which many of the UC hybrid varieties are bred. As the national demand for table wine rises and the university program progresses, this region is turning more and more to make table wine.

Region V (4,001 degree-days or more). Occurs in most of the southern San Joaquin Valley, from Madera to Bakersfield, and much of the Cucamonga district. All of the sherry and port grape varieties carry university recommendations in this region. It will probably always produce a great part of California's dessert wines, but the hybrids and a few other varieties, coupled with advances in vine-training techniques, make table wines a possibility in the warmest of these vineyards.

The trick *is to match vineyard to variety, so that grapes ripen late in their season.*

. . Continued from page 120

most of its wine along the Atlantic seaboard, limiting the home audience to this one outlet. The lone opportunity to taste and buy at the source is congenial.

Thomas Vineyards, in Cucamonga, is housed in the oldest winery building still standing and in use in California. At least part of the adobe structure dates to 1839, when Governor Juan Batista Alvarado of Mexico deeded the property to a winegrower named Tiburcio Tapia. (The east end of the building dates only to 1969, but is a faithful restoration of the original, which washed away in a flood.)

The wines, labeled Thomas Vineyard and Old Rancho, are available for tasting and sale only on the premises. Visitors are free to wander through an aging cellar full of fine old oak ovals, and out back, where there is a modest collection of old winemaking equipment.

Other Than Wineries

The most notable tourist attraction other than wineries in this region is the Annual Los Angeles County Fair. It runs the last two weeks of September, the right time for a companion look at the new vintage in progress. The grounds are located north of Interstate Highway 10 in Pomona.

During the rest of the year, two local picnic parks add greatly to the opportunities offered by the wineries themselves.

Upland Memorial Park, spacious and shady, offers a considerable number of picnic tables to supplement those at the wineries. The town baseball diamond is adjacent. (Since this is Southern California, there are weekend games the year around. Any Sunday afternoon, even in February, the temperature at the seventh inning stretch might reach 80°F/27°C.)

The park flanks Foothill Boulevard toward the east side of town.

Upland-Cucamonga Regional Park, operated by San Bernardino County, has picnic facilities and children's playgrounds on a level, newly landscaped site on Archibald Avenue just a few yards north of the I-10 interchange. There is a minimal day-use fee.

A number of motels and restaurants can be found in the area. For specific information write to the Greater Los Angeles Visitors and Convention Bureau, 505 S. Flower Street, Los Angeles, CA 90071.

Plotting a Route

The towns of Ontario and Upland run into one another so smoothly that the change is imperceptible to all but devoted readers of roadside signs. Together, the communities straddle every major east-west road between Los Angeles and the state line. For visitors to wineries, the most useful of these are I-10 (the San Bernardino Freeway) and Foothill Boulevard, a moderately fast four-lane commercial road that once was part of the much-sung-about Route 66.

The whole district is divided into a tidy gridwork by local roads. The most useful of the north-south arteries are Vineyard, Archibald, and Etiwanda avenues.

Temecula

The Temecula district started all in a rush as a wine-growing area when a real estate development operation turned much of the southwest corner of Riverside County into Rancho California and simultaneously encouraged buyers to plant grapes on their parcels.

Within a fairly short span a dozen growers had 2,000 acres of vines up and going. The first winery came in 1974. At the turn into spring of 1979, the original had gained one neighbor, with a second aborning.

This is relentlessly hilly country. The section where the vines grow is a sort of catch basin for what little runoff water there is from a sparse annual rainfall. It also draws cool, moist sea breezes through a gap in the hills to the west. The combination makes the local climate as pleasant for people as it is for vines. The climate notwithstanding, Temecula has tended to business, rather than developing into a vacation retreat. A pleasant motel welcomes visitors. Otherwise, only the wineries invite passers-through to tarry for pleasure.

The Wineries

The short roster of three cellars offers remarkable diversity of size and style.

Callaway Vineyards and Winery started the new trend in winemaking south of the Tehachapi Mountains. It pioneered the shift toward small, estatelike wineries producing varietal table wines.

Occupying a series of rolling knolls east of Temecula, the winery and vineyards are the property of retired business executive Ely Callaway. The first phase of the cellars was built in 1974 amid vines planted in 1969. Substantial additions have come along since.

The present winery looms up from the top of a sharp rise above Rancho California Road. Its tall, white walls are unbroken by windows except on the west face, where the visitors' hall is a light and airy room. Around back, a short length of metal wall and another of concrete block reveal the original size of the building.

From custom-made crusher to continuous press, stainless steel fermentors, and centrifuge, this is a first-rate example of a modern California winery. Its difference from others is not immediately visible, but differ it does: all of its casks and barrels are of German oak, rather than American, French, or Slavonian. The tour staff gladly explains the hows and whys of it.

Callaway does not offer tasting, except for a fee to organized groups with prior arrangements. The tour is a complete one, though, and picnickers may make use of a well-designed area behind the winery on a first-come, first-served basis (except when it has been reserved for group use).

Wines in the retail sales room include Johannisberg Riesling (regular and late harvest), Sauvignon Blanc, Chenin Blanc (regular and late harvest, the latter known as Sweet Nancy), Cabernet Sauvignon, Petite Sirah, and Zinfandel.

Cilurzo & Piconi Winery was launched in 1978, but its vineyards, the first ones planted in Temecula, go back to 1967.

Garrett's ghost...

After more than a decade of selling their grapes to others, Vincenzo Cilurzo and Dr. John Piconi dug an underground aging cellar for American oak barrels, then built a wood frame building atop that to house stainless steel fermentors and other gear.

The first wines—Cabernet Sauvignon and Petite Sirah—were to be released in spring, 1980.

Mt. Palomar Winery announces itself by means of a loudly painted, upright redwood wine tank perched on a grassy slope above Rancho California Road. The winery proper hides on the reverse slope.

The property of John Poole, Mt. Palomar is set efficiently into a side slope, much as old cellars were in turn-of-the-century Napa or Sonoma. The crusher-stemmer feeds grapes down into a gallery containing stainless steel fermentors and an automatic Vaslin press. This is where the new ends: the fermentors feed new wine into a cave full of venerable oak oval casks and barrels. (Outdoors is a sun-baked solera for sherry types.)

Tours cover all of these points, as well as a small bottling line, ending up in the tasting and sales room. The owner has thoughtfully added a small deli to the tasting room in compensation for the remoteness of his site. Picnic tables outside the cellar door are available to first-comers.

The Mt. Palomar wines available for tasting include Chenin Blanc, Sauvignon Blanc, Cabernet Sauvignon, Petite Sirah, and—rare bird—a dessert Cabernet Sauvignon made after the fashion of Ruby Port.

Plotting a Route

Nothing could be simpler than organizing a day of winery touring in Temecula. Rancho California Road exits east from Interstate Highway 15 about midway between Riverside and San Diego. All of the region's vineyards and wineries lie along that one road, as does the village of Temecula.

Escondido

Escondido is the agricultural heart of San Diego County. A dramatically hilly countryside between sea on one side and desert on the other, it gets enough water to grow avocados, citrus, and some grapes.

Once highly respected for its wines, the district dwindled almost to extinction as a vineyard after Prohibition, but is now making a modest comeback.

It may not be quite winey enough to merit a pilgrimage by a single-minded enophile, but local cellars can be an agreeable part of a day trip out of San Diego.

The Wineries

Escondido has two old-timers, as well as a newcomer that cannot welcome visitors with quite such enthusiasm as the others, though it does welcome them.

Bernardo Winery is one of the old-timers, and a surprising place in almost every respect. Tucked into a narrow draw behind a classy country club development, the property looks a bit like a main street movie set from an old western. More than merely looking the part, the place is actually a village of shops, of which the winery is one.

Visitors can buy indoor plants, worked silver, antique mirrors, and heaven knows what all else in addition to wine. They can also dine in an Italian restaurant.

Winery and tasting room sit on the uphill side of the main street, at its intersection with a side road. Both are wooden buildings, welcoming and more than faintly time-worn. Tours of the cellars are informal, offering an instructive look at a working example of a basket press, and other equipment not often in use these days.

Some long-aged dessert wines lead the tasting room lists.

Ferrara Winery dates from the same era as Bernardo and has a similar cellar full of old upright redwood tanks and some kindred wines. It also has the warm, familial air that makes visitors feel notably welcome.

It differs in singleness of purpose. No galaxy of shops surrounds the winery, which hides away at the end of a quiet residential street not far from the downtown.

Ferrara also differs from Bernardo in having a few surprisingly contemporary touches, not the least of which is an elegant, stainless steel crusher-stemmer.

A small patch of vines marks the property. The winery is tucked in behind the family home and can be seen only from two doorways—one leading to the fermentors, the other to the aging cellar. Tasting goes on in a comfortable building between house and cellar.

San Pasqual Vineyards is the new boy in town, different from its old neighbors in every way.

On the road leading out to the San Diego Zoo's Wild Animal Park, the winery is a plain, fabricated-steel building set atop a knoll at one corner of its vineyards. The vines are within an agricultural preserve in which there is a strict limit on retail activity. Therein lies the limit on San Pasqual's ability to welcome visitors. The proprietors may not sell by the bottle, nor may they operate a tasting room. They may only sell by the case.

Still, serious collectors of California wine will want to visit San Pasqual, which makes only estate-grown, vintage-dated varietal table wines, including Chenin Blanc, Sauvignon Blanc, and Gamay.

The equipment includes a continuous press, stainless steel fermentors, and other modern gear, as well as small oak cooperage for final aging.

Drop-in visitors may buy case lots of wine, but for a look at the cellars, the small working crew needs the courtesy of an appointment.

Plotting a Route

Local vinous geography is almost as simple as at Temecula. The three wineries are accessible via three consecutive exits from I-15. None is more than a mile off the freeway.

For information on accommodations write to the Escondido Chamber of Commerce, P.O. Box C, Escondido, CA 92025. The San Diego Convention and Visitors Bureau, 1200 Third Avenue, San Diego, CA 92101, offers county information.

Los Angeles

Early in the history of wine in California, a sizable vineyard grew where Union Station now stands. Times have moved so far that even the railroad station is now on its way to being a part of the local past.

Los Angeles hardly can be called "wine country" in any general sense. But hardy San Antonio Winery can and does advertise itself in most years as the only producing winery within the city limits of Los Angeles.

San Antonio Winery, with increasing ease, perseveres as a producing winery in spite of its downtown Los Angeles location. The development of field crushing means that the owning Riboli family can bring unfermented grape juice via road tanker from Santa Barbara, Monterey, or other Central Coast vineyards for fermenting in the industrial surrounds of Lamar Street.

The walk-through tour of the winery shows the new developments alongside bits and pieces of equipment from the old days, when they brought whole grapes in trucks from Cucamonga. The clearest evocation of the old era is a big crusher-stemmer, still anchored to its original spot in a room that has been transformed into an Italian restaurant. The clearest evocation of the new era is at the rear of the main cellar: a fermenting room full of stainless steel tanks. Between the two rooms—physically and in time—are the wood aging cellars, filled mostly with redwood tanks, but also including a growing collection of oak barrels.

One of the redwood cellars has an agreeably eclectic collection of old winery tools.

In the tasting room, visitors can assess an extensive line of wines of all types, from varietal table wines to flavored dessert specialties.

A picnic ground with space for 100 adjoins the main cellar. Its tables are available by reservation. The winery also maintains a deli.

San Antonio maintains tasting rooms elsewhere in Southern California. The proprietors will provide a list on request.

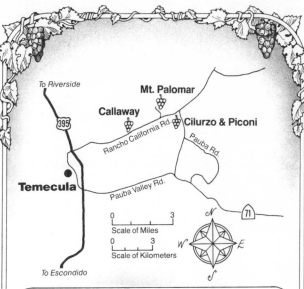

Temecula-Escondido

Callaway Vineyards & Winery. From I-15 Rancho California Rd. exit, E. 4 mi. (PO Box 275, Temecula, CA 92390) Tel (714) 676-4001. Tu-Su 11-4. GT

Cilurzo & Piconi Winery. From I-15 Rancho California Rd. exit, E 6¼ mi., then S ¼ mi. on Calle Contento. (PO Box 775, Temecula, CA 92390) Tel (714) 676-5250. GT by appt.

Mt. Palomar Winery. From I-15 Rancho California Rd. exit, E. 6 mi. (PO Box 266, Temecula, CA 92390) Tel (714) 676-5047. Picnic. Daily 9-5. GT/Ta

Bernardo Winery. I-15 7 mi. S of Escondido, exit Pomerado Rd. to Paseo Del Verano (make U-turn; no left) then to shopping village. (13330 Paseo Del Verano Norte, San Diego, CA 92128) Tel (714) 487-1866. Picnic. Daily 7-6. IT/Ta

Ferrara Winery. W on Felicita from Centre City Pkwy., rt. on Redwood to 15th St. (1120 W. 15th St., Escondido, CA 92025) Tel (714) 745-7632. Daily 9-6:30. IT/Ta

San Pasqual Vineyards. 3 mi. S of Escondido on I-15, exit Via Rancho Pkwy., E. 1 mi. to San Pasqual Rd. (13455 San Pasqual Rd., San Diego, CA 92025) Tel (714) 741-0855. Tours by appt.

Key: GT (guided tour); IT (informal tour); Ta (tasting).

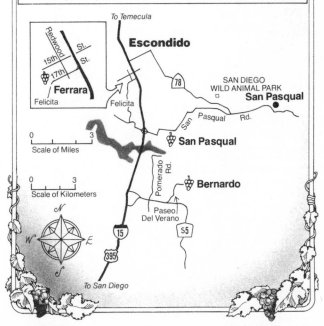

Index

"**When one glass** *of wine invites the second, the wine is good.*" *—Samuele Sebastiani.*

Photographers

David Bartruff: 43 bottom left. **Morton Beebe:** 122. **Ron Botier:** 6 top, 11, 54 bottom. **Gene Dekovic:** 30 top. **Lee Foster:** 62 bottom. **Gerald L. French:** 14 bottom left. **Peter Fronk:** 30 bottom, 71. **D. Gary Henry:** 90 top. **Luther Linkhart:** 51 bottom. **Fred Lyon:** 3, 22 bottom, 43 top. **Jack McDowell:** 79 bottom, 95 right, back cover (left top and bottom). **Barrie Rokeach:** 38 top. **Ted Streshinsky:** 6 bottom, 14 top and bottom right, 19 all, 22 top, 27, 35, 38 bottom, 46 all, 51 top, 54 top, 59, 62 top, 66 all, 74 top, 79 top, 82 all, 90 bottom, 95 left, 103 all, 106 all, 111, 114 all, 119, back cover (top right). **The Monterey Vineyard:** 74 bottom. **Bob Thompson:** 98, 127. **Dick Warton:** 43 bottom right. **Darrow M. Watt:** 87.